PRICING
FINANCIAL
SERVICES

PRICING FINANCIAL SERVICES

G. MICHAEL MOEBS
with
EVA MOEBS

DOW JONES-IRWIN
Homewood, Illinois   60430

ISBN 0-87094-594-7

Library of Congress Catalog Card No. 85–73688

Printed in the United States of America

1 2 3 4 5 6 7 8 9 0 B 3 2 1 0 9 8 7 6

*To my parents who taught me
there are 100 cents in every dollar
and that one cent equals one percent,
and
To my wife, best friend, and partner, Eva,
without whom nothing gets done.*

Preface

This is a book about the pricing of financial services. It could as easily be about the pricing of anything. Services, and in particular financial services, are priced no differently than products or goods. Financial services are subject to the same forces of supply and demand that any free market product is, whether intangible, as in the case of a service, or tangible, as in the case of a good. However, financial services do have their unique characteristics which can wrap a mystical veil around the marketing and pricing of financial services which tends to awe the layman and impress the practitioner. We hope to lift that veil with this book.

If pricing for financial services is not that different from other types of pricing, then what is the need for this book? It has been our observation that the publications currently available generally have fallen short of fulfilling a major market need in the financial service business. Books on this subject can be categorized into two groups: those dealing primarily with microeconomics and the theory of price, and those that are a cookbook on "how to price." Both fall short of providing a single source of theory, practice, and specific tools needed to properly price financial services. Economists generally write the theoretical books on pricing. These provide the background theory for what should be done, but leave the reader hungry for practical suggestions on what to do next and how to implement economic theory. Consultants generally write the cookbooks on pricing, hoping to quickly win fame and fortune for themselves. However, they tend to leave the reader like the seed in the parable which falls on rocky soil and sprouts quickly only to wither away in the heat of the day for lack of substance.

This book is a bridge between theory and practice. It presents both the theoretical aspects and the practical approaches. More importantly, it provides support for the basic symbiosis which should exist between the economist and the practitioner, in that each has aspects needed by the other. The practitioner cannot practice without a working knowledge of the theory, and the economist cannot formulate his theories without feedback from actual implementation. Hopefully this book will allow the economist and the practitioner to cross over into each other's realm, learn the basics of each other's disciplines, shake hands on the way back, and continue to do their jobs better. This is what we intend with this book, and if we accomplish it, we will have achieved our objectives.

To build this bridge on pricing financial services, we present the book in five parts. The first part sets the stage by discussing the nature of financial services as they currently exist in a more or less deregulated environment. In the second part, basic principles and tools are presented. Economics of pricing, or microeconomics, is presented in this part, as is a basic analysis of cost behavior, the fundamentals of present value, asset and liability management, and so forth. Part Three presents a method to combine the theory and tools of Part One and Two in a unique and very practical approach we call Quadratic Pricing. Quadratic Pricing integrates the four basic strategies for pricing with the theory of microeconomics into one process. Part Four details a methodology for implementing what was learned in the previous three sections. It uses a "cookbook" approach for those readers who want "the magic" without the theory; it also refers to other recipes that can be used. Finally, in Part Five, we give some case examples of real life situations to allow readers the opportunity to test the material presented.

The economic background for the book is the financial markets of the United States. We apologize to non-American readers for our bias, but it is under this environment that we learned the business of financial services. We have received insights from subscribers, clients, and friends in Sweden, the United Kingdom, Canada, and South Africa on their markets and economy, and we feel that we have not missed the mark by much in our focus. Research has shown us that financial service pricing, while maybe not universal, is based on identical principles and tools.

To write this book, we have relied on our experience and knowledge gained from over 20 years of pricing financial services or living with the prices set by others. Fortunately, both of us did our graduate work at the Mecca of pricing, the University of Chicago. After this formal training, we worked in several financial institutions, spanning various organizational sizes (money center banks and community banks), organizational structures (branches, unit banks, chain banks, and multibank holding companies), and different regions of the country. Our roles included commercial lending, consumer lending, cash management, operations, data processing, accounting, customer service, management, finance, training, bookkeeping, marketing, auditing, investments, and pricing. In short, we have experience in every functional area of a financial institution. We also continue to assemble a large database on financial service prices which keeps us in touch with thousands of practitioners on an advisory basis.

Our purpose is to provide a single source which will enable practitioners to optimize financial service pricing by bridging theory and practice. During one of our seminars on pricing, one of the participants, a bank president, left early. Later we saw the president in the airport. When we asked him why he had left early, he said, "You didn't give me any magic." In pricing, as in life, there is no magic, except perhaps in Orlando, Florida or Anaheim, California. We hope this book will provide you with what you really need instead.

Michael and Eva Moebs

Acknowledgments

When I was a small boy I remember watching the Academy Awards on TV with my mother. After a seemingly endless stream of recipients went on and on thanking numerous people for their support in winning the Oscar, I said if I ever got an award, I would say I did it all by myself. My mother looked up at me from her ironing with an eye of wisdom and said, "Wait." I never knew what she meant until I did this book.

Pricing of Financial Services is my personal reward; it could not have been done without the help and support of a lot of people.

Paul Judy, retired CEO of A. G. Becker, reviewed some of the first draft and helped solidify my objectives.

Dick Thain, Dean of External Affairs at the University of Chicago, read the manuscript twice and helped give me direction and focus. Dick Thain is a master of marketing and of the English language, but his counsel and support were even more valuable.

Sister Mary Ildephonse provided inspiration and perspective. Her death before the book could be published marred its completion. She will always be remembered.

Eva Moebs, with whom I wrote the book, was a tower of strength in writing, editing, researching, typing, and so on. We kidded that I gave birth, but she nurtured and raised the book. Eva seldom gets credit but she contributes equally with knowledge and toil.

Finally, I would like to thank the numerous employees, officers, and executives of countless financial institutions who provided a testing ground in my many seminars for the material. Their thoughts and suggestions helped form the book.

I now know what my mother meant when she said, "Wait."

Michael Moebs
Little River, California
July, 1985

Contents

Part 1   Introduction

1. **Financial Service Pricing**   3

2. **Pricing = Marketing = Planning**   13
   Research. Product Design. Distribution. Communication.
   Training. Pricing. Planning. Summary.

3. **Pricing Services versus Pricing Products**   32
   Tangibility. Regulation. Marketing Orientation. Proximity. Distribution. Relationships. Price Impact. Uniqueness
   of Financial Services. Summary.

Part 2   Financial Service Pricing Principles

4. **Economics of Pricing**   53
   Transmission of Information. Incentives. Distribution of
   Income. Supply and Demand. Summary.

5. **Cost Considerations**   67
   Cost-Plus. Types of Cost Behavior. Most Costs are Fixed.
   Economies of Scale. Direct and Absorption Costing. Cost
   of Funds. Federal Reserve Functional Cost Analysis.
   Summary.

6. **Fees versus Balances**   **94**
Forms of Payment. Unbundling. Equating Fees and Balances: *Price/Fee. Annualization Factor. Earnings Credit Rate. Adjustments.* Formula for Equating Fees and Balances. Equating a Dollar of Fees. Policy Issues. Summary.

7. **Present Value as a Pricing Tool**   **114**
Future Value. Present Value. Future Value of an Annuity. Present Value of an Annuity. Summary.

8. **Asset and Liability Management Considerations and Risk Assessment**   **131**
Elements of Asset and Liability Management: *Cash Flows. Profits. Rates. Balances. Time.* Gap Analysis. Duration Analysis. Impact on Pricing. Summary.

9. **Account Analysis: The Invoice of Financial Services**   **146**
Interest From Competitors. Comparison to Profitability Analysis. Fees versus Balances: *Changing the Components. Float. Funds Advanced. Reserve Requirements.* General Policy Issues: *Full Disclosure. Accuracy. Indifference Between Fees and Balances. Netting.* Summary.

10. **Pricing Constraints: Laws, Regulations, and Operations**   **160**
Laws and Regulations: *Interstate Banking.* Federal Reserve Regulations: *Regulation D. Regulation J. Regulation Q. Regulation Z. Regulations G, T, U, X.* State Regulations. Specific Regulations: *Depository Institutions Deregulation and Monetary Control Act of 1980. Garn-St Germain Depository Institutions Act of 1982.* Operational Constraints: *Data Processing Constraints. Manual System Constraints. Customer Information File Constraints.* Summary.

Part 3   Pricing Strategies

11. **The Theory of Quadratic Pricing: The Integration of Pricing Strategies**   **177**
Cost-Plus Pricing Strategy. Competition Pricing Strategy. Relationship Pricing Strategy. Value Pricing Strategy. The

Quadratic Pricing Matrix. Product Positioning. The Position of Specific Products: *Passbook Savings Accounts. Basic Checking. Automated Teller Machines. Small Business Loans.* Impact of Marketing Components on a Loan Product. Summary.

Part 4 Implementing Prices

12. Methodology for Implementing Prices   195
Establish a Price List. Conduct a Cost Analysis. Evaluate Competition. Determine Household or Parent Company Positions. Determine Market Position. Prepare Product Line Financial Statements. Conduct an Operational Assessment. Review Applicable Regulations and Operating Policies. Make a Management Decision. Train Staff. Communicate Properly. Monitor Results. Summary.

Part 5 Tactical Pricing Considerations

13. Cases   217
Case A Commercial Savings (Deposit Pricing)
Case B Unsecured Consumer Credit/Credit Card
          (Loan Pricing)
Case C Safe Deposit Boxes (Fee-based Pricing)

Bibliography   231

Index   233

List of Figures

2–1	Consumer Financial Services Life Cycles	18
2–2	Strategic Planning Relationships	25
2–3	The Planning Pyramid	29
2–4	Planning Process Orientation	30
3–1	The Impact on Price of Marketing Components	46
4–1	Classical Supply and Demand Curves	58
4–2	Safe Deposit Boxes Estimated Demand Curve	59
4–3	Printed Checks Estimated Demand Curve	61
4–4	Auto Loans Estimated Demand Curve	62
4–5	Passbook Savings Estimated Demand Curve	63
4–6	Checking Accounts Estimated Demand Curve	64
4–7	Money Market Deposit Accounts Estimated Demand Curve	64
5–1	Comparative Income Statement—All Banks	68
5–2	Price and Cost	69
5–3	Price Does Not Equal Cost	70
5–4	Price Minus Cost Equals Profit	70
5–5	Cost Minus Price Equals Loss	71
5–6	Variable Costs	73
5–7	Fixed Costs	74
5–8	Relevant Ranges	75
5–9	Semivariable Costs	75
5–10	Total Costs	77

5–11	Average Interest Rates	**81**
5–12	Weighted Average Interest Rates	**82**
5–13	Checking Account Cost and Activity	**84**
5–14	Overhead Rates	**85**
5–15	FCA Costs by Function	**86**
5–16	FCA Costs for Regular Checking	**88**
5–17	FCA Costs for NOW Accounts	**88**
5–18	FCA Costs for Regular Savings	**88**
5–19	FCA Costs for Statement Savings	**89**
5–20	FCA Costs for 6-Month $10,000 Certificates of Deposit	**90**
5–21	FCA Costs for Installment Loans for Autos	**91**
6–1	Balance Equivalent for $1 of Fees	**108**
6–2	Median Nonearning Assets for Banks as a Percent of Assets (by state)	**111**
6–3	Median Nonearning Assets for Banks as a Percent of Assets (by size)	**112**
7–1	Present Value Formulas	**115**
7–2	Future Value of $1	**118**
7–3	Present Value of $1	**122**
7–4	Future Value of Annuity of $1	**124**
7–5	Present Value of Annuity of $1	**128**
8–1	Classical Gap	**135**
8–2	Controllable Gap	**136**
8–3	Nonrate Gap	**137**
8–4	Income Gap	**138**
8–5	AL Matrix	**139**
8–6	AL Matrix—Rate Sensitive Gap	**139**
8–7	AL Matrix—Controllable Gap	**140**
8–8	AL Matrix—Nonrate Gap	**140**
9–1	Account Analysis	**149**
9–2	Profitability Analysis	**149**
9–3	Differences Between Account Analysis and Profitability Analysis	**150**
9–4	How Changes in Account Analysis Factors Affect Balance Requirements	**151**
9–5	Funds Advanced	**154**

11–1   The Household Pyramid   **180**
11–2   The Quadratic Pricing Matrix   **184**
11–3   The Quadrants   **185**

12–1   Comparative Financial Report   **202**
12–2   Cross-Sell Account Report   **204**

PART 1

Introduction

1

Financial Service Pricing

This I believe with passionate obsession
And call it wisdom's ultimate advice:
None keeps of life and liberty possession,
But daily pays in sweat and toil their price.

—Sprüche, by Johann Wolfgang Goethe

As the first pricing committee meeting starts, there is general apprehension in the group. Peter, the president, stated in his memo: "I want to establish a permanent committee to review prices for our services and to adjust them if necessary." A simple request, but why now? Before the 1980s, it was pretty simple. A meeting like this would not generally be necessary because price wasn't important. Making loans, taking deposits, keeping the customers happy, showing up for community events, those were the important things. But times change.

The group consists of the major decision makers with some support from marketing and accounting. Lawrence, the head of loans, starts the meeting.

Lawrence: Peter, I think the idea of having a pricing committee and meeting on a regular basis is an excellent one. I'm all in favor of it.

Peter (*the President*): I'm glad you feel that way, Lawrence. In general, what I want to accomplish today is to set an agenda for future meetings and schedule some reviews of our prices. How do you all feel about that?

3

Lawrence: Well, like I said, I'm certainly in favor of it. I'm tired of us giving away our services all the time.

Carl (*the cashier*): I don't know what you mean, giving our services away.

Lawrence: Well, you guys on the consumer side do it all the time. I always see your tellers giving away cashier's checks and other stuff.

Carl: Like you guys in loans don't?

Lawrence: Absolutely not. We negotiate every loan and make a lot of money for this bank. Art, wouldn't you say that loans produce the bulk of the profits in this bank?

Art (*the accountant and controller of the bank*): Yes, they certainly do. In fact, according to my numbers, loans account for 61.3 percent of total revenue for the bank.

Lawrence: See, our area is the big revenue producer. And Carl, your area is the big expense producer.

Carl: What if we include loan write-offs in that, then what do you think the figures would be?

Peter: Now, I don't want to get into an argument about who does what around here. We need to talk in general about our prices.

Martha (*from marketing*): Well, I certainly think we need some discussion about prices. But let's remember that pricing is only one of the four Ps of marketing. As you all know, the four Ps are product, price, promotion, and place. Pricing is certainly important, but research shows that price is not that important to the consumer. In fact, I've brought along with me some new ads for our new self-directed IRA service.

Peter: Martha, I don't think we should talk about your new products right now; let's try to concentrate on the pricing agenda. I'd like to get back to this thought that we might be giving away some services. Is there any particular product we tend to give away a lot?

Art: Well, checking accounts seem to be a bit of a problem.

Peter: Okay, let's start there. What do you think?

Carl (*the Cashier*): Well, we used to have free checking about four years ago, and we lost some customers when we stopped, but we sure gained a lot in profitability. I was even able to eliminate a proof operator because we reduced the number of transactions. Now, prices haven't been changed in four or five years, so we might consider increasing prices a bit.

Martha: But checking accounts are the basic service that both our consumer and half of our business market want. If we increase the prices, we could lose some business.

Peter: Art, what is our cost?

Art: Well, we've participated in the Federal Reserve Functional Cost Analysis for the past eight years. Our costs are pretty much in line with what the national surveys are. We're a little bit under because I think we've got a good shop and we're fairly efficient. Of course, business account costs are kind of all over the board, and we'd really have to take a look at transaction volumes for those.

Peter: Well, what are the prices we're charging? I forget.

Ira (*the investment officer*): Most of our employees do.

Martha: Ira may have a point here. With all the products and services that we sell and all the pricing configurations that we have, it's difficult for the employees to keep track of what's going on. We try to hold training sessions periodically, but with turnover it's difficult for the employees to always know all the checking products we have.

Peter: Well, maybe we should consider consolidating some of these where we might see there's duplication.

Carl: We certainly do have a lot of checking account services. We have a fee account, and when I started with the bank 27 years ago, that was the only kind of account we had. The tellers used to call it a Dime-A-Time account because we charged 10 cents every time you wrote a check. We also have a minimum balance NOW account, where you have to keep $1,000 in the account to get 5.25 percent interest; if you fall below that, we charge you $7 and don't pay you any interest. Then we have a checking account where you get credit for any balances you keep, called our 3–2–1 account. There you get charged $1 if you keep $300, $2 if you keep $200, and $3 if you keep $100. And finally, we have a Super NOW Account where you have to keep a $2,500 minimum where we pay a rate about a point below our Money Market Deposit Accounts, and you pay 50 cents for every check.

Lawrence: Those are a lot of accounts, and isn't there one more for the commercial side?

Carl: Yes, our checking account for commercial customers tracks their fees and gives them an earnings credit of about 4 percent per year for balances, and their balances, hopefully, pay for their fees. But commercial customers aren't really that concerned about our deposit pricing. They really care more about the loan relationship.

Lawrence: I'd fully agree. I think any conversation about repricing commercial accounts, especially on the deposit side, isn't worthwhile. We can give away all kinds of service products to commercial loan customers and still keep profitability.

Ira: Lawrence, you complain that we're giving the show away to the retail consumer. But you're willing to give the show away on all the commercial accounts for the sake of the commercial loan. You forget that over half of our commercial customers don't borrow from us, and they're probably stealing us blind.

Lawrence: Oh, I don't think that's true.

Art: Actually, 55.9 percent of our commercial customers don't have a loan with us.

Lawrence: I don't believe those numbers. You bean counters miss half the stuff you keep track of anyway. I'm telling you the commercial side should be left alone. I'll determine the prices on the commercial side.

Peter: I think you should be a little more open and we should include commercial checking.

Lawrence: Oh, all right. We can take a look at it. It's just that I really know what's going on in this marketplace. Peter, you and I can get together to discuss this later.

Ira: That's what goes on in this place all the time. One or two of you get together and you establish a price. I thought the purpose of this committee meeting was to try to bring some order to this nonsense that we go through all the time.

Peter: Well, I wouldn't call it nonsense, but I would agree that we do have to try to do it more systematically.

Art: Why don't we start by looking at the costs of consumer checking accounts. In the report in front of you, you can see that I've figured out that the average account costs $93.46. We need 22 percent over that to maintain a good profit margin. We can earn about 11 percent gross interest on funds. After taking out 8 percent for reserves and float, net yield would be about 10.1 percent. With $800 average balances, which is what the average customer maintains, that gives us about $81. Since we need about $114 to get our margin, we're short on our average customer by about $33 a year. So it seems quite simple that we have to charge a fee in addition to the balances of roughly $3 a month.

Martha: That's a great analysis, although I didn't follow all of it. But I think you're ignoring a major factor when you just add a profit margin to your costs.

Peter: What's that, Martha?

Martha: I've done a competitive pricing survey every month for all our accounts for the past year, and we are the highest priced checking account in our marketplace. If we double or triple our prices, we're going to substantially lose market share. That's why I suggest we go back to the pricing program we started a couple of months ago which would place us in about the middle of the market.

Peter: So you're suggesting that by increasing our prices, based on what the competition is doing, we would price ourselves right out of the market.

Carl: Yes, but the other thing is that we can't just price based on the competition. Relationships are important, too. We shouldn't forget that the little guy is the one who built this bank. These people come in here when they're young and start a savings account, and then they open a checking account, and then they come in for an auto loan, and then they want a mortgage, and finally, they put money back in with CDs. So these relationships are really important.

Telephone rings. Martha answers the phone, and hands the receiver to Carl.

Carl: Oh, yeah, I know him. Sure, waive the charge on that. He's a good customer of the bank. . . . Now, that's exactly what I'm talking about. Here's a customer who's been with us for 30 years and he's down at the teller line complaining because they were going to charge him for a cashier's check. I went to high school with him, and he's been with this bank longer than I have. Now how could we charge somebody like that? Relationships are important.

Ira: Was that Joe Schmaltz?

Carl: Yeah, it was; how did you know?

Ira: He was in here just three days ago with another request for a cashier's check and raised the same ruckus. I went over after he left and saw who the cashier's check was made out to. Do you know who?

Carl: No, who?

Ira: Merrill Lynch.

Carl: Merrill Lynch!

Ira: Yes, Merrill Lynch. He was moving money out of this bank and taking it to a competitor. And not even an S&L or a bank but one of those brokerage places. So I took a look at his relationship. You know what he has? A tiny little checking account and a tiny little savings account. He's got an old mortgage with us at 7 percent and an auto loan, but nothing else. Most of his deposit business and all his commercial business is with somebody else. Probably Merrill Lynch.

Carl: Gee, I didn't know that.

Lawrence: Martha, your people on the new accounts line probably don't know that either and never asked him to keep his balances here. More than likely we probably screwed up again and he got aggravated with us and moved out.

Martha: My new accounts people do not screw up. We do the best we can with the information we've got. But I think this whole conversation has really gotten off base. All we're talking about is, I the bank this, I the bank that. What about the customer?

Peter: What about the customer, Martha?

Ira: I think what Martha is trying to say is that we've been talking about costs, competition, and relationships, but no one is talking about the customers' needs.

Martha: Absolutely right. We should look at what the customers' needs are and try to satisfy them. I have some research here that indicates that our customers think of us as a very solid, prestigious organization, and they really like us a lot.

Carl: And tomorrow they'll have a bellyache and leave us.

Martha: That's not true. My research is pretty sophisticated. Through it we have found out all about our customers' attitudes and lifestyles.

Lawrence: Sounds like a lot of hogwash to me.

Martha: It's not a lot of hogwash. You guys on the commercial side really think you're something. And I agree with Carl: You're giving the show away.

Lawrence: Now wait a minute. Art said I bring in more than half the revenue for this bank.

Carl: Yeah, but what about those loan losses?

Ira: Or the fact that less than half of your customers are loan customers.

Peter: Wait a minute. Let's get back to these checking accounts. . . .

The door opens and Priscilla, Peter's secretary, motions to him to come out. Peter tells the group to continue. Twenty minutes later Priscilla comes back and tells the group that Peter has a loan prospect on the phone and wants Lawrence to join him immediately. The meeting is over, perhaps to be reconvened later.

*   *   *   *   *

Does this meeting seem familiar? While this is probably a smaller financial institution, this meeting more than likely is representative of what goes on in all types of financial institutions. A group of officers try to get together to make decisions about a fundamental aspect of their business, pricing. As our little vignette illustrates, all the classical rivalries can come out in these committees, and very little may get accomplished.

The business of banking has been changing dramatically lately. And financial institutions have been trying to grapple with a new area they haven't been too concerned about until recently, marketing—and more specifically, pricing.

This is a book about the pricing of financial services. Its objective is to cover all the areas with which a pricer of financial services must be familiar to appropriately price his or her products. Although it would be impossible to cover all these areas in detail, we have tried to present enough material to enable the reader to synthesize the confusing array of theories, principles, constraints, analytical techniques, strategies, and tactics which bombard a pricer these days.

We will be talking about bankers and banking. In actuality, we are referring to all financial institution employees or people involved with financial services. The boundaries are becoming very blurred between institutions and functions, but the shorthand words "bank," "banker," and "banking" are still very useful and appear to be universally understood. We will continue to use them throughout this book.

Prior to 1980, the business of banking had been fairly well controlled by various regulatory agencies. Then, on March 31, 1980, President Jimmy Carter signed the Depository Institutions Deregulation and Monetary Control Act. This act formally started an evolution in the business of banking which is still continuing today. The act had two purposes. One, to deregulate the industry by simplifying many of the rules and regulations that had been in effect since the 1930s. Second, to emphasize monetary control by helping the Federal Reserve control the money supply better.

On December 7, 1981, an article appeared in The Wall Street Journal by Joel A. Bleeke and James W. Goodrich, both with the consulting firm of McKinsey & Company, entitled "Winners and Losers Under Deregulation." Bleeke and Goodrich studied the effects of deregulation on various industries such as insurance, health care, communications, utilities, airlines, securities, and railroads. From their findings it appears that three things happen when an industry goes through deregulation:

1. The performance of firms becomes more variable, with the weak getting weaker and the strong getting stronger.
2. As competition increases because of the lack of regulation and the entry of new firms, the most profitable products (for the depository industry that would be checking accounts) come under severe price pressure.
3. Rapid cost cutting occurs in the industry as firms try to maintain profit positions.

The authors of the article predicted the environment in which newly deregulated firms would find themselves—and this is the environment in which bankers, and we use the term loosely, find themselves today. Bankers suddenly have to price products whereas before prices had been set for them; they now have to control costs when formerly costs had been controlled for them. Pricing is virgin territory for most bankers, and it is often approached with great confusion.

We start by discussing marketing and pricing services in general. In Part Two, we examine some of the fundamental disciplines underlying pricing, like economics and cost. We then present analytical techniques, such as present value, asset and liability management, and account analysis. We also examine some of the constraints to pricing, such as regulation and operations. In Part Three, we discuss the four basic pricing strategies, which, incidentally, can be used to price any product or service. A methodology for implementing prices is presented in Part Four. And finally, we discuss some cases to illustrate some of the pricing principles in actual situations.

This book is based on several fundamental principles, most of which are discussed extensively in the following chapters.

1. Pricing is part of marketing, and marketing is part of planning. They should not—and cannot—be separated. Each is a function of the other two. Planning is the umbrella for everything an institution does, and pricing is one element of marketing, which is the vehicle for the execution of the strategic plans of a business.
2. The theory of pricing is functionally part of economics. Microeconomic theory, or the theory of the firm, deals extensively with the issue of price and the value of services.

3. A uniqueness of banking is that services rendered can be paid for in "hard dollar" fees or with "soft dollar" balances. Only depository institutions are able to accept payment with balances.

4. The time value of money underlies the pricing of interest-bearing financial services. A dollar received today is more valuable than a dollar received tomorrow, and an understanding of the formulas to calculate this value is at the heart of pricing all rate-related services.

5. Banking will always be a regulated business. Government needs to control the monetary situation in any sovereign nation. Also, banking is the intermediary between governments and the public, and between investors and savers. This is also a function that needs to be controlled. Therefore, banking, and pricing of financial services, will continue to be constrained and controlled by government bodies.

6. Four pricing strategies exist for pricing anything, whether a good or a service.

   a. Cost-plus pricing has an internal focus, and adds a profit margin or markup to the production cost of the good or service in order to set the price.

   b. Competition pricing focuses entirely on other firms, examines their prices, and sets prices in order to place one's own firm relative to the competition.

   c. Relationship pricing aggregates all the services used by a household or company and singularly prices the entire amount of services purchased. This pricing strategy allows some products to be priced at a loss, since the relationship as a whole is profitable.

   d. Value pricing is an external strategy which prices products and services based on the perceived value as determined by market research.

   All four pricing strategies need to be considered in pricing any type of good or service. Focusing on one strategy to the exclusion of the others will eventually isolate the firm from its customers, its stockholders, or the marketplace.

7. Finally, financial institutions are in the business to make money. Banks and thrifts often do not have a profit orientation; they are more comfortable with a growth ori-

entation. In today's environment, this must change for financial institutions to survive.

In concentrating on a discussion of pricing, one tends to lose perspective. Keep in mind that pricing is only one part of marketing. For the most part, consumers of financial services are not price sensitive. The person pricing the service tends to be more price sensitive than the person buying the service. Buyers of financial services take into consideration a variety of factors when making their purchase, only one of which is price. Of course, some markets are very price sensitive, such as many commercial customers. Because of the sophisticated users of commercial services and the ability for corporations to seek financial services in an expanded locality, price is much more important to these users. And consumers, gun-shy because of inflation, are becoming more price sensitive, as savers are finding new opportunities for their investment dollars. We will explore the true impact of price on the demand for financial products in the following chapters, and we will discuss how to effectively communicate prices as well as how to actually price.

The book is primarily meant for individuals involved in the pricing, marketing, and management of financial services. This includes *all* employees of a bank, savings and loan, savings bank, or credit union; this includes the frontline loan officers as well as the back room bookkeepers. They all communicate prices. As deregulation continues, functional boundaries become more and more blurred: Banks enter the insurance industry and Sears sells loans. Thus, we are all involved in marketing services, and marketing involves understanding pricing, if not actually determining prices. Our intent is to make your life easier. We hope we succeed.

2

Pricing = Marketing = Planning

Our plans miscarry because they have no aim. When a man does not know what harbor he is making for, no wind is the right wind.

—Seneca (4 B.C.–A.D. 65)

Money won't buy happiness, but it will pay the salaries of a large research staff to study the problem.

—Bill Vaughn

Pricing cannot be examined in isolation. It belongs in the context of a much larger framework and is only one aspect, although a prime one, of the function of marketing. Marketing itself, of course, is part of the overall planning for the organization.

Pricing is the primary expression of a financial institution's marketing plan and is the most direct communication to the marketplace of its philosophy of operations. This philosophy is filtered through and translated into the institution's strategic plan, which can be explicit or implicit. This strategic plan, in turn, then generates or modifies the marketing plan. In this way a circular internal planning process is created with its primary external thrust being the institution's pricing policy.

Strategies are incorporated into this circular planning process, such as an institution's asset and liability management strategy. Why can some financial institutions offer low-rate loans while others can or do not? Why can some institutions offer free checking or checking at very low prices? These marketing strategies are partially the expression of the institution's asset and liability management, and they are the manifestation of the institution's unique funding policies, again generated by its philosophy.

Pricing will often reflect whether an institution is targeting the retail or the commercial market and whether it wants to be a full-service institution offering all services to as many customers as possible or whether it wants to target specific market segments. If it wants to be the dominant market share leader in all of the markets that it serves, then its prices for services and products will reflect this philosophy. For example, the Bank of America in California offers a variety of transaction or checking accounts in order to serve the entire market, ranging from noninterest-bearing fee-based checking to interest-bearing checking with little or no fees if balances are on deposit. This wide product variety helps the Bank of America maintain its leadership in the California market where it is estimated to have 35 percent market share or more.

Historically, the Bank of America, built by the legendary A. P. Giannini, strove to provide services for the "little guy" and the small business. Giannini began his banking career as a member of Columbus Savings, where he disagreed with the directors' orientation toward wealthier clientele and larger businesses. He built his institution, the Bank of Italy, later called the Bank of America, on the philosophy of providing services to the "common man." This philosophy permeates much of Bank of America today, and it is a guiding principal underlying its pricing structure.

Contrast Bank of America's philosophy to that of Morgan Guaranty Bank in New York, which has a selective handful of retail customers in comparison to Bank of America. Morgan's philosophy has been specifically to target the affluent market. Both banks, though very different, are very profitable. Each follows a particular philosophy which is reflected in its pricing policies; the prices of Morgan's services are considerably more expensive than those at Bank of America.

Marketing is the art of integrating customers' needs and wants into the firm's market strategy and producing products and services that will fulfill the customers' needs and wants while making a profit for the firm. This integration and production is done, to a large degree, through the pricing of services. All too often financial institutions encourage their marketing departments to design a product and develop promotional material to communicate the product to the marketplace, and then operations, cashiering, or some other department of the bank prices the product. By conducting their marketing efforts in this fashion, institutions extract the component of price from the marketing formula. This handicaps the marketing personnel and often communicates a disorganized and ineffective strategy to the marketplace.

Marketing, in the classical definition, is often broken down into the "Four Ps"—product, price, promotion, and place. "Product" refers to the design of products and services. "Price" refers to the pricing of products and services. "Promotion" refers to the communication and merchandising of products or services to the customer. "Place" refers to the distribution of products and how products or services will be delivered from the company through sales networks or distribution outlets to the customer.

These classical four Ps can be reorganized into a number of different marketing activities which then would define the entire spectrum of marketing for the organization. These functions include the following:

- Research
- Product Design
- Distribution

- Communication
  Promotion
  Advertising
  Public relations

- Training
- Pricing
- Planning

We will define each of these functions and explore the impact of each on pricing specifically.

RESEARCH

Research constitutes the analytical side of marketing. Thomas R. Criste, formerly Marketing Manager for commercial and consumer products at Wells Fargo Bank in San Francisco and now a partner with Speer & Associates in Atlanta, Georgia, stated, "Given enough of the right data, any dummy can do marketing." The key is the word "right."

Careful analyses of areas such as product design, consumer behavior, current customer purchases, customer attitudes, and demographics is absolutely vital to making appropriate marketing decisions. The use of data to determine the appropriate directions for product design, distribution, communications, training, and pricing, will ultimately lead to a very high assurance of success in decision making.

Procter & Gamble, the consumer products company in Cincinnati, Ohio, has been one of the world leaders in the use of market research to identify all the appropriate components relevant to decisions about its products. Some say that this research and studied application of the data is too slow a process which, in some cases, has hurt Procter & Gamble's market share efforts. But who can quarrel with the success that the company has had with such products as Tide and Charmin? Financial institutions' efforts have been fragmented and sporadic in the use of marketing research, and they have often based their decisions to market and distribute specific products on what they *think* they know about their marketplace and their customers.

In the past, when the financial service business was a highly regulated industry, this approach had furnished financial institutions with sufficient market research. If the banker was wrong, there was little damage done to the institution, either in profitability or in balance sheet structure. Now, with deregulation giving institutions the freedom to set rates and prices without governmental interference, financial institutions can no longer rely on market research based on what they believe their market and customers to be.

Observation as a market research technique is valid for the proper applications, such as when the business is small and the customer base is small or homogenous. The corner shoe store can survive with almost no market research primarily because of its small sales size and its limited customer base. The proprietor knows the types of customers with whom he generally does business, and he orders his shoe inventory accordingly. If the proprietor has no customers with large feet, he will not stock a size 13EE shoe. If he does stock this shoe, he'd better have a refund arrangement with the manufacturer; otherwise, he will always have a size 13EE shoe on his shelf, taking up space and costing him money. The small financial institution, under $25 million in total assets or with less than 1,000 customers, like the shoe store, can suffice with observation as its primary form of market research.

The major drawback to observational market research is that it is highly skewed by the biases of the observer, and thus is not objectively accurate. This research is often limited to those observations personally made by the marketing or chief executive officer between rounds of golf and customer calls. When the business starts to grow, and markets and customer bases start to expand, then more sophisticated techniques are required. Research efforts must become as unbiased and as quantitative as possible and may include elaborate demographic and psychographic (attitudinal) analyses of customer and noncustomer markets.

If the institution does not have available its own in-house capability for market research, then it can readily buy expertise from numerous firms in the field. Trade associations also provide assistance in this area, such as the Bank Administration Institute, the Bank Marketing Association, the U.S. League of Savings Institutions and the American Bankers Association, all of which have seminars, written material, and even specific services for help in demographic and psychographic research for financial institutions.

An interesting example of demographic research is shown in Figure 2–1, a page out of the 1982 American Express annual report which shows consumer financial services life cycles. This chart groups financial services by type and by age group of consumer using that service. On the vertical axis of the graph are the five major product categories of savings, borrowing, insurance products, investment products, and advisory services. On the horizontal axis are age groups or life cycle groups.

According to the research conducted by American Express, for the group under 25 who are "getting started," insurance, borrowing, and savings are the most important services, with some use of borrowing. The 25 to 29 year old group, or the young "empty nesters," appear to buy a good portion of all services except for advisory services. The "borrowing for the future" 30 to 44 year old group have a low usage of investment products and savings but a high need for borrowing because of multiple demands on their discretionary income. This group also builds up their insurance portfolio and uses a smattering of advisory services. The 45 to 54 year olds, the "asset accumulators," require all services with a little less usage of investment products, and again have high demands on their purchasing power. The "preparing for retirement" group, 55 to 64, taper off with their borrowing needs, increase and maintain their savings and investment needs, and start to decrease their insurance requirements except for an increased need for medical insurance. Finally, the older "empty nesters" taper off in all products, especially reducing borrowing with property being paid off.

This approach can be used to guide product offerings. For example, if you wanted to promote credit, you could offer credit

FIGURE 2–1   Consumer Financial Services Life Cycles

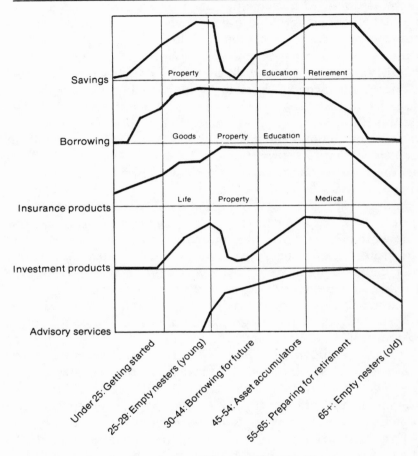

SOURCE: *American Express Annual Report, 1982,* page 18.

for consumer goods, such as stereos, VCRs, or furniture, to the young; you could offer mortgages or home improvement credit to the 30 to 44 year olds; and you could promote educational loans for those in the 45 to 55 year old category whose children are going to college.

How did American Express obtain this data? They conducted extensive research into products, demographics, and attitudes. This approach is the research of the future, and the use of sophisticated research for pricing is invaluable. Research can assist in the identification of perceived value, the relationship position of customers, and the competitive position of the institution, all concepts covered later in this book.

PRODUCT DESIGN

Product or service design, the second element of marketing, can take many forms, ranging from a bundled approach, such as that used by Merrill Lynch with its Cash Management Account, to a relatively simple single product, such as a safe deposit box as offered by many financial institutions. Product design is usually the method used to differentiate a product. However, financial services are relatively fungible in nature and are intangible. Thus, financial "product design" often *is* the price of the service or product.

For example, if a bank were to offer auto loans at 20 percent APR (annual percentage rate), it is highly unlikely that there would be any market at all for its product. If, on the other hand, a bank offered auto loans for 5 percent APR, the market would probably be enormous. For many financial products, the price of the product is the sole determinant for the demand for that product; few other "product design" features are even considered. The price is the product.

DISTRIBUTION

Another element of marketing is the distribution of the product. For tangible products, much greater depth and breadth is available in the use of systems to distribute the product. But the primary method of distributing financial products is personal delivery, consisting mainly of the physical presence of people and buildings. Personal delivery requires face-to-face selling, which is the most costly method of distribution but also the most effective. This takes the form of eyeball-to-eyeball contact, one at a time, with every buyer of financial services.

Because of the personal delivery of financial services, the location of branches and facilities takes on increased importance. For consumers and small business customers, convenience of location is the leading reason why they do business with a financial institution. Is the branch, bank, or brokerage firm convenient for them to use? If it is, the other elements of marketing often take a distant second place in the consumers' marketing decisions.

Mail and telephone are additional forms of distribution and, for the financial products which are transactional in nature and uniform in design, can be an effective method of distributing financial services. Mutual funds have achieved very good results in the use of the mail and telephone to sell their products.

Another form of distribution is through the use of electronic banking, such as automated teller machines (ATMs), direct deposit of payroll, use of a credit card, or wiring funds from one business to another. This form of distribution is increasingly offered by large banks which can afford the enormous costs necessary to deliver these types of services and is becoming quite popular with younger and/or affluent customers who like the convenience of an ATM for emergencies or enjoy using an innovative form of financial transaction processing.

Electronic banking has also become increasingly important for corporate financial services. The growth of cash management, especially wire transfer services for money and information, has become a vital treasury function for most large corporations. The processing of payments in the United States takes the form of physical movement of checks, known as the check clearing system. However, the flow of funds takes place via wires. 97 percent of total dollars moved flow electronically, but this volume is represented by only 3 percent of total transaction numbers.

Once solely the domain of commercial banks, the payment system is being augmented by improved technology fostered by competition mainly from the nonbank sector, such as from General Electric and Automatic Data Processing. Recently, General Electric was awarded the contract by the National Automated Clearing House Association (NACHA) to handle all private electronic intradistrict clearing in the United States, a contract which may have a major impact on the payment mechanism in the United States. In Europe, the Society for Worldwide Interbank Financial Transactions (SWIFT) is somewhat akin to the United States' NACHA. These systems are becoming more interrelated, and advances in telecommunications will further expand the capability of the payment system.

Technology and competition are expanding the distribution choices of those who provide financial services. The use of mail is returning as a cost-effective means to communicate with and promote to customers. The use of the telephone is expanding, and all distribution methods are being aided by electronic banking advances. However, personal face-to-face delivery is still the primary means of distribution and must be the foundation of financial services customer communication.

COMMUNICATION

There are three primary methods of communicating with your marketplace—promotion, advertising, and public relations.

Promotion is an all-encompassing term for all communications with customers for the purpose of selling goods and services. A popular promotional approach was the use of premiums (which are often referred to simply as promos), especially by thrift organizations. Premiums were offered as enticements to customers for them to do business with the institution. Premiums were occasionally so clever that customers bought the financial service just to get the premium. Many thrifts have devoted considerable resources to premiums offered for certain types and levels of deposits or loans. Banks joined the lead of the thrifts with the use of such clever "gifts" as Crocker Bank's Crocker Spaniel in San Francisco and Harris Bank's Hubert the Harris Lion in Chicago. These premiums were very popular and established very positive images for these institutions, especially for parents at Christmastime, who at the last minute stood in long lines to get a stuffed animal for their children. However, as is often the case with a good thing, premiums were abused, and when banks started offering money to new account holders as well as finders' fees to customers who brought in new customers, the regulators imposed limits on the amount and types of premiums that could be used.

Direct marketing, a promotional approach which is sometimes thought of as advertising, was adopted by the banks in the 60s and 70s when banks recognized the success that others such as American Express and the money market mutual funds were having. Direct marketing makes use of such distribution techniques as the mail and the telephone. The extensive use of mail, especially by the credit card companies, led initially to disastrous results in the late 60s as credit card solicitations were sent to prospects without credit screening. But, as the companies learned to effectively target customers who would not abuse credit card privileges, this promotional medium became an effective weapon in the arsenal of obtaining new credit business. Direct marketing is now being used for deposit and transaction products.

The use of the telephone has also been successfully implemented by many of the brokerage firms. Telephone soliciting for financial services is for the most part well done and highly professional. However, one has to do the groundwork. Late one evening the president of one large west coast bank had to soothe the irate chief of police of a small rural area. The chief had received numerous telephone calls from local residents who were being alarmed by telephone solicitations from a local branch of the west coast bank late at night. After this, it was suggested to the president of the institution that he let the local authorities know of any after-hour marketing efforts. Midnight calls to the president always seem to get results.

Advertising is defined as communication with customers or other publics through specific media. In the past, advertising for financial services was limited to mass media such as print, television, and radio, in many cases to the exclusion of more direct promotional methods. Also, advertising tended to be very image oriented; it was common to find ads in newspapers featuring the institution's president flanked by the financial statement or a picture of the building, concentrating on presenting an image. Current advertising tactics often focus on specific products.

The final link in marketing communications is *public relations,* where the target is broader than the customer and the message is image rather than selling. With broadcast journalism often being the only source of daily general information, public relations has become an important element of an institution's communications. The image of the institution is vital and, if not protected, situations such as the run on Continental Illinois in Chicago or the Ohio savings and loan crisis can occur. Public relations communicates the institution's image to its publics which include not only customers but noncustomers, shareholders, regulators, and others, who all have an influence on the position that the institution is able to maintain within its markets.

Marketing communication is a crucial link in a strategic marketing effort. Institutions must accept and become comfortable with the concept that marketing communications are no longer confined to mass media such as television, radio, and outdoor billboards, but also include direct mail, the use of the telephone, and one-on-one sales calls. Also, image building through public relations is important. Promotional strategies, like pricing, are one of the primary means of communicating the institution's policies to the marketplace.

TRAINING

The fifth element of marketing is training. Several years ago, a marketer in a seminar related that the most effective marketing budget was one which allocates 50 percent of the budget to research and the other 50 percent to training the institution's frontline sales personnel to deal effectively with customers. While this allocation may be overstating the case, it is not far off the mark, especially when the distribution of most financial services still takes place on a one-to-one, eyeball-to-eyeball basis.

Training is important not only when communicating product knowledge, but also when pricing services. All too often institutions do not devote the necessary time and resources to training personnel in the implementation of pricing programs. Price changes are passed on to tellers on the day of the change, and often no training takes place as to how to deflect objections or present the price change in a positive light. This creates a situation in which frontline personnel, who are the distribution channel of financial services, may neither understand nor be able to communicate why the institution is changing its prices. All too often I have been told by customer service personnel, when I asked why the price of a particular service was changed, that the price increase was management's decision and nothing further was known. This is a scapegoat tactic and does little to defuse objections. In Chapter 12 on implementation of prices, we will suggest how to effectively train to optimize a price change program. One of the keys to effective pricing is implementation, and that requires proper training of employees.

PRICING

Although pricing is only part of the marketing mix, it can be the most important element. For financial products, price often *is* the product. In spite of its importance, however, price should not be used as a scapegoat for incompetent personnel, poorly designed products, badly communicated information, or poorly researched marketing plans.

Also remember that although pricing is one of the chief ways to communicate the institution's philosophy and strategies, it operates in an indirect fashion. Consumers, for the most part, do not rank pricing as particularly important. Most customers will rank convenience, reputation, and service ahead of pricing. It is important for institutions to research the reasons why customers do business with them in order to quantify the value, through price, that they are providing to customers.

PLANNING

Planning, the umbrella over all the previously discussed functions, is often restricted to include only marketing planning, or only that which is necessary to develop and implement products or services. However, this scope is too narrow. Planning must include all elements of the organization, from asset and liability management to guiding philosophies. Planning must come not only at the end of the process, but must guide the beginning. It relates marketing to the strategies and philosophies of the firm.

Shown in Figure 2–2 are all the strategic planning elements and their relationships with which a financial institution is involved. Strategy, from the Greek, means "the art of the commander in chief." In business today, this definition would change to "the art and science of the chief executive officer." It is the ability of the firm's management to identify the functions of its business and to integrate these functions into an organized structure which directs the firm's efforts.

The figure shows how the various functions feed into and are supported by each other. Strategic planning envelops the entire process. Marketing is in the lower left hand corner of this figure, and it is influenced directly by the overall strategic planning process. Regulation and legislation also have a direct impact on marketing plans, an impact that is explored in greater detail in Chapter 10.

Marketing is also directly affected by capital planning. Depository institutions are directed by regulatory requirements to maintain a certain level of capital as a percent of assets. A good illustration of this relationship was a bank of about $100 million in assets in the Midwest. It had been juggling a dangerously low capital to asset position for some time. When money market deposit accounts were introduced in December of 1982, this bank offered up front a repurchase agreement with an interest rate

FIGURE 2–2 Strategic Planning Relationships

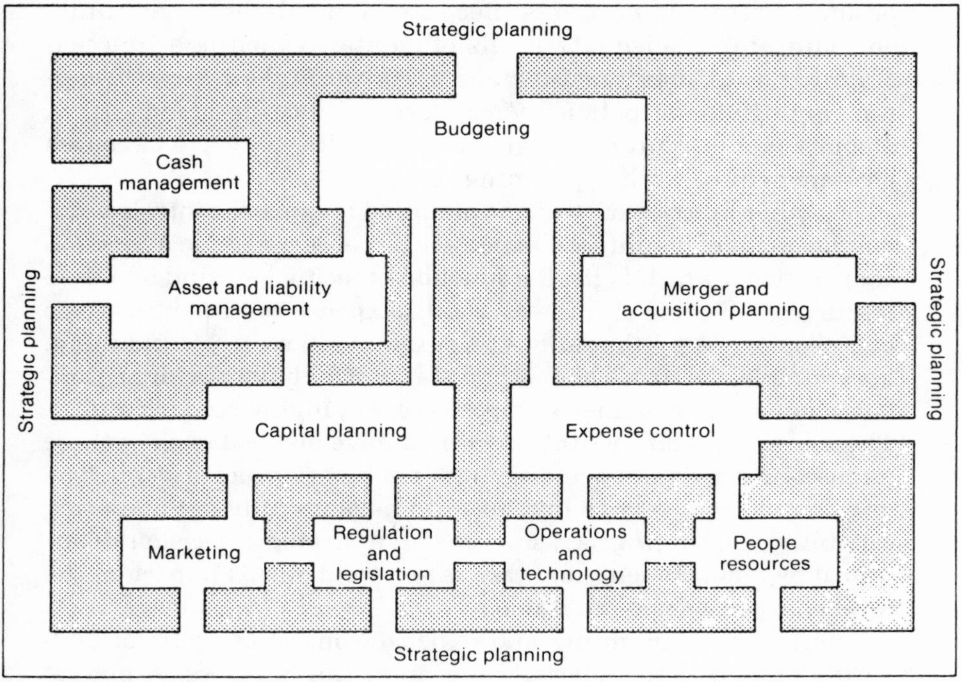

SOURCE: © G. M. Moebs & Associates.

in excess of 20 percent. This repo had a mandatory rollover into the money market deposit account later in December with a guarantee of a similar rate of interest on that account. The bank's marketing decision to aggressively price its repurchase agreements in this way was calculated to get a significant increase in market share of deposits. The institution was highly successful in accomplishing its goal, and was able to substantially increase its total footings (assets) in a matter of days. This, in turn, caused the Federal regulators to shut down the bank's marketing program for this account and strongly urge, as only regulators can, that the bank increase capital. Their potentially dangerous capital position had dipped below acceptable levels because of the increased deposits which could not be deployed fast enough to generate the income to increase capital.

Capital planning is also a direct part of overall strategic planning. For many financial institutions, their only source of capital is internally generated profits in the form of undivided profits or retained earnings. Because of regulatory constraints on maintaining adequate levels of capital, which is a function of growth rate, many institutions must watch their growth, capital, and dividend policies very closely. Since dividends are a disbursement of internally generated profits, they are of course a component of capital planning.

Another function of strategic planning is expense control, or the management of noninterest expenses. Expense control is a function of operations, which is itself a function of technology and of people resources. All three of these elements, expense control, operations and people, are by themselves components of strategic planning. For example, the firm's philosophy may call for having a large number of low-paid personnel as opposed to few, highly paid personnel. There are financial institutions which have adopted each of these philosophies and have achieved high profit performance levels. The decision to use a service bureau or to have an in-house operating capability for check processing is also a strategic decision determined by management, and can have a tremendous impact on the level of expenses and profitable pricing.

Both capital planning and expense control are part of budgeting, which is the short-term plan of the business. A budget is a translation of the firm's strategic plan into an analytical document with a very short, specific time horizon. It becomes a measurement tool for the organization to quantify the results of its efforts to achieve its objectives and goals.

Other elements of budgeting are merger and acquisition planning and asset and liability management. Many watchers of the financial scene believe that the number of depository institutions will substantially decrease by the year 2000 because of merger activities. Since many financial institutions have ownerships which are older and near retirement, this consolidation of financial institutions is a distinct possibility, although not the certainty many predict. But there is no doubt that the demographics of the stockholders can influence merger and acquisition activity for an institution.

One of our recent consulting engagements was to review the prices of a medium-sized Midwestern bank. After a long initial meeting with most of the bank's senior executives, I was asked by the chairman, who was the controlling owner of the institution, to meet with him privately. In that meeting, the chairman indicated that I shouldn't pay any attention to what had been said in the previous meeting; the chairman wanted prices increased across the board because his ultimate intention was to sell the bank. He recognized that the price that he could get for the bank was a function of its level of earnings, and he wanted to increase those earnings to a maximum. He adjusted his prices accordingly and is now in the process of selling his bank for a tidy gain.

Asset and liability management is a daily operation which quantifies the risks involved with managing a firm's assets and liabilities. If the firm views the interest rate environment to be very inflationary, it could decide to go into a short position for most of its earning assets (limit its assets to short-term) and a long position for most of its paying liabilities, hoping to reinvest its assets at higher rates while fixing the cost of its liabilities at lower rates. This could have a dramatic impact on earnings, and strongly influence prices set by the institution.

Related to asset and liability management, cash management is becoming a more important day-to-day element of a financial institution's operations. The management of a firm's daily cash position, focusing on minimizing the nonearning cash levels of reserves, correspondent bank balances, coin and currency, and cash items in the process of collection (float), has become more important as interest rates have increased.

For example, management needs to make decisions regarding the location and the use of clearing services. When Citibank decided to move its headquarters to Midtown in New York City, it ended up maintaining a large operational center in the Wall Street area in recognition of the fact that a lot of time is required at just about any time of the day in New York City to go from Midtown to Wall Street. This is especially acute later in the day when banks are trying to settle daily positions when minutes determine significant impacts to the bottom line. Likewise, when the State of Alaska settled its contracts for oil, which totaled billions, the payment of these contracts came through New York City. The State of Alaska chartered a plane to deliver the payment the same day as the settlement. The cost of the plane was $15,000, and it is claimed that the interest earned by having the chartered plane deliver the money one day earlier was $200,000. A net $185,000 savings—more than sufficient to pay for a State Treasurer's salary.

If one institution has the ability to clear funds faster than a competing institution, it can offer availability of dollars quicker.

This would allow customers, if they are paying in balances for their services, to have more money available to pay for services or to invest. Their cost is therefore lower. Cash management and clearing is examined in greater detail in Chapter 9 on account analysis.

In general, it is beyond the scope of this book to discuss how to do strategic planning. However, there are numerous shortcuts which can help a firm in approaching and performing its overall planning. Figure 2–3 is an exhibit from *Banking Tomorrow,* by Leonard Berry and Thomas Thompson. The chart is a depiction of a process that the authors suggest for describing and structuring the strategic planning process. Most notable, at the foundation of the pyramid is the commitment of management. This commitment is the cornerstone of the pyramid; without it, the structure falls apart. Likewise, successful pricing requires that the strategic direction of management be identified and its commitment secured.

The attitude toward the planning process by an organization can be measured by determining the position of management and the institution, using Figure 2–4. The left-hand vertical scale is a measure of the firm's commitment to two often conflicting groups: stockholders versus the community. Does the institution have a stronger commitment to one or the other? If the institution is more oriented to its stockholders, such as if it were closely held, then a position on the scale toward the stockholder end would be appropriate. If an institution's orientation is toward the community, replacing shareholder interests with community interests, then the institution would score more toward the community end.

On the lower horizontal axis is growth and profits. Is the institution's orientation more toward growth or is it more towards profits? In the past, growth was often the only way to increase the absolute level of profits because of regulated ceilings on prices. Since deregulation, many more institutions have become profit oriented.

On the right-hand vertical axis is a marketing scale. Is the organization myopic in its marketing thrusts, wanting to be all things to all people, as Theodore Levitt delineates in his classic work *Marketing Myopia*? Or, is the organization's marketing orientation more segmented, targeting a limited number of customers that it can service well and profitably?

FIGURE 2–3 The Planning Pyramid

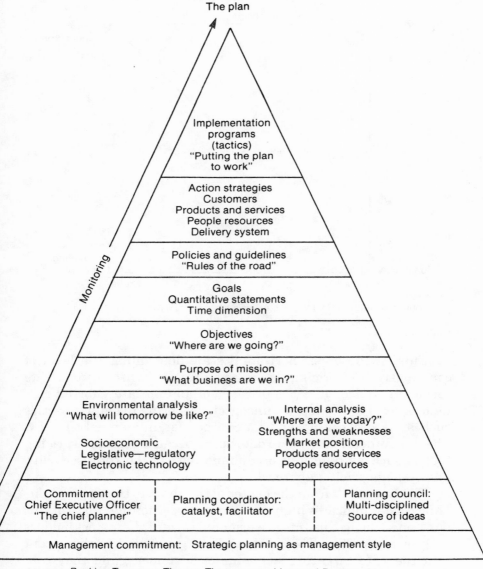

SOURCE: *Banking Tomorrow,* Thomas Thompson and Leonard Berry, p. 24.

FIGURE 2–4 Planning Process Orientation

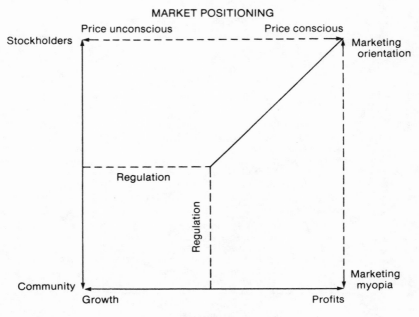

MARKET POSITIONING

SOURCE: © 1985, G. M. Moebs & Associates.

Finally, the upper horizontal scale determines the level of consciousness of pricing. Is the organization conscious of all its services and does it try to price them appropriately for its customers, or is the firm price unconscious, opting to employ tactics such as free checking and no charges for numerous services? This is a difficult position to determine because conscious pricing tactics such as bundling or unbundling can be confused with unconscious pricing approaches.

The line going from the center of the chart to the upper right-hand corner indicates high performance positioning. Institutions positioned along this line are oriented toward their stockholders and toward profits. They are marketing oriented to the extent that they are targeting segments of customers, and they consciously price to provide an optimal balance of pricing with servicing.

Those institutions positioned in the lower left-hand quadrant, defined by "Regulation," although profitable in the past, are coming under severe price pressure in a deregulated environment. They are community oriented to the exclusion of share-holder interests, forsake profits for growth, use a scatter-gun marketing approach in trying to be all things to all people, and are unconscious of their pricing mechanism, giving away many of their services under the guise of satisfying their community and stimulating growth.

SUMMARY

Pricing is a process that must be integrated with marketing and planning. It cannot be achieved without coordination of all marketing functions and all planning elements. Marketing includes research, product design, distribution, market communications, training, pricing, and planning. Planning for the financial institution incorporates marketing, regulation and legislation, operations, people and technology resources, expense control, capital planning, asset and liability management, cash management, merger and acquisition planning, and budgeting. The achievement of an integrated program of pricing, marketing, and planning requires the commitment of management. It is essential for financial marketers to be aware of the position of their firm and its level of commitment. Most important, pricing cannot be done in a vacuum. It is achieved through systematic quantification of the internal and external elements of the business. It is essential in pricing financial services that pricing be viewed as one part of this entire process.

3

Pricing Services versus Pricing Products

All that glisters is not gold—often have you heard that told.
—Morocco, Act II, Scene VII, The Merchant of Venice,
William Shakespeare

Significant differences exist between the marketing and pricing of products as compared to services. The principles covered in the previous chapter—research, product design, communications, distribution, training, pricing, and planning—apply to services also. However, the distinctions that exist between the marketing and pricing of a service versus a product can create generally upward pressure on the prices of services, making services on the whole more expensive than products.

The marketing of services is not as developed as that of products. Financial service industry managements and marketers tend not to have the depth and breadth of experience of their counterparts in product marketing, primarily because financial marketers have lived under the dampening yoke of greater regulation. With usury ceilings imposed by states and Reg Q imposed by the Federal regulators, marketing had been devoted mainly to promoting volume as the only way to increase profits, giving pricing relatively little attention. With half of the arsenal removed from the control of financial marketers, the industry did not attract either the quality or the quantity of marketing talent that a Sears or Procter & Gamble did.

In addition, the operations support for marketing in financial institutions has not been developed sufficiently to give bankers the flexibility and tools they need to do sophisticated market research and analysis, but, rather, has been tailored to support transaction volume.

Now that pricing and the full range of marketing is available to—and sufficiently under the control of—financial institutions, they should guard against adopting wholesale the marketing expertise developed in retail products and applying this expertise "as is" to the very different marketing attributes of services. The attributes that differ between services and products and that have an impact on price are as follows:

- Tangibility
- Regulation
- Marketing orientation
- Proximity
- Distribution
- Relationships

We will explore the implications of each of these differences as they affect the pricing of services. Most of these attributes are double-edged swords in that they carry both advantages and disadvantages. Finally, the finer differences between financial services and other types of services and the impact on financial service pricing will be explored.

TANGIBILITY

Ask any group of people what the primary difference between a product and a service is, and the number one answer would be, "I can pick up and touch and feel a product, but I can't do that with a service."

Tangibility is the key difference between products and services. Products are tangible, services are intangible. The lack of tangibility is the most basic characteristic from which are derived the other characteristics of services.

The lack of tangibility is usually considered a disadvantage for services. But, although tangibility can create a unique market advantage for products in that they are readily definable and easily identifiable, the physical nature of products can also create difficulties.

Perishability is one of these difficulties. Have you ever bought a six-month old potato chip? How about a gallon of two-month old milk, or a ripe four-month old tomato? None of us would enjoy these items or knowingly buy them. Perishability is definitely a problem that product marketers have, particularly with food stuffs.

Services are not perishable. A service may lose its applicability or value to the customer, in which case it can be retailored; but a loan or a checking account, or for that matter a haircut, do not physically spoil.

The tangibility of a product also necessitates carrying costs. A product must be physically inventoried or stored, which involves a cost. At the manufacturer's level, raw materials and work in progress must be stored, while finished goods must be stored at wholesalers and at various retail outlets. Carrying costs can include maintaining or preserving the product, labor and effort to move products in and out of inventory locations, and financing the cash flow shortfalls when suppliers need to be paid before inventory is liquidated. Financial marketers can't produce an inventory of IRA accounts or loans, but on the other hand, they do not have to incur carrying costs, either.

Storage or warehousing leads into the next challenge created by the tangibility of products, transportation. There are costs involved in transporting goods from the manufacturing site to the eventual end user. This cost includes the cost of transport and the cost of refrigeration or additional packaging. Financial service marketers do not face these problems, but they must contend with the other side of the double-edged sword in that their transportation costs as well as their storage costs are embodied in their primary distribution channel—their people—who all walk out the door at closing time every day.

Finally, tangibility allows the unique marketing opportunities inherent in the creation of packaging for products. Packaging, for many consumer product companies, is an extremely important element of product design and promotion. The product marketer has the flexibility of designing attractive and appealing packages that will catch the eye and pocketbook of customers, albeit they also add additional cost to the product. Consider the disproportionate resources allocated to the package of a cereal box as compared to the cost of the product inside. However, how often have you caught yourself saying, "I'm going to take this one, it looks better." This warms the heart of the marketing person who has spent a considerable amount of time and energy to present the product in the most appealing package. This marketing opportunity is not available to service marketers, but the cost is also not necessary.

Of course, the tangible nature of products is not only a challenge but also an opportunity. For example, a physical inventory can be a benefit. Goods can be produced now and sold later. Manufacturers can take advantage of cheaper resources for material and labor and produce a product in one part of the world and ship it elsewhere. Financial service marketers must produce their "product" when and where it is sold.

Most important, the product marketer has the advantage of the physical nature of a product. If you want to buy a clock, you can pick up the various types of clocks, hold them, look at them, see how they work. If they're electric, you can plug them in; if they're mechanical, you can wind them up. And, if you want to, you can bring them back if they don't work and get a refund or an exchange. Ever try to pick up a loan? You can sign the loan document, which is physical, and you can physically receive the check to buy the good or service for which you needed the loan. But you do not usually have the luxury of getting a pile of cash equal to a new car and then taking that cash in bushel baskets to the car dealer and handing it over. Usually you receive a check made out to the dealer in exchange for the new car, a far less satisfying process.

Tangibility of the product or service is, on the whole, a highly desirable attribute which financial marketers have been trying to create for a long time. Some financial institutions have tried to ascribe physical attributes to their checks by personalizing them in various ways, or to their certificates of deposits by offering embossed imitation parchment copies.

Insurance firms probably have the biggest problem because of the nature of their product. Although the checks that a customer uses from the bank may not seem very tangible, they are still more tangible than the insurance policy a customer buys once and files in a drawer somewhere. Some insurance products are so intangible, they are almost non-products. If the customer buys term life insurance, he builds up no cash surrender value, and, if he doesn't die within the term of his insurance, he sees no tangible return whatsoever. He may have eliminated risk for himself and his family, but he did so at the uncomfortable cost of purchasing an expensive, essentially invisible product.

To counter this difficult image, most insurance companies have adopted the strategy of establishing an image of the company rather than the service in the minds of consumers. When the word *Prudential* is mentioned, the Prudential Insurance Company would love for you to think of the Rock of Gibralter. When the word *Kemper* is mentioned, the Kemper Insurance Company wants you to think of the Kemper cavalry. When you hear *Sentry,* Sentry Insurance Company would like for you to envision the colonial sentry on duty, standing vigil for you. When you see the good hands, you will hopefully think of the good hands of the Allstate Insurance Company.

Several years ago, in a program sponsored by an insurance trade association, I had the opportunity to debate one of the top lawyers from one of the largest insurance companies. At one point in the conversation, he turned to me and said, "Look at what you bankers are doing with your passbooks. You're trying to get rid of them. You're lowering the rates and various other things to try to get existing passbook customers to move to statement savings or other savings accounts. But what have you got in that passbook? Tangibility! In the insurance industry, for decades we've been trying to achieve some form of tangibility so that the customer would perceive a higher value for our services. Why do you think we have the good hands of Allstate?"

This lawyer recognized one of the great mysteries in financial service marketing when he focused on the substitution of statement savings accounts for passbook savings accounts. With deregulation and the resulting closer examination of internal cost structures, the 5.5 percent savings account has not retained the popularity it once had under the auspices of Regulation Q. Now bankers and thrift executives and credit union personnel are industriously trying to eliminate the passbook because of operational cost considerations, claiming it is more costly to service a passbook than a statement account.

But this claim is questionable. After considering the cost of handling a monthly statement, the cost of postage, and the increased interest rate that most depository institutions offer for statement savings as a supposed inducement for customers to accept this "lower cost" product, it is doubtful whether the cost is less for a statement savings account. A statement savings account is definitely more cost effective in those cases where businesses receive a single statement for all their accounts or where consumers receive a unified statement that includes all products for the household, such as checking accounts, CDs, or an auto loan. But this argument can only be applied to a small fraction of all savings accounts.

Even if, for the sake of argument, we were to submit that the statement savings account is cheaper to sell and maintain, we would still argue that under no circumstances should a bank relinquish the passbook account, and certainly not aggressively market the statement savings account in lieu of a passbook savings account. Why? Because the passbook account is a tangible product!

For those of you over the age of 30, what was your first interface with a financial service? It was probably similar to my own. Back when you were about seven or eight years old, your Dad might have said, "Let's go to the bank." You jumped into the car or possibly the bus, or maybe even the trolley car, and the next stop was the bank. And you were impressed. It was probably the first time you were in a business establishment, and for many of you it was the biggest and the quietest building you had seen. All the people were dressed in what appeared to be their Sunday best, and it was air conditioned. The banking lobby looked as neat as your front room, where you generally weren't allowed.

Your Dad might have gone up to a teller and completed a transaction and then said, "Come on, son, we're going over here to open an account for you." And what type of an account was it? A passbook savings account. And what did you do with that passbook that the teller gave you? I remember clearly that I took mine home and stuck it under my pillow for the first night. Then the next day I took it outside and showed it to all my buddies and impressed them with my tale of the bank I had visited and how great my Dad was.

And now what do we as bankers and thrift industry officials and credit union personnel want to do? Take the passbook away. Is that what the customer wants? Is that good marketing? No.

If it is truly the case that passbook accounts are less cost effective than other accounts, especially statement savings accounts, what can we do? What would a product marketer do? First, sell the tangible nature of the account. Market the fact that you will give the customer a book where she can look up what her balance is at any time, to see her record of savings and her accumulation of interest. She can keep the passbook wherever she wants. Second, charge more for a passbook, by having a lower rate of interest or perhaps imposing a fee.

Both of these moves are simple, straightforward marketing moves that supply the customer with what is wanted—tangibility and a feeling of security—and achieve for the depository institution what it wants, customer satisfaction at the best cost/ benefit combination available.

Another example of tangibility is the brick and mortar of which institutions are so proud. This, however, is an example of tangibility which institutions often market well. When you think of a bank, what do you think of? Brick and mortar. Financial executives talk about the high cost of brick and mortar, but it also has high tangibility. When people think of a bank, they think of pillars and bars and brick, and most important, security. It is exactly for the very reason that stone and brick are most secure that most high security buildings such as banks and thrifts are made of brick and mortar. So, financial service organizations, whether depositories, insurance company headquarters, or brokerage firms, use tangibility to establish security as part of the image of their institutions in the minds of the consumer.

Interestingly, it has been observed that when a bank encounters financial difficulty, it will inevitably feature a picture of its building, signifying security and tangibility, on the front of its annual report.

Lack of tangibility is the key characteristic of services. This attribute causes other auxiliary characteristics to be attached to services in a chain of cause and effect. Lack of tangibility causes services to be highly regulated, which in turn causes a lack of marketing orientation among service industry executives. Lack of tangibility also causes the purchase of a service to be based on trust, which necessitates close, personal selling, which ultimately dictates the most successful form of service marketing—a relationship orientation. These characteristics are examined in detail below.

REGULATION

The second major difference between service and product marketing is regulation. Because of the intangible nature of services, which are therefore difficult for the consumer to judge accurately, services are for the most part more regulated than products.

Every spring, in Professor Richard J. Thain's marketing class at the University of Chicago, when I make this statement, it is guaranteed to raise the hackles of the students who insist on at least a half-hour debate. Although it is true that product companies are regulated and under the auspices of such governmental bodies as the Federal Trade Commission, the Federal Drug Administration, and the Security and Exchange Commission, for every product regulation or regulatory body, one more regulator could probably be named for a service.

Services by their very nature need to be regulated. They lack substance and physical presence, and therefore create uncertainty in the customer's mind as to whether the service is going to be performed as contracted. It is not possible to return a service if dissatisfied, and it is seldom possible to sample a service before purchasing. Similarly, it is not possible for the seller to repossess a service if the customer doesn't pay.

Regulation can take several forms. Many services need to be licensed. Barbers, beauticians, bartenders, mechanics, all of these trades are licensed in one form or another and display their licenses in their establishments.

Another form of regulation is the requirement of credentials. Many service companies and their professional employees must have formal degrees and/or a specified number of years of experience in order to be allowed to offer their services. Certified public accountants, lawyers, doctors of medicine, all need to go through a rigorous formal education process and, in most states, must have a number of years of experience before they can obtain the formal credential necessary to perform their service.

Examination is yet another way regulatory bodies exercise control over services. CPAs must pass a rigorous, 17-hour examination in order to be allowed to perform their service. Lawyers also need to pass an examination ranging from 12 to 18 hours in order to achieve their professional credential and be allowed to offer their services to the public. Most MDs need to be certified through examination by regulatory boards which are usually sponsored by the state. All these examinations are forms of regulation.

Finally, the Federal government directly regulates services. Perhaps the most familiar set of regulations for financial institutions is the Federal Reserve Board Regulations, including Reg Q on interest rate ceilings, and Reg Z governing truth in lending.

In addition, government requires some formal chartering procedure for most financial institutions. Depository institutions are chartered at the federal and/or the state level; investment firms are chartered at the federal level; and insurance firms, at the state level.

In Chapter 10, we explore in some detail the legal and regulatory parameters which act as constraints on the service marketer, specifically on his freedom to exercise flexibility in pricing.

MARKETING ORIENTATION

The management of most service firms, in comparison to the management of most product firms, is not marketing oriented and has a minimum of marketing experience. Most commercial banks are run by lending personnel who have achieved their position of leadership in the organization through training other than marketing. The training of lending officers consists primarily of credit analysis and the development of credit judgement. These officers tend to be financially oriented and have often earned formal credentials and advanced degrees in the field of finance. They have not been trained in marketing. Although credit judgement is absolutely essential for a loan officer, a credit orientation is quite different from a marketing orientation. Even more important, financial service executives have usually not picked up informal marketing experience in their way up the ladder. It is only in the last five years that a significant number of institutions have hired professional marketing officers for their staffs.

This combination of lack of formal training and lack of experience is rarely evident in product companies' managements. In product companies, executives have often achieved the leading management position in their firms precisely because of their expertise in the marketing function, and few have made it to the executive level without a foundation in marketing. For example, Procter & Gamble is one of the classic instances of a company in which most of its senior executives have been groomed on the marketing front lines.

Marketing expertise is lacking in financial service firm executives not only because the majority of them have risen through the ranks of corporate lending, but also because of the approach to profitability forced upon financial institutions by regulation. As mentioned before, innovative approaches, or even the classical approaches, to product design and to pricing were strictly constrained; the only way financial institutions could increase profits was to increase size. This fostered the mentality of "growth for growth's sake" which is still driving much of the marketing in financial institutions today. This desire for growth manifested itself in offering free products in the hopes of building volume, the old "loss leader" idea. Banks offered a free checking account in the hopes of getting loan or savings business, which was an acceptable strategy in the world of regulation and low interest rates when balances had relatively little value but is a difficult strategy to follow competitively today. Investment banking firms offered research and other advisory services free if underwriting revenues could be obtained from a client. Savings and loans grew rapidly by giving away ancillary services to their primary product of mortgages, such as continuous compounding on savings accounts.

Thus, marketing was a neglected discipline. If one is constrained from offering innovative products, or offering innovative pricing structures, marketing expertise becomes an underappreciated talent. As regulation diminishes, financial service executives will become more oriented toward and concerned about the marketing aspects of their firms, and marketing credentials and experience will become highly valued.

PROXIMITY

The closeness of the manufacturing site of a product to the purchaser is irrelevant. Distribution systems can deliver products anywhere in the world. Catalogs give the widest possible range to the customer base of any product. However, how far will you travel to get your hair cut? Most people keep services within a rather closely defined geographical area. Services need to be nearby because their selection and use is primarily based on convenience. You generally want your dry cleaner, your barber, your auto mechanic, to be within a convenient distance. This same selection criteria of convenience has also been proven to apply to financial institutions. Most people want their bank or savings and loan to be conveniently located, in the form of a building, a drive-in facility, or an ATM. Firms interested in offering you their services need to be located relatively close to you.

Proximity is necessary because the primary delivery method of services is personal; distribution is accomplished through individuals directly selling to other individuals. The cost of transporting that salesperson becomes incorporated into the cost of transporting the service, so that transportation is, in effect, subsidized by the purchaser. If the transportation subsidy becomes significant and the total cost of the service, including the transportation cost, rises too high, then the buyer will seek this service closer to home.

Many financial service firms without established geographical networks in locations of interest to them are targeting customers in these areas nonetheless. This strategy flies in the face of established marketing wisdom. The consumer wants most services, including financial services, to be available with a local telephone call or a local visit to the office. Financial, brokerage, or insurance services that are provided over a long distance usually end up being transferred to a more local office.

Those financial service firms that attempt to go against this marketing precept fight an uphill battle. They must use such distribution methods as electronics and shared networks for ATMs in order to provide to their customers the proximity which is natural to most services. However, these means of distribution, although proximate, violate the other precept, personal delivery, which we examine in greater detail later in this chapter. Thus, these methods will have limited success.

In the corporate credit market, there are exceptions to this. It is not unusual for large corporations to get credit lines from out of state sources. But they also will generally have their main banking relationship with a large local bank. When comparing the location of the headquarters of a Fortune 1000 company and the location of the headquarters of its lead bank, there is a high corollation of geographical proximity. On the consumer side, this same relationship holds.

Yet many financial service firms are trying to end run this very basic rule of selling services with the use of artificial transplants such as electronic banking. Although these methods are occasionally successful, they are difficult, they go against proven marketing research, and they will have limited appeal.

DISTRIBUTION

Distribution systems for services is another basic difference between products and services. The market penetration of most services, as we've mentioned, is a function of a physically convenient location because delivery is accomplished through eyeball-to-eyeball contact with the customer. For example, most dry cleaning establishments require that you come in to deliver and pick up the garments that you wanted cleaned. Some establishments pick up the garments and deliver them back to you, but this is the limit of extended distribution. If you are a dry cleaner in San Francisco with customers in New York, the use of a local physical facility is necessary; otherwise, you are subject to the whims and costs of United Parcel Service and Federal Express, not to mention the unique handling services of the U.S. Postal Service.

Services are heavily dependent on trust because of their intangible nature and are purchased on a direct contact basis. Since you cannot sample or test a service before you purchase it, you must trust the sales delivery tool that the service will perform what it is supposed to perform. The best way to gauge trustworthiness is in an in-person discussion with a representative of the service firm, thus necessitating the personal delivery system of service industries.

This is especially true as the purchase value of the service, and specifically financial service, increases. If a financial transaction is very expensive, relative to the financial standing of the customer, then this transaction almost always takes place on a personal basis with a representative of the financial institution. For example, would you invest $200,000 of your personal funds in a unknown bank that is located 2,000 miles away? Some people would, through electronic banking via wire transfers, but only if the distant bank is known to them, and usually only if they can deal directly with officers known to them. Most people, however, would seek out a financial institution in their immediate area and personally deliver the funds.

In contrast, would you buy clothes manufactured in a distant country, by workers not one of whom is known personally by you? Of course you would; we all do it all the time.

In addition, most financial services are sold one at a time. If you want to open five checking accounts, you have to fill out the identical paperwork for each of the accounts; they cannot be aggregated so you sign only one signature card and fill out only one corporate resolution. The reason for this is that financial transactions are of a liquid nature. Transfer of value is accomplished easily. Because of this highly liquid nature, the potential for fraud is great. To guard against abuses, control is tight and forms and documents to be filled out in person proliferate. Therefore, the distribution once again has to be on a very personal one-on-one basis. Without this control, the financial institution leaves itself open to security problems and losses due to fraud.

Although proximity and personal distribution is necessary, it is possible to lever current distribution systems to sell financial services. Companies can utilize current distribution systems which are already on a person-to-person basis, thus presenting the financial service as a "tag along" service.

A company that is using this approach is Sears, with its numerous retail stores and locations of Dean Witter, Coldwell Banker, and Allstate. If any one of these locations desires to sell the services of any of the subsidiary companies, it has a built-in advantage because of the presence of salespeople already in place. The on-site locations coupled with these salespeople allow Sears to lever its current situation to successfully offer financial services.

American Express is another company that uses an in-place personal sales system as leverage. It uses agents in the form of other financial institutions to distribute one of its main products, travelers checks. Tellers at numerous depository institutions are, in effect, the sales personnel for American Express. Understanding the basic characteristics of services, they mainly distribute their product not through the mail and not through electronics, but through this personal distribution network. American Express does have numerous direct offices of their travel company, and, with the addition of Shearson and Lehman Brothers investment bankers, has auxiliary locations through which to distribute their travel products and credit cards. But their primary method of distribution is through agents such as other depository institutions.

Citibank is attempting to distribute its services through both direct and indirect means. For a direct presence in its target markets, it has purchased several savings and loan associations—Fidelity Savings and Loan in Oakland, California; First Federal Savings and Loan in Chicago; and New Biscayne Federal Savings and Loan in Miami, Florida. And Citibank is also utilizing electronic distribution such as the arrangements it has made with the MPACT system in Texas and the Norwest Bank Corp. system which operates in the upper Midwest. In both cases, Citibank is sharing an ATM network. The next step may be for Citibank to utilize this system to sell its services for transactional accounts such as checking accounts, NOW accounts, and other depository products.

The distribution of services, and especially financial services, is most successfully accomplished on a person-to-person basis. Attempts to bypass this approach will be limited in success to those products or customers that do not need or want the personal trust and confidence achieved through person-to-person contact.

RELATIONSHIPS

The intangible nature of services requires close, personal selling to establish trust, the most appropriate form of which is the relationship approach. Services tend to be purchased from the same supplier more than once. How often have you changed your dry cleaner, barber, auto mechanic, or specifically, financial institution in the past year? Service vendors usually try to maintain an ongoing relationship with their customers, and the customers, in turn, try to stay with their current service vendor. Personal acquaintance with the supplier, therefore, tends to drive purchasing behavior, which therefore revolves around relationships.

An on-going relationship allows various pricing options. A service firm can afford to sell specific services at or below cost in order to secure an on-going relationship which is profitable. An auto mechanic may sell an oil change and a grease job at a very low price to help establish a relationship which will include a future tune-up job or other high ticket service work. The selling of more than one service to the same consumer is another important aspect of relationship selling. This is especially true with financial services where profitability is based on selling a combination of services, such as a transaction account with a savings account and a loan.

For most service firms, the customer relationship determines the nature of the product configuration. Because of the relationship orientation, the options available for pricing can be more numerous than for the product firm. The service firm can thus discount certain products in order to maintain profitability of the overall relationship. A product firm usually regards each sale purely on a one-time transactional basis.

PRICE IMPACT

The differences between products and services have major impacts on price. In Figure 3–1 is depicted the effect on price of the factors of intangibility, regulation, lack of marketing ori-

FIGURE 3-1 The Impact on Price of Marketing Components

	Presence		Effect on Price	
Characteristic	Service	Product	Service	Product
Tangibility	No	Yes	Decrease	Increase
Regulation	Strong	Weak	Increase	Decrease
Marketing Orientation	Weak	Strong	Variable	Variable
Proximity	Necessary	Unnecessary	Increase	Decrease
Distribution	Personal	Impersonal	Increase	Decrease
Relationship	Emphasized	Irrelevant	Variable	Variable

entation, proximity, distribution, and relationships. Let's examine the effect of each of these factors.

Tangibility tends to increase the price for a product and the lack thereof decreases the price of a service. All other things being equal, if two financial institutions offer the same service, but one offers tangibility, that second institution can raise the price charged or lower the rate offered. In a nonfinancial realm, an educational institution which is accredited and offers a diploma, a tangible product certifying an intangible service, can charge more. Anytime a service is guaranteed in writing, a tangible evidence of worth, it is valued more highly by the consumer.

Thus, if financial marketers can achieve tangibility, then they can raise their prices. For example, customers who want a passbook account would be willing to accept a lower rate for the tangible satisfaction of having the passbook.

Regulation increases the price for services in relationship to products. Licensing, professional credentials, examination, and formal government regulation at both the federal and state level all increase price. As Milton Friedman says in his book *Free to Choose,* there are no free lunches. Regulation has a cost, the payment of which is incorporated into a higher price to the consumer.

The changing orientation of service industries toward marketing has an effect similar to duck hunting when the sky is filled with ducks. When you fire, you are bound to hit something. But as the number of ducks diminishes, your chances of being successful also diminish. Similarly, the managers of service industries going through deregulation, such as the airline industry, trucking, banking, and brokerage, face a situation in which their initial forays into marketing should enjoy a high degree of success. Customers in these industries are not used to formal marketing strategies and therefore should respond positively to even the most rudimentary marketing attempts.

But as deregulation continues, service marketing will have to improve in sophistication. For example, in the past, free checking accounts were widely available, and the marketing of the account was simple. Today, although the environment is much more complicated, offering free checking is still a viable strategy, if managed wisely and combined with a sophisticated marketing plan that takes into account all elements of distribution, research, training, and pricing.

In general, the still prevalent lack of marketing expertise in financial institutions will have a mixed effect on price. In some cases, it will drive prices up if management targets high value segments which are not price sensitive; in other cases, prices will drop because of management's inability to judge the value of new products or the strength of competitors and their impact on marketing directions.

Proximity generally increases the price for a service. Proximity is accomplished through either transporting the service to the customer or building a facility close to the customer. Both these options are high cost to the provider of the service, a cost which is passed on to the consumer.

The distribution methods most successful for financial services raise prices. Trained individuals are the most effective and the most expensive form of distribution, making services highly labor intensive. The cost of hiring, training, and perhaps transporting these sales personnel is passed on to the customer.

Finally, a relationship orientation has a mixed effect. The prices of individual products and services tend to be pushed down, but the overall price, or the profitability for the entire relationship, increases with a strong relationship. Customers who buy large volumes of products, or who buy a number of different products, generally are offered volume discounts or the supplier's best prices. The same holds for services, where the price of an individual service may be lower. However, the lower price is offered only because the seller can make high profitability on overall volume or by cross-selling other products or services.

The discounting of some services by financial institutions in order to obtain extensive relationships with particular households or companies is a frequent strategy. Consequently, some service products may have very thin or no profit margins while other service products have very profitable margins. Relationship pricing allows the financial service marketer this flexibility. If a customer is price sensitive on a particular service, then the bank or savings and loan can lower prices on that individual service. In the aggregate, however, the overall relationship would be profitable.

In summary, the differences between services and products impact marketing and pricing in a variety of ways. The impact of intangibility, regulation, marketing management, proximity, distribution, and relationships must be considered in total and factored into the overall pricing of financial products. Lacking an understanding of these differences or ignoring them can produce inappropriate pricing decisions.

UNIQUENESS OF FINANCIAL SERVICES

Not only do financial services differ from products but they differ from other services as well. These differences can be summarized into two unique characteristics:

- Financial service firms, especially those with lending powers, have the ability to create money.
- Financial service firms, especially those capable of taking in deposits, have the ability to accept balances as payment for services rendered.

Depository institutions have the unique ability to create money through what is called the multiplier effect. In its simplest form, the multiplier effect works as follows. Consumer X deposits $100 in Bank A. Bank A, after putting 8 percent of the deposit aside for reserves, lends out $92 to Consumer Y. Consumer Y takes the $92 and deposits it in Bank B. Bank B, after reserving 8 percent, lends out $84.64 to Consumer Z. And Consumer Z puts the $84.64 into Bank C. Now $276.64, or $100 plus $92 plus $84.64, is in circulation, all from the original $100. Thus the banking system has created money, an ability unique to the financial service industry.

In Chapter 6, we discuss the other unique characteristic of the financial service industry, and specifically depository institutions, that fees can be translated into deposit balances to pay for services. In financial service jargon, this is the ability to pay for a service with "soft dollars." Try to identify some other industry that has the ability to collect payment for its services in this form. The ability to use "soft dollars" or a compensating balance to pay for financial services is a unique characteristic of the industry.

These characteristics of the creation of money and the ability to pay for services with compensating balances are truly unique features which separate the financial institution industry from all other service industries. I have been told by an executive of a large non-bank firm that is heavily involved with financial services nationwide that one of the major reasons they wanted to get into the financial service business was because they could then accept payment in the form of compensating balances. This firm understands the uniqueness of banking.

SUMMARY

The differences between services and products present both opportunities and challenges to financial service marketers. The lack of tangibility creates the unique distribution system with its necessity for proximity and personal contact. The same lack of tangibility coupled with the highly liquid nature of most financial products created strong regulation, which in turn created a marketing myopia on the part of financial institution managements while they concentrated on growth. Finally, the personal selling requirement lends itself to the relationship approach often used by service industries. Firms that market financial services using approaches that deviate from these basic precepts will encounter difficulty.

These various characteristics tend, in general, to raise the prices of services. If financial institutions can manipulate the characteristics of services, they can keep profitability intact.

Finally, financial services differ from other services in that depository institutions can create money and can accept balances as a form of payment. These two unique characteristics affect price and can be used to the advantage of financial service pricers.

PART 2

Financial Service Pricing Principles

4

Economics of Pricing

If the nation's economists were laid end to end, they would point in all directions.

—Arthur H. Motley

Economic theory underlies pricing of any product or service including financial services. Microeconomics—the theory of the firm—and the theory of price are part of the general discipline of economics. The pricing principles derived from microeconomics are reflected in the classical supply and demand curves drawn by economists, which will be reviewed later in this chapter.

This book concentrates specifically on financial service pricing. There is no intention to supply a definitive work on either microeconomic theory or price theory; many books are available on general economics and price theory, from Dow Jones-Irwin and other publishers, a few of which are listed in the bibliography. Rather, some of the broader concepts of economics are covered here, focusing on those principles which are of primary importance when pricing financial services. First, the role that prices play in economic decisions will be discussed. Second, demand curves will be estimated for some financial services to help in understanding microeconomic theory as it applies to pricing financial services.

Since in financial services the product often *is* the price, pricing is the primary communication to your customer and the marketplace, and it is therefore vital to understand the impact of prices on volume and the development of demand curves which represent buying behavior of customers. An understanding of the behavior of the supply curve, which represents the intentions and behavior patterns of those who supply goods and services, is also important. However, the demand curve development and understanding is of more relevance to the pricing equation for you, the suppliers of financial services, and it is here where we will concentrate our efforts.

Milton Friedman, a Nobel laureate in economics, and his wife Rose, in their book *Free to Choose,* devote their first chapter to understanding the role of prices in economic theory. *Free to Choose* is the Friedman's personal statement about the explosion of laws, regulations, and government intervention in the "free market" economy and how these have constrained the freedom and prosperity of Americans. The Friedmans indicate that the role of prices is three-fold:

1. Transmission of information;
2. Incentives; and
3. Distribution of income.

TRANSMISSION OF INFORMATION

The transmission of information is "the ability to know." Information is needed to properly allocate resources, and this information is transmitted through the price mechanism. As prices rise, this transmits information that demand has risen. The information contained in prices tells you that someone is willing to pay more, so you may want to produce more to make more money. For financial products, transmission is relatively easy because of organized money markets. In the past, of course, prices may not have reflected accurate information because of regulatory interference with the free transmission of information. Does 5.25 percent really reflect the worth of deposits?

John Naisbitt in his popular book *Megatrends* stated, "One way to think of banking is as information in motion." If banking is information in motion, and one of the roles of pricing is to transmit information, then much of banking is defined by the prices of its products and services. When government Treasury bills are offered at a discount, for example, the essence of the product is money. The price conveys information concerning the value of money. Because a financial product often is price, its exchange—every time it's bought or sold—will transmit information. Many financial service products are defined by how they are priced.

The ability to know, or the transmission of information, is an essential role of pricing. Picture yourself driving down the highway. You look at the gas gauge and you see that you need gas. Your thoughts are then transferred to looking for information about where you can get gas. As you drive down the road, you see a sign that indicates a gas station is coming up where gas is $1.50 per gallon. You look at your gauge and think, I can drive a little bit further because the price is too high. Further on, you see another sign indicating a price per gallon of $1.40. You decide that this is an acceptable price and pull off. As you approach the exit, you see a sign that indicates that past this exit, a mile down the road, you can get a gallon of gas for $1.25. But you'll have to drive two miles out of your way for this gas. You decide that's OK to get another $.15 off on a gallon. The process could continue as you see more signs indicating lower prices. What is happening is that information is being transmitted via the price, which is creating incentives to deviate from your course of travel for the reward of paying a lower price for a resource you need.

In financial services, the transmission of information takes place constantly, such as by telephone between traders on the international level, or in its most common form, in the lobbies of most branches and facilities of banks and savings and loans. It is hardly possible to walk into a financial institution without seeing a lobby sign indicating the prices of various deposit services. Several companies are now providing an attractive and functionally efficient signage for financial institutions to transmit price information to their customers. Hopefully, this price information will give the customers incentives to act with that particular institution because they see that the price is better. In addition, the transmission of information is being done in a highly efficient manner, enabling the "information in motion" to move even faster.

INCENTIVES

Prices also furnish an incentive, which is "the ability to act." Once information is obtained, the consumer is presented with alternative actions. These actions are decisions that allow consumers to use information and make decisions that enable them to act in a way that they find economically advantageous. Price information gives the incentive to make decisions to allocate resources to the satisfaction of consumer needs. Knowing the information is generally not sufficient to precipitate action. A consumer must also have the incentive to act on the price information. Thus, the role of pricing is very much a relative position. That is, consumers have incentives when they know two or more prices for the same service. Consumers can then make a decision to accept that price which would give them the greatest benefit.

Going back to the auto example, you have now finally decided what price you're going to pay. As you pull into the gas station, you see that the price of $1.25 would be lowered to $1.20 if you pump the gas yourself. Do you pump gas to save another nickel? You have an incentive, furnished by price information, from the gas station owner, because if you pump your own gas, he can reduce his labor costs. Therefore, there is an incentive on both sides; the buyer saves money by pumping his own gas, and the supplier is willing to lower the price to keep labor costs down.

Of course, price is not the only incentive determining behavior. Satisfaction, ego, image, and risk all play a role. It is rare that the driver of a Cadillac will pump his own gas, or that people pump their own gas in the driving rain, or that a woman in a suit will pump her own gas.

Price incentive is the profit motive. It is the reward for seeking out the right product or service. After determining the highest interest rate being offered on a money market deposit account, you can act by opening an account at the selected depository institution. You are then rewarded by the interest income earned from the money market deposit account less the resources you've expended, such as time or transportation dollars, to gather the necessary information to open the account. So, the price must be sufficiently low to compensate for the extra effort and time required to seek out the information and to respond. Your reward is profit.

For example, many shoppers with frugal intentions will spend hours shopping every week to buy groceries at three or four different stores in an effort to pay the lowest price on a good or to use a coupon that reduces the price. These people don't factor in the added traveling costs involved to get these lower prices, namely, gasoline, wear and tear on the car, and time expended which might be more profitably put to use. For them, the reward is getting the lowest price at any cost. This illustrates the fact that rewards can be both financial in the form of increased profits and personal in the form of satisfaction. People will stay on a job that they don't like because they like the people they work with or the job is located in an area they like. So the profit motive is not the only incentive; there are many other determinants of behavior.

DISTRIBUTION OF INCOME

Finally, the distribution of income is "the ability to be rewarded" for what is valued most highly. Income distribution is based on the prices for your services or the capital resources you own. If your services are valued more highly, you will be paid more, and the prices of your services will reflect this. If the capital resources you own are valued more highly, then you will be paid more for the use of those resources. Prices distribute wealth into those areas which are valued more highly.

The reward a supplier or buyer receives closely relates to the distribution of income function of prices and the incentive function of prices. Not only does a manufacturer have the incentive to produce more for higher prices, but if he does produce more than the competition, he will get a bigger slice of the pie and receive more income.

These three functions of price work in tandem to produce buyer and supplier behavior. With financial services, buyers can "shop" for rate. They first get information on the level of prices, and if the price information is sufficiently attractive to them, they will buy that financial service. Those consumers with a larger amount of money, which is more highly valued by the industry than a smaller amount of money, will receive a better rate, and so the distribution of income will be in their favor. Suppliers, on the other hand, receive information on the general level of prices of money, and what they may have to pay. They have the incentives to structure their balance sheets in such a way as to fund as cheaply as possible and invest as dearly as possible. Those institutions whose services are more highly valued can get better rates for loans and so receive a larger share in the distribution of income.

FIGURE 4–1 Classical Supply and Demand Curves

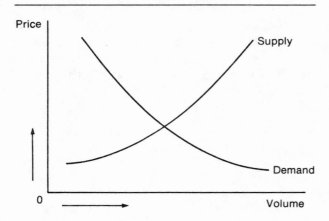

Thus, the three roles of prices are intertwined to produce economic behavior. Prices affect both buyers of financial services, or the demand side, and sellers of financial services, or the supply side. To further understand the economic role of prices, let's examine in greater detail the mechanics of supply and demand.

SUPPLY AND DEMAND

Shown in Figure 4–1 is the classical configuration of the downward sloping demand curve, from left to right, and the upward sloping supply curve, from left to right. Two variables, price and volume, define the behavior of buyers (who determine the demand for products and services), and sellers (who determine the supply of products and services). In supplying a service, financial institutions would like to sell as much as they can for the highest price they can get. Consumers of financial services, conversely, would like to get as much of a financial service as possible for as low a price as possible; they want high interest rates on deposits, no service charges, and low cost loans. A financial institution needs to decide at what level of volume it can supply the services to cover its costs and also provide a profit to itself as well as income to the owners of the financial institution.

If consumers demand more services than are supplied, the price will rise. If institutions provide more services than are

FIGURE 4–2 Safe Deposit Boxes
Estimated Demand Curve

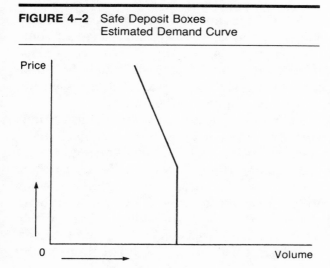

desired, the price will fall. The point at which the demand exactly matches the supply is called market equilibrium and is the point where the two curves cross. It is only at this point that price stabilizes or remains constant.

Let's use this basic economic theory of supply and demand, using the variables of price and volume, to examine the price behavior of several services offered by financial institutions.

Shown in Figure 4–2 is an estimated demand curve for *safe deposit boxes*. On the vertical axis is the price, increasing as one moves up the axis. On the horizontal axis is the volume, increasing as one moves to the right. The origin would indicate $0 price and 0 volume. As price increases from $0, volume remains steady at the capacity of the vault. As price moves even higher, volume starts to drop slightly.

The almost vertical line indicates that price has little effect on safe deposit box purchases by customers. As the price increases or decreases, there will be very little effect on volume. Economists call this "inelasticity of demand" or "price inelasticity," meaning that there is very little slope in the demand curve, and a price movement upward or downward will have little effect on volume.

The demand curve is shaped as it is because financial institutions are usually limited in the amount of space that they have available for vaults, and the vaults are limited as to the number of boxes available. This capacity problem is represented by the straight vertical portion of the demand curve. At some point, however, as the price rises, the line does start to slope toward the left, indicating decreased demand. Demand shrinks because, as the price increases, there are fewer customers willing to pay for the security of putting valuables in a box.

It is certainly incongruous that many financial institutions that offer safe deposit boxes will not use the price mechanism to adjust capacity constraints. They substitute waiting lists instead. Rather than increasing the price for a safe deposit box, the institution will keep the prices the same and make people wait in anticipation for someone to either leave the area or to die. This is communism at its best. The Soviet Union loves to dictate what it believes is proper allocation of goods and services. In the case of safe deposit boxes, financial institutions using waiting lists fall victim to the Marxist method of fixing prices and then allocating resources by edict instead of using the free market price mechanism to allocate. If institutions would raise their prices, demand for safe deposit boxes would start to taper off as customers began to explore alternative safe keeping services, thus easing the capacity constraint. In addition and most importantly, the institution would make more money through higher fees.

The demand for *printed checks* is estimated in Figure 4–3. The line is perfectly vertical, indicating that price has no effect on volume. As in the case of safe deposit boxes, volume is fixed regardless of price. In the case of deposit boxes, the position (not the slope) of this line was determined by the capacity of the financial institution; in the case of printed checks, the position of the line is determined by the number of checking accounts in the institution. It is extremely rare to have a customer close a checking account and leave a financial institution or not start a relationship with a financial institution because the price of printed checks, one of the components of a checking or NOW account, is too high. Many executives of financial institutions have found that the price of printed checks is almost perfectly inelastic.

It is interesting that some financial institution executives have found that when they raise the price of printed checks, it is not the customer who complains but rather the supplier of the printed checks. One institution doubled the price of its printed checks, which produced a substantial increase in fee income and

FIGURE 4–3 Printed Checks
Estimated Demand Curve

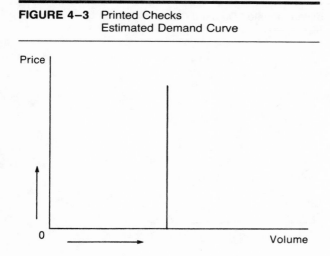

few complaints from customers. But the printer of the checks, a large national check printing firm, sent several of its people to the financial institution with questions regarding the level of price. It was in the check printing company's interest to keep check prices to the consumer as low as possible because substitutes were possible. If the price rose too high, the consumer might use less checks and use ATMs instead or other forms of electronic banking, lowering the income to the check printing company. The three functions of prices—information, incentive, and rewards—interacted here to produce very specific price behavior.

In Figure 4–4 is an estimated demand curve for *auto loans.* This is the classically shaped curve. At the top of the demand curve, the buyer of auto loans will seek substitute products, or sources of funds, perhaps getting the money from friends or relatives or not buying the car. At the other end of the curve, the cost of money is so low that a mad dash occurs to get auto loans, with people buying second cars they may not need, or trading in old cars ahead of their usual time.

In the early 1980s, with very high short-term interest rates, the auto markets were substantially affected. In addition, ancillary auto market products, such as gas and oil, were being affected by the oil embargos, which also caused consumers to curtail their buying decisions for automobiles. The automobile manufacturers in the early 80s tried to give the consumer an

---

FIGURE 4–4   Auto Loans Estimated Demand Curve

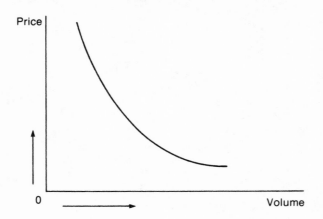

incentive to purchase autos by offering very low financing, such as 7.7 percent annual percentage rate. In most cases, this was successful because the auto manufacturers were able to counter their losses on financing by increasing the price of the car. This is an example of how the price for a good or service can be influenced by the price of another good or service.

In Figure 4–5, *passbook savings,* we have an example of price fixing. Through Regulation Q, federal regulators of banking services limited the amount of interest that is paid on savings accounts. Thus, price could not vary and therefore had no effect on volume. The economists would say that the price is totally elastic, meaning that any changes in volume are totally independent of price. Government in this case dictated what the price for a particular service could be. The effect of this was that bankers were used to obtaining low-cost funds. In the 60s and the 70s, the cost of a savings account was 3 percent to 5 percent.

However, with the advent of deregulation in March of 1980, many of the restrictions of Regulation Q were eliminated. What bankers and especially executives in the savings and loan industry saw was a substantial decrease of deposit money at low rates. This money transferred to higher rated certificate of deposit accounts. Simultaneously, the savings and loan industry had locked in long-term, fixed rates on mortgages. The result

FIGURE 4–5 Passbook Savings
Estimated Demand Curve

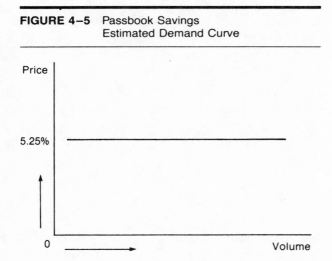

was a narrowing, and in many cases a reversing, of the spread that savings and loans had traditionally enjoyed between the dictated low-cost money under Regulation Q and what they could lend money for. Thus, as the "price fixing" behavior was eliminated for this product, about 25 percent of the savings and loan industry was consolidated or liquidated.

In Figure 4–6 is depicted *checking account* behavior. The convex curve flattens out both at its top and bottom. At the top end of the curve, consumers resist the high price and most find substitutes, such as cash or money orders. As the price slowly starts to decrease, volume picks up quickly as checking accounts are priced at the highest acceptable level. In the center of the curve, behavior is much like with other products, in that a decrease in price will result in an offsetting increase in volume. At the lower end of the demand curve, a vertical flatness appears, because even when checking account services are offered for free, there is a limit to how much demand exists; a consumer can use only so many checking accounts. Volume in total can now only increase by capturing customers from neighboring institutions. This is a limited tactic, however, because then the convenience/location factor comes into play. The incentive of having a free checking account will not induce all of the United States to go to the same financial institution, as other factors affect the incentive structure.

FIGURE 4-6 Checking Accounts
Estimated Demand Curve

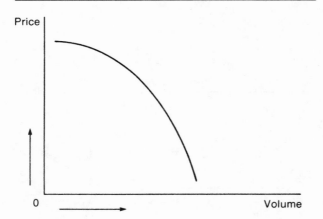

Our last figure, Figure 4-7, depicts the estimated behavior of *money market deposit accounts*. Here the financial institution is the buyer and establishes the demand, and the depositor is the seller and establishes the supply. When the interest rate on the account is very low, or approaches 0 percent, the demand from financial institutions is infinite as they compete to get these very low-cost deposit dollars. As the interest rate rises, the demand drops off. Finally, when the interest rate equals the price of other short-term funding available to financial institutions,

FIGURE 4-7 Money Market Deposit Accounts
Estimated Demand Curve

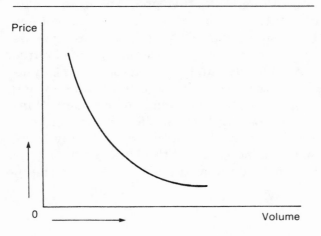

the demand virtually stops. So the demand has a definite cap or ceiling.

Other deposit products are similar. When the cost to financial institutions for funds is low, demand is very high. But as the rate institutions have to pay to secure funds rises, and as the rate approaches alternative sources of funds, the economic behavior of substitution appears with a vengeance.

There are short-term exceptions to this behavior. When money market deposit accounts were introduced in December of 1982, there were several depository institutions in the country which offered very high rates of interest, up to 40 percent, to provide incentives to consumers to move their money to those particular institutions. The strategy was to pay a high initial rate on the assumption that the money would stay with the institution at a much lower rate in the future.

In general, however, there are ceilings and floors to the demand for financial services. These must be understood and taken into consideration when estimating demand for services and when setting prices.

SUMMARY

In this chapter, we have described the role of prices in defining economic behavior. The role of pricing takes three forms: the ability to know or the transmission of information, the ability to act or incentives, and the ability to be rewarded or the income distributing role of prices.

Microeconomic theory, or the theory of price, is based on the theories of supply and demand, and is represented by supply and demand curves. Estimated demand curves were developed for several basic financial services which showed different aspects of consumer behavior. In some cases, the demand curves were inelastic because of capacity constraints or because only so much of the service could be used. In other cases, demand curves were very elastic, as in the case of governmentally established prices for savings accounts. A third type of behavior was examined for deposit products, depicting how rates for deposits begin to be edged out at the top end of the curve by alternative sources for funds, creating a very real ceiling on prices but one created by the free market mechanism rather than by "price fixing."

Economic behavior caused by supply and demand interaction was also examined. When prices are too high, substitution takes place. Capacity constraints can influence behavior, and capacity limitations are often inappropriately priced by using waiting lists rather than the price mechanism. Even a free product does not have infinite demand as consumers can stockpile only so much of a good or use only so much of a service. Finally, the price of ancillary products can also strongly influence the demand for the primary product.

Microeconomics is covered in great detail by many other books, and we suggest that the interested reader explore further. However, what has been covered here are the fundamentals of the very important effect on price caused by customer demand and the role of prices in determining consumer behavior. Much of what a financial marketer does revolves around the determination of quantifying customer demand for the services sold; therefore, it is highly useful to understand the underlying economics.

5

Cost Considerations

Kids are not encouraged to open savings accounts anymore because the banks say it costs them too much money to teach the kiddies savings habits.

Bill Granger, columnist, Chicago Tribune, 6/24/83

Winston Churchill, an eminently quotable statesman, was seated next to a woman at a state dinner who was considered a very attractive member of nobility. As the evening wore on, he found that the woman's intelligence and charm did not match her beauty, and Winston became disenchanted and bored. It was Mr. Churchill's style to consume large amounts of brandy normally, but on this occasion, he imbibed a bit more than usual. Finally, in the midst of a particularly boring discourse from the lady, he said, "Lady, you're ugly." To which the lady turned to Winston and said, "Sir Churchill, you are drunk!" Winston Churchill replied, "Yes, but in the morning I will be sober!"

Cost is the ugly side of the business, for both services and products. But it is essential in overall planning and for appropriate pricing. In our examination of cost, we will look at the position of costs in the pricing scheme, the common cost-plus pricing strategy, and the behavior of costs in financial institutions. We will concentrate on the economic side of costing rather than the accounting side, and will conclude with the implications of financial service costs on financial service pricing.

FIGURE 5-1   Comparative Income Statement—All Banks (Percent of Assets)

	1983	1982	1981	1980	1979
Interest income	11.06%	12.32%	12.03%	10.18%	8.85%
Interest expense	6.31	7.44	7.15	5.38	4.22
Net interest margin	4.75	4.95	4.93	4.83	4.65
Noninterest income	.57	.48	.54	.49	.47
Expense:					
Salaries	1.61	1.63	1.63	1.59	1.55
Occupancy	.46	.45	.43	.41	.39
Other	1.05	1.04	.99	.97	.93
Total expense	3.65	3.65	3.59	3.50	3.37
Net income	1.03	1.11	1.17	1.20	1.16

SOURCE: *U.S. Bank Performance Profile*, Bank Administration Institute, 1979–1983.

Joel Bleek and Jim Goodrich, in their *Wall Street Journal* article of December 7, 1981, called "Winners and Losers Under Deregulation," indicated that they and their colleagues at McKinsey & Company had found that a major trend of industries going through deregulation is that they exhibit rampant cost cutting. This was true for the airline, trucking, and security industry. But is it true of the banking industry?

Shown in Figure 5–1 are ratios on a consolidated basis for the entire banking industry for the years 1979 through 1983. The figures show that cost control appears to be present. From 1979 to 1980, costs rose over 11 percent; the next year, costs rose 3 percent, the next 2 percent, and the next year costs leveled off. So, although costs had been rising sharply, the cost control aspect of deregulation is beginning to apply to the banking industry as well. Cost cutting has not been dramatic, but it does appear to be present.

COST-PLUS

As will be explained in Chapter 11, where we discuss Quadratic Pricing, there are four major strategies of how to approach pricing. Cost-plus, where a profit margin is added to the cost of production, is one of these strategies, and a very common one. But is cost-plus a sound way to price? If General Motors were to build the best car they could, regardless of what the consumer wanted, their cost might be $30,000. It would probably be an outstanding car, but how many would GM sell if it were priced

FIGURE 5–2 Price and Cost

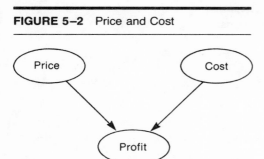

at $40,000? An understanding of consumer desires and the value attached to these are vital. And cost has no relation to this necessary external marketing analysis.

Costing is an internal analysis devoted to aiding the firm in its product planning, and it should be used primarily to answer the question of whether the company should be in this business or produce this product. If costs for producing a service are substantially above the rest of the suppliers of the service, then the firm must decide whether it is able to maintain a profit margin in relation to prices to competitively stay in the business. It could be that costs are substantially higher because the service is substantially better than what is being offered by the competition. This may limit the market for the sale of the good, but still may give the producer an opportunity to compete profitably. Rolls Royces, Cadillacs, and Lincoln Continentals are examples of products that are very costly to produce, are very expensive, and have limited markets. Yet these companies survive primarily because they produce a high-quality product.

Another way to look at the interaction of price and cost to determine profitability is shown in Figure 5–2. "Price" equals the revenue that the firm generates from the sale of its products or services. "Cost" equals the expenses that the firm incurs to produce those products or services. No linkage exists between price and cost, and they are not directly related. They are indirectly linked through profit and are essential components for determining profitability and the strategic direction of the firm. But they have no relationship directly, as shown in Figure 5–3.

Unfortunately, too many firms, not just financial institutions, operate under the assumption that costs plus a markup should equal their price. But this approach is devoid of all marketing

FIGURE 5–3 Price Does Not Equal Cost

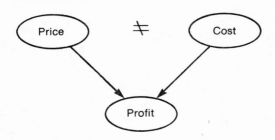

or customer satisfaction orientation. Government uses the cost-plus approach. Municipalities and Federal departments allow suppliers of goods and services to bid for projects based on their costs plus an allowable profit margin. This may be an acceptable approach for a nonprofit organization concerned with public policy, but it is not the way the free market works.

A further examination of the relationship between costs, prices, and profitability is shown in Figure 5–4. Price is the largest of the concentric circles and cost is the smallest of the circles. What is left over between the largest circle of price and the smallest circle of cost is profit. If the cost circle is larger than the price circle, as shown in Figure 5–5, a loss is generated.

If the cost is greater than the price, the firm can either raise its prices, lower its costs, or discontinue producing the product.

FIGURE 5–4 Price Minus Cost Equals Profit

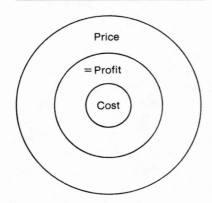

FIGURE 5–5 Cost Minus Price
Equals Loss

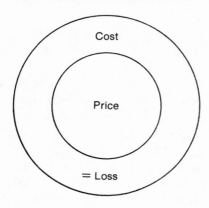

Raising prices is a marketing decision. Decreasing costs is an internal administrative decision. The firm could decide to do both, which are budgetary tactical decisions.

Or the firm could decide to sell this product or service at a loss under the strategies of either bundling or loss leader. Bundling has been, and to a large extent still is, a common strategy in financial service marketing. It is defined as the pricing concept that groups several different services or products and sells them for one price. Common in the brokerage industry for many years was the practice of offering research with transaction processing for one price for buying and selling securities. In the commercial banking industry, it was common for many years, until the mid to late 70s, to charge one price based on a loan rate and include operational and cash management services as part of the package. When using this bundled approach, it is possible to offer some products at what would be a loss on an individual basis.

The loss leader strategy is one which is very prevalent in the grocery industry. Milk and eggs are generally sold close to cost or below, because these items are needed on a day-to-day basis by most consumers. Grocery stores will boldly advertise the cost for milk and eggs because this draws customers into the store. The marketing tactic is to then induce the customer to buy other items with higher profit margins while in the store.

The loss leader strategy works well in a high transaction business. It can be deadly in businesses such as financial services which are more relationship oriented rather than transaction oriented. I used to have a manager in a large money center bank who always wanted to offer our operational services as loss leaders. His marketing memos would always include the fact that we must have "lost leaders." We did; the bank eventually got rid of him.

Numerous financial services are sold at very minimal margins or below costs at many financial institutions. For example, discount brokerage is gaining popularity with depository institutions. The commission structure for discount brokerage ranges from 20 to 40 percent of the total commissions being earned by the depository institutions that do not have their own discount brokerage operation. This is a skinny margin. In addition, those institutions that do have their own discount brokerage, such as Bank of America with Charles Schwab and First National Bank of Chicago with Pershing, are finding that these operations are very expensive because of the personnel and resources necessary to run the operation efficiently. They also find that revenue is barely able to cover costs.

Does that mean that these institutions should get out of this business? Most would say no. The discount brokerage service can be viewed as an opportunity to cross-sell other financial services such as self-directed IRA accounts which could substantially increase the profitability of the customer relationship.

For many years, banks offered free checking accounts as loss leaders in order to attract customers which they hoped would use other services of the bank. Also, many smaller banks offered trust services as loss leaders, which are expensive because these services are very labor intensive. The banks were trying to attract the high net wealth individuals of their marketplace in order to cross-sell other services.

It is common practice for the large money center banks to offer loans below market to their best customers. How can institutions offer these sub-prime loans? Because the loan is bundled into a relationship. The institution is usually obtaining other business in the form of balances or service fees sufficient to cut the rate to the customer and still make a profit. This is a technique often used with commercial customers, but it has seldom been used with consumers.

Cost-plus pricing is not an appropriate strategy for pricing products or services—especially financial services which are relational rather than transactional. *Costs should be used to calculate profit, but costs should not be used to set price.* Costs are important for planning to determine strategic directions for the financial institution and its products, but it is easy to get caught up in the intricacies of analyzing costs and make the great leap

---

FIGURE 5–6 Variable Costs

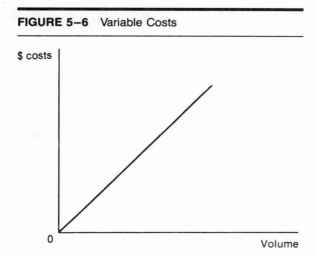

over the theoretical cavern to the conclusion that these theories pertain also to price. This assumption is invalid. The analyses of the behavior of cost is important for understanding how profitability is affected by different levels and types of costs as well as different levels and types of prices. But we reemphasize that costs are not directly related to pricing.

TYPES OF COST BEHAVIOR

In order to adequately control the profit margin with minimal risk, price behavior should generally follow cost behavior. There are three types of behavior which costs can exhibit: they can be variable, fixed, or semivariable.

Variable costs vary with the level of goods or services produced or sold. In Figure 5–6, for every unit increase in volume, quantity, or activity, total costs rise $1, creating a 45-degree angled line. The slope of this line can be different, of course, but the line always slopes upward as variable costs increase proportionately with volume increases.

For variable costs, total costs will increase in direct proportion to volume. But the cost of one unit will remain constant and, in our example, will always cost $1.

Examples of variable costs are part-time employees' salaries, electricity, postage, some data processing charges, and forms.

FIGURE 5–7 Fixed Costs

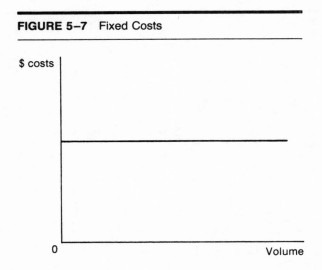

Fixed costs do not vary with volume. They remain fixed over a period of time and do not increase as the quantity of services sold or produced increases. Figure 5–7 shows fixed costs.

For fixed costs, total costs remain fixed as volume increases. But the cost of one unit decreases as volume increases. If costs are fixed at $10, the cost of one unit is $10. But the cost of two units is $5 per unit, and the cost of five units is $2 per unit.

Fixed costs for financial institutions include building, computer equipment, furniture, fixtures, software programs, the president's salary, and janitorial expense.

One of the key concepts of fixed costs is that they remain fixed only over a relevant range. If volume increases over that range, then costs jump up a tier. For example, a bank president's salary is considered relatively fixed, except for occasional salary adjustments, with a very wide relevant range. It will only vary perhaps five years from now when the bank holding company buys another institution, requiring a second president. A proof machine is also considered a fixed cost, but it has a much smaller relevant range. The cost of the machine doesn't vary as volume increases, but in six months, when volume has increased sufficiently to require a second machine, the cost doubles, creating a step function as illustrated in Figure 5–8.

Semivariable costs (sometimes called semifixed or mixed costs) include both fixed and variable elements. A good example is data processing costs. The cost of acquiring the computer hardware

FIGURE 5–8   Relevant Ranges

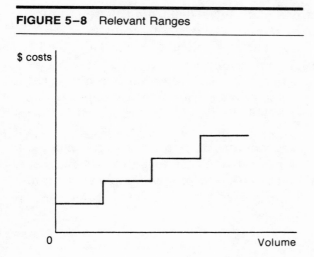

and software is fixed, not varying as use of the computer in-creases. However, on-line hookup to a data processing service or operation is usually charged based on the on-line time used. This is a variable cost. Thus, total data processing costs would dem-onstrate behavior as shown in Figure 5–9. Other examples of semivariable costs may include equipment rental, telephone costs, and salaried personnel subject to overtime.

Salary, wages, and benefits are included in all three types of cost behavior. This is because personnel expenses can vary con-

FIGURE 5–9   Semivariable Costs

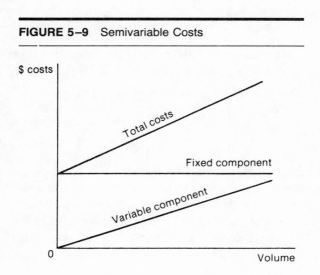

siderably. The bank president is needed from the time the bank opens until it closes. He or she is the chief executive officer and determines the strategy and the policy. But you only need two presidents if you acquire a second bank. In this case, salary is a fixed cost. Part-time tellers, on the other hand, are brought in to handle peak levels of activity throughout the business cycle. Sometimes they are needed, sometimes not, depending on the level of activity. Here, wages are a variable cost. If the bank requires a training program and hires a consultant for a fee to train employees in its newest IRA offering, this is a fixed cost. If that consultant also charges additionally based on the number of people who go through the program, this cost becomes a semi-variable personnel expense.

MOST COSTS ARE FIXED

Many costs for financial institutions are fixed, and constitute somewhere in the range of 20 to 60 percent of the total cost structure of most financial institutions. This means that volume considerations, which may change the relevant range or significantly increase or decrease the cost per unit, can have dramatic effects on the level of cost for a particular product.

For example, assume that the following conditions exist at a particular institution:

$$
\begin{aligned}
\text{Variable costs} &= 10{,}000 \text{ accounts} \times \$2 = \$20{,}000 \\
\text{Fixed costs} &= \$30{,}000 \\
\text{Total costs} &= \$50{,}000 \\
\text{Cost per account} &= \$5.00
\end{aligned}
$$

If the level of activity increases to 15,000 accounts, then the cost structure, as shown in Figure 5–10, would change as follows:

$$
\begin{aligned}
\text{Variable costs} &= 15{,}000 \text{ accounts} \times \$2 = \$30{,}000 \\
\text{Fixed costs} &= \$30{,}000 \\
\text{Total costs} &= \$60{,}000 \\
\text{Cost per account} &= \$4.00
\end{aligned}
$$

Since fixed costs represent such a high proportion of total costs, and since the behavior of fixed costs is such that unit costs decrease as activity increases, total costs per unit can also be expected to decrease as activity increases. Thus, the level of activity can have a dramatic impact on the cost per account assuming the relevant range is not exceeded.

FIGURE 5–10 Total Costs

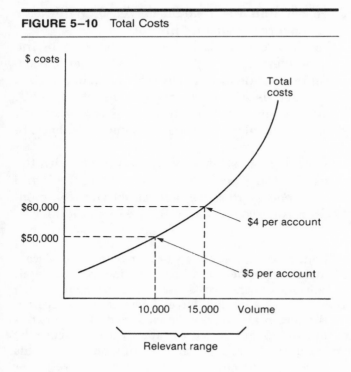

In Figure 5–10, notice that as we approach the right side of the graph, total costs begin to slope sharply upward. This is the point at which we encounter the top boundary of the relevant range. If we continued to increase volume, costs would jump to a higher tier and again exhibit a concave slope as volume approaches the next relevant range boundary.

The implications for a financial institution are that high volume is important to cover fixed costs. As volume increases, costs per account, per loan, or per investment offered decrease. This cost efficiency can then either be passed on to customers or can contribute to greater profitability for the institution.

ECONOMIES OF SCALE

Because many of the costs in banking are fixed costs, and therefore increases in levels of activity will decrease unit costs, the theory that there are economies of scale in banking has frequently been advanced. With ever larger amounts of deposits, fixed costs could be spread over a greater transaction and deposit base and therefore per unit costs would decrease. While this theory holds to some degree, it has its limitations.

Economies of scale are limited in banking because of the necessary personal delivery system discussed in Chapter 3. Also, the theory of economies of scale ignores the constraint of relevant range; when volume increases beyond certain transaction levels, fixed costs will also increase. And of course, as is the case with other types of firms, financial service institutions are subject to the law of diminishing returns.

If economies of scale do exist, it is more than likely with the smaller institutions. Preston Martin, Vice Chairman of the Board of Governors of the Federal Reserve, addressed the Commonwealth Club of San Francisco on March 9, 1984 as follows:

> The jury is still out on the question of whether economies of scale are generally important to the overall banking industry. In retail banking with multiple branches, costs have mitigated against such economies. However, some studies have shown that average operating costs (as a percentage of assets) appear to decline in banks with deposits of up to $75 million. Thrifts appear to experience the same phenomena until deposits reach $500 million. ... At this stage, however, the case has not yet been made conclusively that bigger is necessarily better in all submarkets."[1]

DIRECT AND ABSORPTION COSTING

Once costs have been classified by behavior, whether fixed or variable, they need to be aggregated to allow reporting by function. In order to do this, first a cost must be identified as a direct or an indirect cost.

Labor directly attributed to the production of a product is called direct labor. Material directly attributed to a product is called direct material. All costs not easily traceable to a product are called indirect costs or overhead. Overhead can be either fixed or variable. Examples of variable overhead include supplies or indirect labor. Examples of fixed overhead include rent, insurance, taxes, depreciation, and management salaries.

---

[1]Federal Reserve speech, "Darwinism and the Economic Evolution," March 9, 1984.

Direct costing is a method of determining the profitability of a product by taking into account only those costs that are directly attached to the production of the particular product. Therefore, to find the profitability of a product, only direct labor and direct material are subtracted from total revenue. For example, to find the profitability of cashing checks using direct costing, the direct costs of teller and teller supervisor salaries, and the costs of direct material in the form of supplies, forms, and perhaps the use of teller equipment would be subtracted from total revenues.

Absorption costing, also called full costing, determines the profitability of a product by taking into account all costs, including labor, material, and overhead. Overhead is "absorbed" or allocated to products by using various methods too detailed to present in this limited space.

The major difference between direct costing and absorption costing is that direct costing does not take into account overhead as a cost attributable to a product or service. Rather, direct costing concentrates on the "contribution" that is made by each unit, which is then used to cover total overhead.

Unfortunately, using direct costing for determining profitability of products and services emphasizes a short-term focus and can be misleading. The temptation is to establish prices which cover only direct costs of labor and material. However, most costs for financial institutions are fixed, and many of them are fixed overhead. Excluding overhead thus usually means that most costs will be excluded when determining profitability for a product. On the other hand, financial institutions should understand that fixed overhead is spread over a lot of different products, and eliminating a product that is unprofitable will usually not eliminate the fixed costs.

There is the case of a large regional bank that did not understand its internal cost structure. It had been very successful in providing correspondent banking services. Management determined that on a direct costing basis, in the short run, the service was making a contribution that could be applied to total overhead costs, and thus the service could be considered profitable. But in the long run, on an absorption basis, there appeared to be no profitability. The decision was made to leave the correspondent banking business, after providing this service for many years. It was assumed that the costs for this function would then be eliminated.

Some employees were laid off and some equipment was sold. Some costs did go down. However, most of the costs incurred by the correspondent banking function were fixed overhead costs such as building space, vice presidents' salaries, and furniture and fixtures. These costs did not go down, but rather had to be absorbed by other products of the bank. Consequently, since a revenue source had been eliminated but most of the fixed costs remained, total profitability was reduced. It was extremely difficult to correct this strategic mistake and reenter the market, and attempts since then have met with little success.

COST OF FUNDS

So far we have discussed primarily noninterest costs. However, the bulk of costs and most of the revenue of a financial institution are related to interest bearing instruments. The costs of these instruments is called the cost of funds. The cost of funds can be related to interest earned in two ways—using spread or using margin.

Spread is the weighted average difference between the interest rates associated with specific earning assets and paying liabilities. Net interest margin is the weighted average difference between the interest rates associated with all assets and all liabilities plus capital.

It is important to understand the difference between average and weighted average. Shown in Figure 5–11 is a balance sheet listing various interest rates for all assets and all liabilities and equity. The average rate for the assets, shown at the foot of the second column, is 11 percent. The average rate for the liabilities is 8 percent. Subtracting 8 percent from 11 percent gives us a margin of 3 percent. However, this figure has not been weighted for the dollar amounts in each category.

In Figure 5–12 is the same balance sheet with assets and liabilities broken into two columns, one for earning assets and paying liabilities, and one for nonearning and nonpaying. Earning assets total $90 million. Paying liabilities total $78 million. Weighting the rates of the earning assets by their dollar amounts, we get a rate of 11.09 percent. Weighting the paying liabilities, we get a rate of 7.90 percent. Since we are only dealing with earning assets and paying liabilities, subtracting these two rates will give us the weighted average spread of 3.19 percent.

FIGURE 5–11 Average Interest Rates

Assets:	Amount in $millions	Interest Rate
Cash and due from	$ 6	—
Fed funds	2	11%
Treasury bills	10	9
Agencies	10	10
Corporate	8	12
Commercial loans	30	13
Mortgage loans	20	8
Installment loans	10	14
Other assets	4	—
	$100	77% ÷ 7 = 11%
		= average rate
Liabilities/Equity:		
Demand deposits	$ 15	—
NOW accounts	8	5%
MMDA accounts	30	8
Savings	8	5
CDs	20	8
IRAs	4	10
Jumbo CDs	8	12
Capital	7	—
	$100	48% ÷ 6 = 8%
		= average rate

To calculate net interest margin, we include all assets and all liabilities and capital. Now the weighted average interest rates fall to 9.98 percent for assets and 6.16 percent for paying liabilities and capital, or a net interest margin of 3.82 percent. This is an increase of 82 basis points from our original un-weighted calculation and an increase of 63 basis points from the weighted spread calculation. When calculating rates, it is important to be clear about whether you're calculating spread or margin.

Spread is of course part of margin. Since spread includes only those assets and liabilities that are earning or paying an interest rate, and since net interest margin would include these items plus all other assets and liabilities and capital, then, by definition, spread is part of margin. Margin, as seen by the examples, can be heavily influenced by the nonrate elements of the balance sheet. Spread is only concerned with earning assets and paying liabilities.

FIGURE 5–12 Weighted Average Interest Rates

Assets:	Earning Assets in $millions	Nonearning Assets in $millions	Interest Rate	Weighted Average Rate
Cash and due from	—	$ 6	—	—
Fed funds	$ 2	—	11%	22
Treasury bills	10	—	9	90
Agencies	10	—	10	100
Corporate	8	—	12	96
Commerical loans	30	—	13	390
Mortgage loans	20	—	8	160
Installment loans	10	—	14	140
Other assets	—	4	—	—
	$90	$10		998

Weighted Average Rate to Calculate Spread = 998 ÷ $ 90 = 11.09%
Weighted Average Rate to Calculate Margin = 998 ÷ $100 = 9.98%

Liabilities/Equity:	Paying Liabilities in $millions	Nonpaying Liabilities in $millions	Interest Rate	Weighted Average Rate
Demand deposits	—	$15	—	—
NOW accounts	8	—	5%	40
MMDA accounts	30	—	8	240
Savings	8	—	5	40
CDs	20	—	8	160
IRAs	4	—	10	40
Jumbo CDs	8	—	12	96
Capital	—	7	—	—
	$78	$22		616

Weighted Average Rate to Calculate Spread = 616 ÷ $ 78 = 7.90%
Weighted Average Rate to Calculate Margin = 616 ÷ $100 = 6.16%

For pricing purposes, spread is a more appropriate measure to determine cost of funds. It is less subject to the fluctuations of nonearning assets and nonpaying liabilities or to the distortions caused by nonearning assets being supported by paying liabilities. A few examples will clarify the distorting influences upon margin.

If an institution can free up $1 million of nonearning assets by a reduction in float and invest those funds in earning assets with rates approximately equal to the weighted average rate, spread will remain the same. However, margin will increase because nonearning assets have been reduced and more assets now carry interest rates. Likewise, switching nonpaying liabilities to paying liabilities will reduce net interest margin. A common example is a reduction in demand deposit accounts, a nonpaying liability, with the full reduction going into an interest paying account such as a NOW account. Here, spread increases somewhat, but margin decreases significantly.

Margin is heavily influenced by nonearning assets and liabilities which do not carry a rate and therefore cannot be priced. These assets and liabilities should be excluded from rate related analyses. Therefore, it is more appropriate for the financial marketer to concentrate on spread, rather than margin, since the calculation of spread includes only those interest rate bearing assets and liabilities which are available for him to price.

FEDERAL RESERVE
FUNCTIONAL COST ANALYSIS

For 25 years, the Federal Reserve has been collecting the costs of financial services in banks of various size categories for the purpose of producing an analysis of costs by functions. The report of these analyses has come to be called the Federal Reserve Functional Cost Analysis. In 1984, over 500 banks and 60 savings and loans participating furnished data which the Federal Reserve used in its national study. This study is also summarized and tabulated for the individual banks for their use.

The Functional Cost Analysis (FCA) is a completely voluntary service. Institutions which participate must provide data in a stipulated form to the Federal Reserve. The data is collected by fiscal years and includes information on assets, income, expenses, and item counts collected by the institutions under the guidance of uniform procedures.

The FCA, although highly useful, does have some problems. First, the figures represent a sample rather than the total universe of all banks. Second, much of the data collection is performed by junior management or supervisory personnel. Third, the cost data is subject to judgment because many of the volumes are estimates. It can be difficult, especially in smaller institutions, to get accurate item counts of transactions, such as the number of checks that are cashed over the teller line. Finally, the costs are based on ledger balances, and ledger balances ignore such balance sheet items as cash items in the process of collection.

FIGURE 5–13   Checking Account Cost and Activity for Banks $50 to $200 Million in Deposits

Monthly cost:	1984	1983	1982	1981	1980	1979
On-us debit	15.9¢	15.9¢	15.3¢	13.4¢	11.8¢	11.0¢
Deposit	32.7¢	32.6¢	31.5¢	27.6¢	24.4¢	22.5¢
Transit check deposited	8.8¢	8.8¢	8.5¢	7.4¢	6.6¢	6.1¢
Account maintenance	$4.42	$4.40	$4.24	$3.67	$3.24	$2.98
Check cashing	29.1¢	28.9¢	27.8¢	24.3¢	21.5¢	19.8¢
Monthly activity:						
On-us debit	22.1	22.1	21.2	21.8	20.6	21.1
Deposits	4.1	4.1	3.9	3.9	3.6	3.7
Transit checks	20.8	21.8	22.2	21.5	19.6	20.4

SOURCE: *Functional Cost Analysis.* New York: The Federal Reserve, 1979–1984.

However, the FCA is the only viable analysis available on costs in the industry. While the FCA is subject to the flaws and errors of individual institutions, many institutions invest considerable time and effort to produce very usable data. The validity of the data due to the size of the sample is fairly accurate, costs and item counts are usually checked by senior officers, and variances are generally within plus or minus 10 percent of an institution's true costs.

The FCA analyzes individual financial products. For example, in Figure 5–13 are the Functional Cost Analysis checking account costs by different item costs for the last six years. Listed are on-us debits (checks from this bank), deposits, transit checks (checks from another bank), maintenance, and the cost of cashing checks in person. The difference in cost between an on-us debit from 1979 to 1984 is 4.9 cents, or approximately a 45 percent increase in check processing costs in this six-year period. The trends for other costs are very similar. Thus, it appears that the costs for checking accounts have been increasing, but the rate of increase is slowing, as discussed earlier in this chapter. In addition, the trend indicates that banks must keep a careful eye on the prices to their customers if they are to maintain profitability. If your prices for the processing of checking accounts have not increased at least 45 percent between 1979 and 1984, then, assuming your costs closely match the FCA costs, the profitability of your checking account service could be narrowing.

In addition, Figure 5–13 shows activity for checking account transactions. The number of checks written on the average account has risen slightly to just over 22. Thus, customers are not

---

FIGURE 5–14 Overhead Rates

	Under $50 million deposits	$50–$200 million deposits	Over $200 million deposits
Personal checking account	46.6%	48.8%	53.2%
NOW account	52.9	49.5	50.5
Special	42.9	51.1	44.7
Commercial	23.6	19.4	19.3
All transaction accounts	45.9	42.1	40.9

SOURCE: *Functional Cost Analysis*. New York: The Federal Reserve, 1984.

---

giving up paper checks, and the much ballyhooed checkless society predicted in the 60s, 70s, and 80s is far from a reality. The implication for pricing is that the paper check will be with us for a long time, and bankers should price this product accordingly. Also, pricing of electronically based products such as ATM accounts is difficult since acceptance of the paper check is still very strong.

Another use of the Functional Cost Analysis is to analyze overhead rates. As overhead is usually fixed, an analysis of fixed costs can estimate overhead. Dividing the account maintenance cost by the total expense for a transaction account gives a close approximation of fixed checking costs, and therefore overhead. In Figure 5–14 are listed these overhead percentages, by three different size institutions, for personal checking accounts, NOW accounts, special accounts (where fees are charged for all checks written), commercial accounts, and for total transaction accounts.

Notice that overhead for checking accounts in general is a smaller percentage of costs for larger institutions than for smaller. This is primarily because larger institutions have a much higher concentration of activity in commercial accounts, which produce lower fixed costs and more variable costs.

Another use of the Functional Cost Analysis is to compare the different amount of costs connected with the various functions in an institution. Shown in Figure 5–15 is a breakdown of costs, such as salaries, data processing, and marketing, by size of institution. When these cost categories are compared across sizes, it is interesting to note that external expenses, such as computer service bureaus, are higher for the smaller banks since the larger banks have access to their own staffs.

FIGURE 5–15 FCA Costs by Function

Expense Detail	Net Earning Summary 145 Banks Deposits Up to $50M		280 Banks Deposits $50M–200M		84 Banks Deposits Over $200M	
	Percent of Operating Expense					
Operating Expenses						
1 Officer salaries	$ 254,973	18.63 %	$ 785,803	17.62 %	$ 3,175,142	15.58 %
2 Employee salaries	240,966	17.61	880,682	19.74	4,518,548	22.17
3 Fringe benefits	109,837	8.02	383,374	8.59	1,818,348	8.92
4 Salaries and fringe, subtotal	$ 605,776	44.27 %	$ 2,049,861	45.96 %	$ 9,512,039	46.67 %
5 Off-premise computer expense	$ 67,028	4.89 %	$ 176,270	3.95 %	$ 725,554	3.56 %
6 Furniture and equipment	89,230	6.52	314,483	7.05	1,468,275	7.20
7 Printing, stationery and supplies	41,327	3.02	131,115	2.94	609,894	2.99
8 Postage, freight, and delivery	31,147	2.27	90,041	2.01	430,346	2.11
9 Publicity and advertising	33,215	2.42	111,447	2.49	548,772	2.69
10 Fees, legal & other (incl hold co mgmt fees)	24,577	1.79	115,818	2.59	656,587	3.22
11 Telephone and telegraph	17,665	1.29	67,257	1.50	400,003	1.96
12 Occupancy	98,717	7.21	374,320	8.39	1,667,086	8.18
13 External examinations and audits	19,967	1.45	53,135	1.19	119,301	.58
14 Director fees	20,379	1.49	47,208	1.05	107,019	.52
15 FDIC insurance	24,204	1.76	77,910	1.74	326,643	1.60
16 Other insurance, except realty, life,etc	13,368	.97	29,601	.66	81,754	.40
17 Travel	10,246	.74	32,002	.71	157,746	.77
18 Dues and memberships	7,497	.54	20,898	.46	65,017	.31
19 Donations and gifts	5,411	.39	14,869	.33	53,836	.26
20 Books, period., info. svcs	3,554	.26	12,365	.27	38,803	.19

21	Loan losses	121,256	8.86	400,978	8.99	1,569,134	7.70
22	Computer software expense	3,629	.26	9,470	.21	69,060	.33
23	All other expenses	130,010	9.50	330,494	7.41	1,772,704	8.69
24	Total operating expense	$ 1,368,213	100.00 %	$ 4,459,550	100.00 %	$ 20,379,584	100.00 %
	Memoranda						
25	Off-premise computer expense	$ 67,028	4.89 %	$ 176,270	3.95 %	$ 725,554	3.56 %
26	Computer software expense	3,629	.26	9,470	.21	69,060	.33
27	*On-premise computer expense	37,705	2.75	228,177	5.11	1,731,370	8.49
28	Total expenditure for data services	$ 108,362	7.92 %	$ 413,919	9.28 %	$ 2,525,985	12.39 %
	Interest Expense						
29	Demand deposit interest	$ 266,710	.702 %	$ 731,678	.581 %	$ 2,293,176	.419
30	Time deposit interest	1,995,640	5.252	6,291,291	4.995	25,607,123	4.682
31	Non-deposit interest	367,391	.967	1,761,645	1.399	9,429,156	1.724
32	Total interest expense	$ 2,629,743	6.920 %	$ 8,784,615	6.975 %	$ 37,329,457	6.825 %
	Miscellaneous Data						
33	Personnel / $million A/F	.82		.80		.84	
34	Number of banking offices	2.04		4.53		21.35	
35	3 year loan loss avg / avail funds	.297 %		.283 %		.262 %	

*Included in several operating expenses.

SOURCE: *Functional Cost Analysis.* New York: The Federal Reserve, 1984.

FIGURE 5–16 FCA Costs for Regular Checking
($50–200 million deposit size banks)

	Cost	Monthly Activity	Cost times Activity
On-us debit	$.16	18	$2.88
Deposit	.33	3	.99
Items deposited	.09	3	.27
Checks cashed	.29	1	.29
Account maintenance	4.42	1	4.42
Total cost			$8.85

SOURCE: *Functional Cost Analysis*. New York: The Federal Reserve, 1984.

FIGURE 5–17 FCA Costs for NOW Accounts
($50–200 million deposit size banks)

	Cost	Monthly Activity	Cost times Activity
On-us debit	$.16	16	$2.56
Deposit	.33	3	.99
Items deposited	.09	3	.27
Checks cashed	.29	1	.29
Account maintenance	4.42	1	4.42
Total cost			$8.53

SOURCE: *Functional Cost Analysis*. New York: The Federal Reserve, 1984.

FIGURE 5–18 FCA Costs for Regular Savings
($50–200 million deposit size banks)

	Cost	Yearly Activity	Cost times Activity
Deposit	$.80	6	$4.80
Withdrawal	1.54	5	7.70
Interest posting	3.02	4	12.08
Account maintenance	20.48	1	20.48
Total cost			$45.06

SOURCE: *Functional Cost Analysis*. New York: The Federal Reserve, 1984.

Cost information is useful for determining profitability of products, as mentioned earlier. In Figures 5–16, 5–17, 5–18, 5–19, 5–20, and 5–21 are examples of product costing using the Functional Cost Analysis.

FIGURE 5–19 FCA Costs for Statement Savings
($50–200 million deposit size banks)

	Cost	Yearly Activity	Cost times Activity
Deposit	$.80	6	$4.80
Withdrawal	1.54	5	7.70
Interest posting	3.02	12	36.24
Account maintenance	20.48	1	20.48
Total cost			$69.22

SOURCE: *Functional Cost Analysis*. New York: The Federal
Reserve, 1984.

In Figure 5–16, average monthly activity in a checking account is multiplied by the costs reported in the Functional Cost Analysis. Total cost for an average checking account for a bank between $50 and $200 million in deposits is $8.85. The average cost for a NOW account, shown in Figure 5–17, is $8.53, or about 4 percent lower. Although the FCA does report the interest expense associated with a NOW account, the figures used here report only the noninterest expense; if interest expense were added in, it would substantially increase the cost for the NOW account. Annualizing these figures, checking and NOW account costs average over $100 yearly.

Figures 5–18 and 5–19 list the costs for regular (passbook) savings and statement savings. Passbook savings costs total $45.06, while statement savings costs total $69.22. The difference in cost is caused by the different number of interest postings. Passbook interest postings are quarterly, while statement savings are usually posted monthly, adding costs of over $24. It has been argued that a passbook savings account has higher interest posting costs, but when mailing and handling costs of a statement savings account are added, statement savings is probably more expensive. Noted in previous chapters was our skepticism with the common belief that passbooks can no longer be offered because of their higher expense; the Functional Cost Analysis supports our conclusion.

Shown in Figure 5–20 are the costs of a six-month $10,000 Certificate of Deposit (CD) for banks between $50 and $200 million in deposits. The costs include opening and closing, the initial deposit, the withdrawal at the end of the period or the month, interest posting, and account maintenance for one-half year. Total costs for a CD with interest paid at maturity are $20.08,

FIGURE 5–20 FCA Costs for 6-Month $10,000 Certificates of Deposit ($50-$200 million deposit size banks)

	Interest at Maturity			Interest Monthly		
	Cost	Activity	Cost times Activity	Cost	Activity	Cost times Activity
Account opening	$ 4.88	1	$ 4.88	$ 4.88	1	$ 4.88
Deposit	.79	1	.79	.79	1	.79
Withdrawal	1.54	1	1.54	1.54	6	9.24
Account closing	2.84	1	2.84	2.84	1	2.84
Interest posting	3.02	1	3.02	3.02	6	18.12
Account maintenance	14.02	.5	7.01	14.02	.5	7.01
Total cost			$20.08			$42.88
Interest equivalent			.40%			.86%

SOURCE: *Functional Cost Analysis.* New York: The Federal Reserve, 1984.

FIGURE 5–21 FCA Costs for Installment Loans for Autos
($50–$200 million deposit size banks)

	Paper Payment	Electronic Payment
Cost to make	$ 74.18	$ 74.18
Cost to collect—48 × $5.79	277.92	138.96
	$352.10	$213.14
Interest equivalent (reduced yield)	2.20%	1.33%

SOURCE: *Functional Cost Analysis.* New York: The Federal Reserve, 1984.

while the cost of processing a monthly check for this same CD increases the cost to $42.88.

Shown at the bottom of Figure 5–20 is the interest equivalent of these noninterest costs, which was calculated by dividing the cost (times 2 to annualize it) by $10,000. For the CD which pays interest at maturity, the interest equivalent is 40 basis points, while for the CD which pays interest monthly, the interest equivalent is 86 basis points.

In order to maintain profitability on CDs, this processing cost must be taken into consideration. Customers who prefer interest monthly could be offered a lower interest rate. Here is an example where cost-plus pricing considerations provide useful insight to allow the marketer to influence pricing behavior.

Finally, in Figure 5–21, the costs for processing an installment loan, assuming a 48-month term, total $352.10. If customers agree to have payments deducted automatically from a checking account, this is estimated to reduce the cost to collect by 50 percent, lowering the total costs to $213.14. If we assume that an automobile costs approximately $10,000, which is what the Federal Reserve statistics indicate, and the monthly down payment is 20 percent, which has been found by "Pricing $trategy" newsletter to be the most common down payment percentage, and if the term is 48 months with a rate of 12 percent interest, then a rough calculation for the interest equivalent for the cost to process an installment loan would be 220 basis points [($352.10 ÷ 4 years) ÷ ($8,000 ÷ 2)]. For the electronic payment, the interest equivalent is 133 basis points [($213.14 ÷ 4 years) ÷ ($8,000 ÷ 2)].

Again, the implications for the financial marketer are numerous. Can the customer be persuaded to pay for auto payments with automated debits to a checking account? If so, value to the institution in the form of reduced costs is present which can be passed on to the customer in the form of a reduced rate. If the customer prefers a coupon book, this higher cost loan should carry a higher interest rate to protect the yield to the bank.

Also, the cost to process an installment loan is probably more expensive than financial institutions realize. This cost reduces profitability unless prices can be increased to compensate. With the strong competition from the captive auto finance companies such as GMAC providing low rates of interest, financial institutions may want to consider their strategies in the auto loan market.

The FCA can be used in a variety of ways to assist in pricing of products. While it has its limitations, these can be overcome with appropriate use of the analysis. The FCA can be used strategically for evaluating the implications of costs and cost control, for product planning to determine whether or not institutions want to stay in particular product lines, and finally as input into what the appropriate pricing behavior can be for products based on their use and value to the consumer.

SUMMARY

Costs are a key component for determining profitability. But they have no direct relationship to prices. Although a cost-plus pricing approach can be useful for analyzing profitability, it is not an appropriate pricing strategy for financial products.

Costs can demonstrate variable behavior, fixed behavior, or semivariable behavior. Most of the costs for financial institutions are fixed and are included in overhead. The pricing of products should cover these fixed costs.

Direct costing, which considers only those costs directly attributable to a product or cost center, is useful for determining the incremental contribution generated by a product or service. But its use should be restricted to internal applications. Absorption costing, which assigns all costs including overhead to products, is far more useful for financial institutions, especially since so many of their costs are fixed overhead.

The use of spread takes into account the weighted average rates of interest for earning assets and paying liabilities. Spread, as well as net interest margin, is a major tool for pricing purposes.

Finally, financial institutions have a decided advantage when performing cost analyses because of the availability of the Functional Cost Analysis. This analysis provides a good approximation of costs by size of institution and for various types of products, and can be used not only for product analysis but also for strategic analysis.

An analysis of cost behavior can furnish information to financial institution marketers of how costs will affect profitability. Also, the behavior of costs can be examined in conjunction with the use of products by the consumer to analyze behavioral patterns which can then be used for pricing purposes.

In conclusion, analysis of costs is necessary and useful, but it should be remembered that costs have no direct relationship to price.

6

Fees versus Balances

We all know how the size of sums of money appears to vary in a re-markable way according to whether they are being paid in or paid out.

—Julian Huxley

In 1975 my wife and I moved from Illinois to California for a few years. Even though we had been married only three years, we had accumulated what I called a lot of junk and what she called "memorable treasures." We had to reduce our load to bring it within the acceptable weight limit for the move. We came up with the idea of having a party for our friends, which would get us all together for the last time and, unknown to them, solicit their help in parting with some of our junky treasures. We wrapped our life jackets, rattan baskets, and dart boards in news-paper, and as each guest arrived, they received one of these presents.

However, few were fully pleased with what they had acquired through the luck of the draw. Each guest started eyeing someone else's treasure. Very few had much cash on hand, so alternative forms of payment had to be found. Everyone started to barter. Long chains of negotiations took place. Some doctor friends of ours had received a small vacuum cleaner for which they had no use. But they wanted the two brand-new life jackets which they could use on their brand-new boat. Unfortunately, the cou-ple who had the life jackets were not interested in the vacuum cleaner. Neither of them had cash to use in the transaction. The doctor couple was determined and set out during the evening to find out what the people who had the life jackets wanted. It turned out that what they wanted was a leather bowling ball bag, but not the bowling ball inside. The doctors figured out that the people who had the leather bowling ball bag really wanted a crocheted pillow. But the people who had the crocheted pillow didn't want the leather bowling ball bag either; they wanted a metal mailing container. And so it went all evening. The doctors figured out a chain of about five transactions which eventually got them their life jackets.

Just as these party guests used an alternative form of payment, financial institutions, as mentioned earlier, also have the ability to accept an alternative form of payment. Their customers can pay not only directly with coin or currency, but indirectly with balances that are kept on deposit. Balances are an indirect form of payment rather than a direct exchange, and financial institutions are the only businesses that can use this payment mechanism.

FORMS OF PAYMENT

Payment for goods or services can take many forms. Bartering is but one way to pay for goods. It is probably the oldest form and still exists today, although the more sophisticated term of "counter-trade" is now used. According to a report prepared in May of 1984 for the members of the General Agreement on Tariffs and Trade (GATT), barter may represent as much as 40 percent of world trade.

Coin and currency are the most classical form of payment. Coin (gold and silver minted pieces) is probably as old as bartering as a way to transfer value. Currency (paper specie signifying a promise to pay by a government) is one of the easiest forms because the difficulty of storage and bulk is eliminated. This way is sometimes too easy when the printing presses start running quickly.

Another form of payment is by check or draft. The personal check mechanism has only come into relatively common usage since the end of World War II. Official item checks are similar, such as cashier's checks, money orders and certified checks, most of which are required when the payor is unknown to the payee.

Drafts also fall into this category; a draft differs from a check in that a draft is not as closely defined and is a more flexible instrument. It does not have to be drawn upon a bank but rather may direct one party to pay another; it may not be a negotiable instrument in that it does not meet the "four corners rule," which specifies that in order to be negotiable a draft must specify no conditions that extend beyond its own four corners; and it may be payable on demand or at a specified time in the future.

Credit cards constitute another form of payment. Originally started by retail merchants to stimulate sales of their goods, credit cards such as MasterCard, Visa, and American Express now account for a huge percentage of transaction business worldwide. While the credit card was intended to be, as its name implies, a device for accessing a line of credit which would enable the buyer to purchase a good or service, it has become a transfer of value mechanism. About 50 percent of credit card transactions do not constitute credit. That is, the purchaser has no intention of paying interest for the use of another's money to make a purchase, but rather is using the credit card to facilitate a transaction. Many financial service companies find that a credit card is used for a third purpose, that is, as a means of identification of the customer.

Another method to make payments is via electronics. Automated teller machines allow customers to cash a check and make payments, such as for loans or utility bills. Point of sale devices are very similar in nature. Also, preauthorized drafts can automatically charge a checking account, using a paperless debit, at a financial institution based upon a standing authorization from the customer.

Finally, a requirement for payment can be met via credit, using either a direct loan for personal or commercial purposes or, as we noted above, a credit card. In addition, many people use unsecured credit with financial institutions by using float, which is cash items in the process of collection. The classical example of using float happens every Friday when customers bring in their paychecks at the end of the day. Financial institutions, usually the depository for the customers, take part of the paycheck in as a deposit and in many cases give part of it back as cash. This is known as a "split deposit with cash back." But when do most of those paychecks clear through the payment system? Often not until Tuesday morning. These customers, from Friday night until the bank receives payment on Tuesday almost two and a half days later, have enjoyed a loan from the bank which was not applied for or approved on a formal basis.

All of these mechanisms of payment are direct means. Barter, coin, currency, check, credit card, electronic debit, and loans are termed "hard dollar" payments for services and goods that are purchased. "Hard dollar" signifies that some form of direct payment must be received for the transaction.

If the supplier of the service is a financial institution with depository capabilities, then an additional form of payment, called "soft dollars," is available. If an institution requires that a customer leave noninterest bearing balances, or balances that carry less than a market rate of interest, then value is given to the financial institution because it can invest these balances in earning assets to earn additional revenue. The value received by the financial institution can be accredited to the depositor and used to offset charges for services.

This, fundamentally, is the concept of fees and balances. It is the concept which makes the business of banking unique from all other types of services. A financial institution can require that a balance be maintained for a period of time in an account that does not bear interest or is below the market rate of interest and can structure the arrangement in such a way that it can achieve the same level of compensation as it would through direct payment. This uniqueness of banking was first identified in Chapter 1 and is fundamental to pricing financial services.

The use of balances is the major reason why many nonbanking firms want to get into the banking business. Think of the possibilities for Sears if their customers, 36 million American households, were able to pay for goods and services with excess balances maintained with the Sears Financial Network. For example, if a customer had overpaid his credit card account with Sears on which, let's assume, Sears was allowed to pay interest or give an earnings credit, then the customer may not have to pay in hard dollars for the next item purchased.

William F. Ford, past president of the Atlanta Federal Reserve Bank, in a speech at the American Bankers Association's correspondent banking conference, suggested some slogans for Sears:

"Buy your stocks where you buy your socks."
"If you lose your shirt, we'll sell you another one."

"Chop your taxes where you buy your axes."
"Buy your house where you bought your blouse."[1]

Other nonbanking firms wanting to expand into the banking business have the same motive. Merrill Lynch has already initiated a market thrust with their Cash Management Account. Think of the endless possibilities that Merrill Lynch can offer its customers with this concept of maintaining a level of balances in some depository account directly controlled by Merrill Lynch. For example:

- You want financial advice; just leave $5,000 in a noninterest bearing checking account with Merrill Lynch.
- You do not want to pay transaction fees for stocks and bonds purchases; just leave $30,000 in a noninterest bearing checking account.
- You want research available to diagnose various investments; just leave $10,000 or more in a Merrill Lynch checking account.

Using balances to pay for services of course requires that the customer maintain a noninterest bearing, or low-interest bearing, checking account. Then, the interest the institution earns from investing the balances can be split between the depositor and the institution. If the institution were to pay the depositor a money market rate of interest, there would be no interest earned left for the benefit of the institution.

Offering this payment mechanism to a purchaser of financial services has other benefits besides payment for services. It requires that a checking account be opened. This means that the depositor purchases an additional product from the financial institution, strengthening the relationship. This concept of relationship selling will be explored further in Chapter 11 on Quadratic Pricing.

Although this pricing mechanism can be used as a unique advantage, it is sometimes overlooked. In the May 1984 issue of "Pricing $trategy" newsletter, it was noted that approximately 2 percent of the banks that had offered noninterest bearing checking accounts no longer did so, and that 80 percent of the savings and loans that could offer this account did not do so. This ignores one of the most fundamental principles of banking, and fails to exploit this unique advantage. The use of balances

---

[1]"Fed's Ford Provides Light Touch with Upbeat Speech to Conference," *American Banker,* November 23, 1981.

as a form of payment is an attractive option for many customers. It is also a concept that has been limited to the commercial side in the past, where this form of payment is called "compensating balances." Thus, unexplored opportunities exist on the consumer or retail side.

UNBUNDLING

In their landmark work in 1972 Bryan and Clark, officers of the State Street Bank in Boston, published an article which was later transcribed into a book, called "Unbundling Full Service Banking." Bryan and Clark suggested that banks should start to "unbundle" or charge explicit prices for all commercial services and products being offered. This concept was applied by many banks on the corporate and commercial level by taking a product perspective and pricing individual services on a stand-alone basis.

There are three basic arguments for the payment of fees instead of balances for services, as suggested by Bryan and Clark. First, a treasurer could employ cash balances more profitably in other ways than to pay for services. Since 1962 when Citibank began offering the large denominated negotiable certificate of deposit, a wide variety of instruments has been made available to corporate treasurers for short-term investment. Many of these instruments, especially in the 1970s and the early 1980s when rates were at very high levels, offered corporate treasurers better returns for their balances than the earnings credit that the banks were giving for compensating balances. The second argument states that, when a payment is made by leaving balances, the customer can lose tax benefits. If a fee is paid, then the corporation can apply its tax rate to reduce the impact of the fee. Finally, the fractional reserve system of the United States produces friction in the system. All depository institutions are required to maintain reserves with the Federal Reserve, as dictated by the Depository Institutions Deregulation and Monetary Control Act of 1980, enacted in March. Thus, when you leave balances with your bank, the bank sets aside a percentage of the balances (up to 12 percent) as a reserve with the Fed, and then gives you earnings credit on the remainder. You thus lose getting full benefit for every dollar left with a bank or thrift.

These are valid points against using balances as a form of payment, but there is another side to the coin. Although companies can invest their dollars elsewhere, some companies do not have the time, inclination, or ability to invest their excess dollars properly. In addition, some companies do not have the sizable amounts needed to earn market rates of return for their short-term investments. Much commercial paper and other short-term investments offer market rates only for multiples of $1 million. Under this level, rates are less and do not equate to market returns.

Second, although fees are tax deductible and balances are not, if a corporation is not in a fully taxable position, or pays no taxes, then the tax advantage of paying a fee as opposed to leaving balances is reduced or lost.

Finally, the fractional reserve system does produce a "friction" in the system, and thereby requires more balances to equate with the comparable fees. This is probably the most legitimate argument against the use of balances. But this impact can be offset by those institutions that do not have high levels of reserves because of a small amount of transaction accounts, such as demand deposit accounts, and who pay for reserves with vault cash.

Thus, a strong case can be made for offering the balance payment mechanism to smaller commercial firms that do not have the expertise or amount of investment dollars to earn truly competitive market yields on their excess funds, are not in a fully taxable position, or deal with institutions which pay very little or nothing in reserves.

EQUATING FEES AND BALANCES

There are four components necessary to calculate the equivalency of balances and fees. These components will be defined and explained in detail. The interrelationships among them and the impact of each factor will be discussed. And finally, the formulas used to equate a fee into a balance and vice versa will be presented.

The four components, or independent variables, required to equate a fee into a balance are:

- The price or fee;
- An annualization factor, which is a constant, to equate all terms to the same time frame;
- An earnings credit rate;
- Adjustments.

Algebraically, if the values for these four are known, the fifth or dependent variable, the balance equivalent, can be calculated. To calculate a fee as the dependent variable, the balances maintained substitute for fees as the first independent variable.

Price/Fee

The first component of the equation is the price of the service or product. If you were to pay hard dollars in the form of check or currency, then what would be the fee that you would have to pay? If the service being purchased is a checking account and the fee is $5 per month, then the fee to be used in the equation is $5.

Annualization Factor

Two of the factors, the earnings credit rate and the adjustment percentage, are usually stated as yearly figures. Therefore, in order to place all components of the formula on the same time basis, it is necessary to have an annualization factor for periodic payments. If a checking account has a $5 monthly fee, to equate this into a balance equivalent, the annualization factor of 12 is needed to increase the monthly periodic fee to an annual charge. Another way to equate all factors would be to divide the earnings credit rate and the adjustment percentage by 12 to get a monthly rate. But tradition has dictated that the fee, which is usually on a monthly basis, be multiplied to an annual basis.

Earnings Credit Rate

The earnings credit rate represents the value the institution is willing to give for the balances left to pay for the fee. This value is reflected in an annual percentage rate. The earnings credit rate often is confused with interest rates on earning assets. When an interest rate on earning assets is used to equate a balance, this is done for profitability analysis to give full value to the balance as though it were being employed by the institution as an earning resource. But this rate is incorrect for valuing balances that are used for payment of fees.

Balances that are left to pay for fees should be valued at a rate that represents what the firm would need to pay to obtain the balances in the market. A marginal purchased cost of funds rate would be most appropriate. Some financial institutions use the average cost of funds, but it is most appropriate and theoretically correct to use a marginal cost of funds rate.

When setting an earnings credit rate, an institution should ask itself what it would have to pay for balances in the market place. For a bank, the basic standard could be a demand deposit account; for a thrift institution, a NOW account; for a credit union, a share draft account; and for a brokerage, a margin account.

Adjustments

The fourth factor for the equation is adjustments. Most financial institutions do not have all of their assets earning revenue for the firm. Nonfinancial firms, on the other hand, have the vast majority of their assets deployed in the making of their income producing product. On a cost accounting basis, a product firm using absorption costing allocates all of the costs of assets to its products, including the fixed assets of building and equipment, the cost of money for carrying receivables, the cost of inventory, and the cost of any idle cash, in determining product profitability. A financial institution would follow the same procedure. However, a financial institution traditionally has not factored some balance sheet items into the overall price of its products and services.

Adjustments for a financial institution constitute the following balance sheet items:

- Coin and currency
- Reserves with the Federal Reserve system
- Correspondent balances with banks
- Cash items in the process of collection (float)
- Nonaccruing earning assets
- Accrued interest receivable
- Other nonearning assets
- Fixed assets

Some of these adjustments, such as reserves for transaction accounts, could be allocated to specific services. Also, some items such as fixed assets might be allocated to product costs.

In order to properly equate a fee to balances, nonearning assets must be factored into the balance equation. This is accomplished by reducing the earnings rate by that percentage of assets which constitute nonearning assets. For example, if non-earning assets are 10 percent of total assets, then balances should be reduced by 10 percent. This is calculated by multiplying the earnings rate by $(1 - .10)$ or .9 to obtain the adjusted earnings credit rate.

Some depository accounts have specific nonearning assets which can be directly associated with these accounts. In particular, cash items in the process of collection, or float, can be directly allocated to transaction accounts such as DDA, NOW, and Super NOW accounts. Most savings and investment accounts carry a very small amount of float.

Another specific adjustment attributed to transaction accounts is for reserves. Depending on the size of the institution, this could be considerable. Under current reserve requirements, as discussed in Chapter 10 on legal and regulatory parameters, 3 percent reserves are required on total transaction balances of $28.9 million or less and 12 percent on balances over $28.9 million.

When items such as reserves and float can be specifically associated with one type of account, then these adjustment items should be deducted only from the deposit account that is involved.

FORMULA FOR EQUATING FEES AND BALANCES

The above components are incorporated into an algebraic equation as follows:

F = Fees or Price
E = Earnings Credit Rate
A = Adjustments
B = Balance Equivalent
C = Annualization Factor (constant)

The formula for translating a fee into a balance equivalent is as follows:

$$\frac{\text{Fees} \times \text{Constant}}{\text{Earnings Rate} \times \text{Adjustments}} = \text{Balance Equivalent}$$

or

$$\frac{F \times C}{E \times (1 - A)} = B$$

To equate a balance to a fee, the formula would be adjusted as follows:

$$\frac{\text{Balances} \times (\text{Earnings Rate} \times \text{Adjustments})}{\text{Constant}} = \text{Fee}$$

or

$$\frac{B \times [\, E \times (1 - A)\,]}{C} = F$$

The best way to understand the use of these formulas is to calculate some examples, such as a noninterest bearing deposit account, a NOW account, and a certificate of deposit.

Noninterest Bearing Deposit Account Example:

Fees = F = $5
Earnings Credit Rate = E = 9.5%
Adjustments = A = 10%
Annualization Factor = C = 12

The formula then would be:

$$\frac{\$5 \times 12}{9.5\% \,(1 - 10\%)} = B = \text{Balance Equivalent}$$

B = $702

A $5 monthly fee would equate, therefore, to $702 in balances. This is an average balance which has been adjusted for nonearning assets such as float and reserves; therefore, it is an investible, collected balance. If the customer leaves $702 for one month, that would be the equivalent of $5 in fees per month.

The formula can be worked backwards as a check. Substituting the same values into the fee formula rather than the balance formula, the equation becomes:

$$\frac{\$702 \times [\, (9.5\% \times (1 - 10\%)\,]}{12} = F = \text{Fees}$$

F = $5

NOW Account Example:

Fees = F = $15
Interest on the transaction account = 5.25%
Earnings Credit Rate = E = 9.5% − 5.25%

Adjustments = A = 10%
Annualization Factor = 4

In order to equate the value of balances in an interest-bearing account to fees, it is necessary to substract the interest paid for the balances from the earnings rate given. In this example, the earnings rate is 9.5 percent, but the customer is receiving 5.25 percent interest on the balances deposited. This reduces the value of the balances by the cost that is paid in interest earned. It is important when using interest-bearing deposits or other paying liabilities in payment for fee-based services, that the value given to customers includes only that portion that has not already been paid to them in the form of interest received.

Now the equation becomes:

$$\frac{\$15 \times 4}{(9.5\% - 5.25\%) \times (1 - 10\%)} = B = \text{Balance Equivalent}$$

B = $1,569

If the customer wants to pay for service fees of $15 per quarter with a NOW account or other interest-bearing transaction account which pays 5.25 percent, then she would have to leave $1,569 per year. This is an average collected balance net of float, reserves, and other nonearning assets. To work the formula backwards again, substitute the values into the fee formula:

$$\frac{\$1,569 \times [\,(9.5\% - 5.25\%) \times (1 - 10\%)\,]}{4} = F = \text{Fee}$$

F = $15

Certificate of Deposit Example:

Fees = F = $5
Interest on CD = 9%
Earnings Credit Rate = E = 9.5% − 9%
Adjustments = A = 1%
Annualization Factor = C = 12

The formula becomes:

$$\frac{\$5 \times 12}{(9.5\% - 9\%) \times (1 - 1\%)} = B = \text{Balance Equivalent}$$

B = $12,121

As in the case shown previously with the NOW account, the earnings rate is net of the interest that is paid on the certificate of deposit. While the higher rate for a CD substantially reduces the net of the earnings rate, there is also a substantial reduction in the amount of adjustments, to 1 percent. A certificate of deposit does not require adjustments for float and reserves as in the previous two examples, and adjustments are estimated to be 1 percent. The earnings rate nets out to .495 percent, with a balance equivalent of $12,121.

The implications of these fees and balances formulas are intriguing. Note that if a CD paying 9 percent interest is maintained with the financial institution for at least $12,121, the institution could afford to forego charges worth $5 to customers on a monthly basis. This may be the equivalent of the monthly checking account charge and could be a pricing opportunity. There may be a reduction in fee profit if you forego $5 of fees for the checking account, but you are compensated instead by the $12,121 kept in the certificate of deposit. The institution is therefore indifferent between fees and balances if the formulas are correctly applied. In addition, the banker now has secured a better relationship by having two accounts with the same customer. This is relationship pricing built on fees and balances, a concept to be explored further in Chapter 11 when we discuss Quadratic Pricing.

EQUATING A DOLLAR OF FEES

Another approach to help understand the equating of fees and balances is to use $1 as the monthly fee and equate this to a series of different balance levels. In Figure 6–1 is shown the different balances required at various earnings rates and adjustment percentages. Adjustments can vary by size of institution or by type of account. The earnings rate would be net of any interest being paid on the balances maintained.

The mathematics underlying Figure 6–1 are based on using the numerator of the basic equation, which is fees annualized for periodic payments. Since only $1 of monthly fees is used, the constant becomes $1 times 12 months or $12. The only factors that change, therefore, are the earnings rate and the adjustment percentage.

An example will illustrate the use of this chart. Using an 8 percent earnings rate and an adjustment factor for nonearning assets of 10 percent, then the equivalent balance that is needed each month to pay for $1 of monthly service fees would be $167. If you wanted to pay 5.25 percent interest on this account, then the net earnings rate will be 8.00 percent minus 5.25 percent, or 2.75 percent. With the same adjustment percentage of 10 percent, the balance equivalent is now $485, a $318 increase.

This chart graphically illustrates the impacts of adjustments and earnings rates on balances required. If, for example, your institution has adjustments of 10 percent and a competitor has adjustments of 12 percent and your prices are the same, there will be a difference in the level of balances required from the customer. At an 8 percent earnings rate, with 10 percent adjustments, the balance equivalent for $1 of fees is $167; but at 12 percent adjustments, balances required are $170, a $3 difference. For a commercial customer shopping the local banks for the best deal, this means a 2 percent higher price at the competitor's institution.

Remember that adjustments include float. Therefore, if one bank is better at clearing its items than another bank, this can be reflected in a higher earnings rate being paid for balances. Smaller financial institutions vary considerably in their efficiencies of clearing items. Customers who pay for their services with balances receive a real benefit from the bank that is more efficient, which can be used as a competitive marketing advantage.

POLICY ISSUES

Some issues exist when equating fees with balances that should be integrated into overall company policies.

First, financial institutions should equate their fees and balances so the institution is indifferent as to the form of payment. In some cases, financial institutions may want to offer an incentive for customers to pay in one form or another and may increase or decrease their prices accordingly. But this is a deliberate strategy to introduce differences. In general, it is important that an equilibrium be maintained. If fees do not equal the balance equivalent being requested, then customers, especially commercial customers, will quickly seek out the lower form of payment and adjust to the institution's unconscious policies. A bias will be built up in the institution against the form of payment with the lower yield; this should not happen. For

FIGURE 6–1 Balance Equivalent for $1 of Fees

Earnings Rate	Adjustments Percentage											
	5%	6%	7%	8%	9%	10%	11%	12%	13%	14%	15%	20%
0.25%	$5,053	$5,106	$5,161	$5,217	$5,275	$5,333	$5,393	$5,455	$5,517	$5,581	$5,647	$6,000
0.50	2,526	2,553	2,581	2,609	2,637	2,677	2,697	2,727	2,759	2,791	2,824	3,000
0.75	1,684	1,702	1,720	1,739	1,758	1,778	1,798	1,818	1,839	1,860	1,882	2,000
1.00	1,263	1,277	1,290	1,304	1,319	1,333	1,348	1,364	1,379	1,395	1,412	1,500
1.25	1,011	1,021	1,032	1,043	1,055	1,067	1,079	1,091	1,103	1,116	1,129	1,200
1.50	842	851	860	870	879	889	899	909	920	930	941	1,000
1.75	722	729	737	745	754	762	770	779	788	797	807	857
2.00	632	638	645	652	659	667	674	682	690	698	706	750
2.25	561	567	573	580	586	593	599	606	613	620	627	667
2.50	505	511	516	522	527	533	539	545	552	558	565	600
2.75	459	464	469	474	480	485	490	496	502	507	513	545
3.00	421	426	430	435	440	444	449	455	460	465	471	500
3.25	389	393	397	401	406	410	415	420	424	429	434	462
3.50	361	365	369	373	377	381	385	390	394	399	403	429
3.75	337	340	344	348	352	356	360	364	368	372	376	400
4.00	316	319	323	326	330	333	337	341	345	349	353	375
4.25	297	300	304	307	310	314	317	321	325	328	332	353
4.50	281	284	287	290	293	296	300	303	307	310	314	333
4.75	266	269	272	275	278	281	284	287	290	294	297	316
5.00	253	255	258	261	264	267	270	273	276	279	282	300
5.25	241	243	246	248	251	254	257	260	263	266	269	286
5.50	230	232	235	237	240	242	245	248	251	254	257	273
5.75	220	222	224	227	229	232	234	237	240	243	246	261

6.00	211	213	215	217	220	222	225	227	230	233	235	250
6.25	202	204	206	209	211	213	216	218	221	223	226	240
6.50	194	196	199	201	203	205	207	210	212	215	217	231
6.75	187	189	191	193	195	198	200	202	204	207	209	222
7.00	180	182	184	186	188	190	193	195	197	199	202	214
7.25	174	176	178	180	182	184	186	188	190	192	195	207
7.50	168	170	172	174	176	178	180	182	184	186	188	200
7.75	163	165	166	168	170	172	174	176	178	180	182	194
8.00	158	160	161	163	165	167	169	170	172	174	176	187
8.25	153	155	156	158	160	162	163	165	167	169	171	182
8.50	149	150	152	153	155	157	159	160	162	164	166	176
8.75	144	146	147	149	151	152	154	156	158	159	161	171
9.00	140	142	143	145	147	148	150	152	153	155	157	167
9.25	137	138	139	141	143	144	146	147	149	151	153	162
9.50	133	134	136	137	139	140	142	144	145	147	149	158
9.75	130	131	132	134	135	137	138	140	141	143	145	154
10.00	126	128	129	130	132	133	135	136	138	140	141	150
10.25	123	125	126	127	129	130	132	133	135	136	138	146
10.50	120	122	123	124	126	127	128	130	131	133	134	143
10.75	118	119	120	121	123	124	125	127	128	130	131	140
11.00	115	116	117	119	120	121	123	124	125	127	128	136
11.25	112	113	115	116	117	119	120	121	123	124	125	133
11.50	110	111	112	113	115	116	117	119	120	121	123	130
11.75	108	109	110	111	112	113	115	116	117	119	120	128
12.00	105	106	108	109	110	111	112	114	115	116	118	125

financial institutions to fully avail themselves of the unique advantages of payment with balances, it is important that both forms of payment be equally acceptable to the institution.

Second, given that financial institutions are indifferent as to the form of payment, which form will customers choose? Probably fees, unless adjustments for nonearnings assets are zero, because of the friction caused by balance adjustments. This friction, caused by nonearning assets such as float, reserves, cash, and correspondent banking balances, reduces the value of balances as represented by the earnings rate. Thus, balances must be higher in order to maintain equivalency with fees to compensate for adjustments. Fortune 1000 corporations and many other companies recognize the friction in the banking system; therefore, there is a growing movement to fee-based payments.

This friction in the system due to adjustments for nonearning assets can be reduced by efficiency of operation. If one institution can maintain a higher level of efficiency in keeping these adjustments to a lower level, then it has a competitive advantage over others. Nonetheless, some level of adjustments will still exist. While adjustments are truly a negative in balance equivalency, they represent a marketing challenge for financial institutions to preserve their unique payment system as a competitive advantage over nonfinancial institutions.

A third issue is the level of adjustments themselves. Shown in Figures 6–2 and 6–3 is the level of nonearning assets for banks by state and by size. As can be seen, there is a significant difference among states and even among sizes of banks, with smaller banks tending to reflect a lower level of adjustments due to a lower level of reserves. Lower reserves for smaller banks is inherent in the regulatory system but is also due to greater efficiency in cash management. Variances in the levels of adjustments can also be caused by the proportions of different types of accounts, since many savings and investment accounts do not carry reserves.

Also, note in Figure 6–3 that the level of nonearning assets has been decreasing in almost all size categories since 1980 because of the Fed's efforts to reduce the float in the system.

Another policy directive should be that transaction accounts be allocated the specific nonearning assets that can be attributed directly to them. In the case of transaction accounts such as checking accounts, NOW accounts, Super NOW accounts, or share draft accounts, collection of deposits is required, which incurs

---

FIGURE 6–2   Median Nonearning Assets for Banks as a
Percent of Assets (by state)

Alabama	11.32%	Missouri	9.85%
Alaska	14.75	Montana	10.66
Arizona	13.54	Nebraska	8.60
Arkansas	11.49	Nevada	16.48
California	16.85	New Hampshire	13.58
Colorado	13.69	New Jersey	11.32
Connecticut	11.43	New Mexico	13.32
Delaware	7.35	New York	10.60
Dist. of Columbia	14.30	North Carolina	10.92
Florida	12.55	North Dakota	9.25
Georgia	11.12	Ohio	9.52
Hawaii	13.03	Oklahoma	11.18
Idaho	12.09	Oregon	14.51
Illinois	10.17	Pennsylvania	8.91
Indiana	9.32	Rhode Island	16.40
Iowa	8.41	South Carolina	11.36
Kansas	8.75	South Dakota	8.53
Kentucky	9.23	Tennessee	10.65
Louisiana	12.63	Texas	14.49
Maine	12.05	Utah	15.42
Maryland	9.71	Vermont	8.73
Massachusetts	11.00	Virginia	10.27
Michigan	11.36	Washington	13.88
Minnesota	9.24	West Virginia	8.84
Mississippi	11.33	Wisconsin	9.55
		Wyoming	12.97
All States	10.75		

SOURCE: *U.S. Bank Performance Profile*, Bank Administration
Institute, 1983.

---

float, and by regulatory fiat these accounts have reserve requirements. Therefore, these accounts should bear a higher level of
adjustments. Accounts that do not have these specific conditions
should have lower adjustments.

The fifth issue that must be considered when deciding on a
fees and balances policy is that balance equivalents will only
work where the earnings rate for the balances is greater than
interest paid on interest-bearing accounts. If the earnings rate
offered for a balance equivalent is less than or equal to the
interest paid to the customer on his account, then no value remains and the customer cannot be given credit for balances toward fee-based services. Some institutions, because of their asset
and liability structure, can support paying liabilities and bor-

---

FIGURE 6–3   Median Nonearning Assets for Banks as a Percent of Assets (by size)

Asset Size	1983	1982	1981	1980
Under $10 Million	10.75%	10.28%	10.61%	11.17%
$10–$25 Million	10.78	10.16	10.36	10.60
$25–$50 Million	10.56	10.67	10.91	11.26
$50–$100 Million	11.05	11.26	11.55	11.78
$100–$500 Million	10.21	10.44	11.27	12.14
Over $500 Million	12.84	13.88	15.52	16.27
All Sizes	10.76	10.63	10.95	11.31

SOURCE: *U.S. Bank Performance Profile*, Bank Administration Institute, 1983.

---

rowed funds at very high levels of interest. In this case, it should be recognized that these funds cannot carry double duty and also be allowed to be used for balance equivalents. It is only excess value that should be given for balances, above what is already paid out in interest.

Finally, the concept of fees and balances directly affects the pricing of services which historically have not been fee-based, such as loans. In the past, corporate loan customers had been required to maintain compensating balances, which increases the cost of borrowing. In the past 10 years, pressure has been mounting to eliminate this practice. The compensating balances approach follows the theory of bundling, where the value of deposit balances is used to produce a higher yield on the earning asset. While price sensitivity in the commercial market may reduce use of this type of "bundled pricing" and, in fact, has already reduced its usage appreciably for consumer accounts, this form of pricing is still an effective means to increase yield.

SUMMARY

The concept of the equivalency of fees and balances is fundamental to the pricing of financial services. Balances are considered "soft dollars" rather than "hard dollars" such as coin, currency, checks, credit card, electronic debits, or even bartering. Many competitors to depository institutions understand the uniqueness of soft dollar payment, and firms such as Merrill Lynch and Sears are using it with products such as the Cash Management Account and even nonfinancial products.

Equating fees to balances requires four factors: The price for services, an annualization factor which equates all terms to an annual basis, the earnings rate which values the balances at the rate at which a firm would have to borrow to replace these funds, and, finally, adjustments which represent friction and reduce the total balances on which credit can be given. Several examples were cited which used the formulas for equating fees into balances and balances into fees, including a noninterest-bearing transaction account, a NOW account, and a CD investment account. Finally, a chart was presented which equates $1 of fees at various levels of earnings rates and adjustments.

Policy issues related to the pricing of fees and balances are numerous. Financial institutions should state their prices to promote indifference between balances and fees so that customers can pay in either form. Customers will always prefer to pay a fee, all things being equal, due to the friction of adjustments. The level of adjustments varies considerably by type of institution, size of institution and type of account. Transaction accounts which can be specifically associated with particular nonearning assets should be adjusted accordingly. Equating of fees into balances only works where the earnings rate given for balances is greater than interest paid on interest-bearing accounts used to pay for fees. Finally, the concept of equating fees and balances is important in the other pricing aspects of the financial institution, such as with relationship pricing and loan pricing.

7

Present Value as a Pricing Tool

Compound interest is the most powerful force in the world.
—Benjamin Disraeli

Present value is a generic term used to designate the value of money held over time, the time value of money. It involves a series of mathematical formulas which allow the user to calculate value given certain interest rates and time periods. The term "present value" can either refer to the general time value of money or it can refer to one of the four specific formulas used to calculate time value.

The specific use of the term "Present Value," as opposed to the general use of the term, refers to calculating the value of future money brought back to the present, either for a lump sum or for a series of payments (annuity). Future value, which can also be calculated either for a lump sum or an annuity, involves determining the value of money in the future which is held now.

All rate-related asset and liability calculations performed by the financial institution executive use these basic formulas. Compounding to obtain yields on deposits uses one of the two future value formulas. Discounting a loan uses one of the two present value formulas.

Benjamin Disraeli, the Prime Minister of England at the turn of the century, stated that present value was the most powerful

---

FIGURE 7–1   Present Value Formulas

Factors

P = Known present value of money
F = Known future value of money
R = Interest rate
N = Term

Future Value $= P(1 + R)^N$

Present Value $= F\left[\dfrac{1}{(1 + R)^N}\right]$

Future Value of an Annuity $= \left[\dfrac{(1 + R)^N - 1}{R}\right]$

Present Value of an Annuity $= \left[\dfrac{1 - \left(\dfrac{1}{(1 + R)^N}\right)}{R}\right]$

---

force in the world. Yet, in the past ten years, during my numerous speeches and seminars on the subject of pricing of financial services, it has become apparent to me that the vast majority of people attending these seminars do not really grasp present value theory and are uncertain how to best apply present value to pricing deposits and loans.

In Figure 7–1 are presented the four basic formulas. The variables for the formulas are very simple. They consist simply of interest rate and term, and the known present or future amount(s).

The first formula, Future Value, can be used to determine the compound value associated with any type of deposit. A lump sum of money is deposited now, and you want to know what it will be worth in the future; hence the use of Future Value. The second formula, Present Value, can be used to discount the face value of a loan or a government Treasury bill. With a T-Bill, you are buying the promise to receive a set amount in the future, and you want to know what you need to pay today to secure that future promise; hence the use of Present Value. The third formula, the Future Value of an Annuity, can be used to calculate the total sum of IRA (Individual Retirement Account) contributions over a series of years. Money is periodically deposited into an IRA through a stream of payments. You want to know what that series of payments will be worth in the future. The fourth formula, the Present Value of an Annuity, can be used to determine installment payments required for loans such as auto loans and mortgages. You know the total that you want to have received in the future. You need to calculate what series of payments is necessary to reach that sum in the future.

Each one of the results of these calculations is often called a "factor." Thus, we speak of the present value factor or the future value factor. This factor is always calculated for the value of $1. For example, a "yield" is a stated rate that has been compounded, or to which a present value factor has been applied.

In this chapter, we will review the basic present value formulas and apply them to examples of pricing financial service deposits and loans. Tables will be presented showing the results of the various formulas, and methods of manipulating the data in these tables will be explained. As an aside, formulas connected with any spreadsheet type software program on a personal computer can produce the same tables shown in this chapter.

FUTURE VALUE

Future value is probably the most common of all the present value formulas. Almost every person who deals with financial services, whether as an buyer or a seller, will have some interface with this particular algebraic formula. The calculation multiplies the known current value of money by one plus a rate for the particular period of time raised to an exponential power for the number of periods to be analyzed.

In Figure 7–2 are calculated future value factors of $1. Across the top are listed the various interest rates we've chosen to analyze, and along the side are listed the various number of periods. Applying the future value formula for, say, 5.25 percent compounded daily for one year, or 365 periods, the following calculation is computed:

$$F = \$1 \ (1 + 5.25\%)^{365}$$
$$= 1.05390$$

If the deposit totals $100, by applying the future value factor you can calculate that at the end of one year the deposit will be worth $100 times 1.05390, or $105.39.

In contrast, the same rate compounded quarterly is listed in Column 3 of the table. Now the following is calculated:

$$F = \$1 \ (1 + 5.25\%)^4$$
$$= 1.05354$$

Now the same $100 deposit is worth less, at $105.35. The yield due to paying interest on interest quarterly for four quarters is 5.35 percent while the stated rate is 5.25 percent.

The difference between compounding 5.25 percent daily and compounding it quarterly is .00036, or approximately 4 basis points. (A basis point is equal to 1/100th of a percent, not to be confused with the loose usage of "point," which usually means 100 basis points.)

A difference of 4 basis points doesn't seem like much. But what if an institution had $100 million dollars in savings accounts that were paying 5.25 percent, and it was trying to decide whether it should pay interest on a daily or quarterly basis. The 4 basis point difference now amounts to .0004 times $100 million dollars, or $40,000. That may pay for at least one teller a year at many institutions!

Since savings rates have been changed to 5.5 percent, we've included columns in Figure 7–2 for 5.5 percent compounded daily and 5.5 percent compounded quarterly. Here the difference is exactly 4 basis points. As the interest rate increases, the impact of compounding differences will increase.

For example, assume that a money market deposit account is paying 8 percent. An institution is trying to decide whether to pay daily, monthly, or quarterly compounded interest on $25 million of money market deposits. What would the difference be? Looking at Column 5 of the chart, the yield from daily compounding for 365 periods would be 8.328 percent. Compounding on a monthly basis, listed in the next column, yields 8.300 percent or 2.8 basis points less. Quarterly compounding, from Period 4 of Column 7, yields 8.243 percent or a net of 8.5 basis points lower than daily. This results in paying $7,000 less in interest for monthly compounding and $21,250 less for quarterly compounding for the total $25 million on deposit.

This $21,250, for the average $100 million institution with about 25 percent of its assets ($25 million dollars) in money market deposit accounts, represents, on a before-tax basis, an increase of almost 2 percent profitability measured by return

FIGURE 7–2 Future Value of $1

Period	(1) 5.25% Daily	(2) 5.50% Daily	(3) 5.25% Quarterly	(4) 5.50% Quarterly	(5) 8.00% Daily	(6) 8.00% Monthly	(7) 8.00% Quarterly	(8) 10.00% Monthly	(9) 12.00% Monthly	(10) 14.00% Monthly
1	1.00014	1.00015	1.01313	1.01375	1.00022	1.00667	1.02000	1.00833	1.01000	1.01167
2	1.00029	1.00030	1.02642	1.02769	1.00044	1.01338	1.04040	1.01674	1.02010	1.02347
3	1.00043	1.00045	1.03989	1.04182	1.00066	1.02013	1.06121	1.02521	1.03030	1.03541
4	1.00058	1.00060	1.05354	1.05614	1.00088	1.02693	1.08243	1.03375	1.04060	1.04749
5	1.00072	1.00075	1.06737	1.07067	1.00110	1.03378	1.10408	1.04237	1.05101	1.05971
6	1.00086	1.00090	1.08138	1.08539	1.00132	1.04067	1.12616	1.05105	1.06152	1.07207
7	1.00101	1.00106	1.09557	1.10031	1.00154	1.04761	1.14869	1.05981	1.07214	1.08458
8	1.00115	1.00121	1.10995	1.11544	1.00175	1.05459	1.17166	1.06864	1.08286	1.09723
9	1.00130	1.00136	1.12452	1.13078	1.00197	1.06163	1.19509	1.07755	1.09369	1.11004
10	1.00144	1.00151	1.13928	1.14633	1.00219	1.06870	1.21899	1.08653	1.10462	1.12299
11	1.00158	1.00166	1.15423	1.16209	1.00241	1.07583	1.24337	1.09558	1.11567	1.13609
12	1.00173	1.00181	1.16938	1.17807	1.00263	1.08300	1.26824	1.10471	1.12683	1.14934
13	1.00187	1.00196	1.18473	1.19427	1.00285	1.09022	1.29361	1.11392	1.13809	1.16275
14	1.00202	1.00211	1.20028	1.21069	1.00307	1.09749	1.31948	1.12320	1.14947	1.17632
15	1.00216	1.00226	1.21603	1.22733	1.00329	1.10480	1.34587	1.13256	1.16097	1.19004
16	1.00230	1.00241	1.23199	1.24421	1.00351	1.11217	1.37279	1.14200	1.17258	1.20392
17	1.00245	1.00256	1.24816	1.26132	1.00373	1.11958	1.40024	1.15152	1.18430	1.21797

18	1.00259	1.00272	1.26455	1.27866	1.00395	1.12705	1.42825	1.16111	1.19615	1.23218
19	1.00274	1.00287	1.28114	1.29624	1.00417	1.13456	1.45681	1.17079	1.20811	1.24655
20	1.00288	1.00302	1.29796	1.31407	1.00439	1.14213	1.48595	1.18054	1.22019	1.26110
21	1.00302	1.00317	1.31499	1.33213	1.00461	1.14974	1.51567	1.19038	1.23239	1.27581
22	1.00317	1.00332	1.33225	1.35045	1.00483	1.15740	1.54598	1.20030	1.24472	1.29070
23	1.00331	1.00347	1.34974	1.36902	1.00505	1.16512	1.57690	1.21031	1.25716	1.30575
24	1.00346	1.00362	1.36745	1.38784	1.00527	1.17289	1.60844	1.22039	1.26973	1.32099
30	1.00432	1.00453	1.47874	1.50635	1.00660	1.22059	1.81136	1.28270	1.34785	1.41620
36	1.00519	1.00544	1.59908	1.63498	1.00792	1.27024	2.03989	1.34818	1.43077	1.51827
42	1.00606	1.00635	1.72921	1.77458	1.00925	1.32190	2.29724	1.41701	1.51879	1.62769
48	1.00693	1.00726	1.86993	1.92611	1.01057	1.37567	2.58707	1.48935	1.61223	1.74501
54	1.00780	1.00817	2.02211	2.09058	1.01190	1.43162	2.91346	1.56539	1.71141	1.87078
60	1.00867	1.00908	2.18666	2.26909	1.01324	1.48985	3.28103	1.64531	1.81670	2.00561
66	1.00954	1.00999	2.36461	2.46285	1.01457	1.55044	3.69497	1.72931	1.92846	2.15016
72	1.01041	1.01091	2.55704	2.67314	1.01590	1.61350	4.16114	1.81759	2.04710	2.30513
78	1.01128	1.01182	2.76514	2.90140	1.01724	1.67913	4.68612	1.91039	2.17304	2.47127
84	1.01215	1.01274	2.99016	3.14915	1.01858	1.74742	5.27733	2.00792	2.30672	2.64938
90	1.01303	1.01365	3.23350	3.41805	1.01992	1.81849	5.94313	2.11043	2.44863	2.84034
96	1.01390	1.01457	3.49664	3.70991	1.02126	1.89246	6.69293	2.21818	2.59927	3.04505
180	1.02623	1.02749	10.45552	11.68305	1.04024	3.30692	35.32083	4.45392	5.99580	8.06751
270	1.03960	1.04152	33.80794	39.93320	1.06096	6.01362	209.91640	9.39969	14.68152	22.91443
365	1.05390	1.05654	116.68278	146.13914	1.08328	11.30515	1377.40829	20.67785	37.78343	68.97089

on assets. According to the Bank Administration Institute's U.S. Bank Performance Profile and other analyses of the average return on assets, a bank of about $100 million in total assets for 1984 earned almost 1 percent on average assets. With this change in compounding, that same average bank could raise its ROA to about 1.02 percent.

PRESENT VALUE

The present value formula calculates the value today of money to be received in the future. Note that the present value formula is very similar to the future value formula except that the discounting factor becomes the denominator rather than the numerator. Present value, which is used to discount loans and government securities, calculates the current value for money which will be received in the future, for which the future amount is known.

How much money would you have to give a financial institution today to receive $1 one year from today, assuming that that institution were paying 5.25 percent compounded daily? If you go to Column 1 of Figure 7–3, and go down to period 365, you see that you would have to give the banker 95 cents ($.94886) today in order to receive $1 one year from today.

As was the case with future value, the higher the interest rate the greater the differential between compounding methods. Let's try a problem:

> A new father walks into a bank and, after giving a cigar to the new accounts salesperson, says, "I want to put enough money into the bank today so I'll have $20,000 for my new son 18 years from now when he's ready for college." The new account sales representative says, "For long-term money, we're paying 8 percent quarterly." How much money would the new father have to put into the bank today in order to return 18 years from today and pick up $20,000 (assuming no taxes) for his new son's college education?

If you go to Column 7 of Figure 7–3, which is 8 percent compounded quarterly, you get your answer. Quarterly compounding for 18 years equals 72 periods, and the factor is .24032. This factor is the current value of a dollar received 18 years from now compounded quarterly at 8 percent. In other words, if you left 24.032 cents with an institution today, 72 quarterly periods or 18 years from now you could walk in and receive $1, or more than four times the value you had left with the institution. Using the formula, the following would be calculated:

$$\frac{1}{(1 + R)^N} = .24032$$

therefore,

$$P = \$20,000 \ (.24032)$$
$$= \$4,806.40$$

So the new father needs to deposit $4,806.40, or less than one fourth of the $20,000, today in order to have $20,000 18 years from today.

This form of present value calculating is called discounting. It is used on the deposit side for what is called a zero coupon CD or bond.

FUTURE VALUE OF AN ANNUITY

The future value of an annuity, or the value in the future of a series of payments made over time, is again a restructuring of our basic future value formula from Figure 7–1. The future value of an annuity table, Figure 7–4, assumes that the payment will be received at the end of each period (in arrears); therefore, all factors for the future value of one payment, shown in Period 1, since the payment is received at the end are 1.00000.

Proceeding through these formulas, you will notice that the formulas become more convoluted. But they work the same. Let's go through an example to see how these tables are related. Assume an interest rate of 5.25 percent compounded quarterly. If you were to receive $1 every quarter, looking at Period 4 of Figure 7–4 (for four quarters) and Column 3 (for 5.25 percent quarterly), at the end of four quarters you would have $4.07944.

Now, going back to Figure 7–2, you can calculate each of these four payments individually: $1 received at the end of one period (not compounded) is 1.00000; $1 compounded for one period (Period 1, Column 3 of Figure 7.2) is 1.01313; $1 compounded for two periods (Period 2, Column 3) is 1.02642; and $1 compounded for three periods (Period 3, Column 3) is 1.03989. Adding these four figures together, you get 4.07944, the same as the factor calculated in Figure 7–4.

The future value of an annuity is an important table for calculating the accumulation of money received on a periodic

FIGURE 7-3 Present Value of $1

Period	(1) 5.25% Daily	(2) 5.50% Daily	(3) 5.25% Quarterly	(4) 5.50% Quarterly	(5) 8.00% Daily	(6) 8.00% Monthly	(7) 8.00% Quarterly	(8) 10.00% Monthly	(9) 12.00% Monthly	(10) 14.00% Monthly
1	0.99986	0.99985	0.98705	0.98644	0.99978	0.99338	0.98039	0.99174	0.99010	0.98847
2	0.99971	0.99970	0.97426	0.97306	0.99956	0.98680	0.96117	0.98354	0.98030	0.97707
3	0.99957	0.99955	0.96164	0.95986	0.99934	0.98026	0.94232	0.97541	0.97059	0.96580
4	0.99942	0.99940	0.94918	0.94684	0.99912	0.97377	0.92385	0.96735	0.96098	0.95466
5	0.99928	0.99925	0.93688	0.93400	0.99890	0.96732	0.90573	0.95936	0.95147	0.94365
6	0.99914	0.99910	0.92474	0.92133	0.99869	0.96092	0.88797	0.95143	0.94205	0.93277
7	0.99899	0.99895	0.91276	0.90883	0.99847	0.95455	0.87056	0.94356	0.93272	0.92201
8	0.99885	0.99880	0.90094	0.89651	0.99825	0.94823	0.85349	0.93577	0.92348	0.91138
9	0.99871	0.99864	0.88927	0.88435	0.99803	0.94195	0.83676	0.92803	0.91434	0.90087
10	0.99856	0.99849	0.87775	0.87235	0.99781	0.93571	0.82035	0.92036	0.90529	0.89048
11	0.99842	0.99834	0.86638	0.86052	0.99759	0.92952	0.80426	0.91276	0.89632	0.88021
12	0.99828	0.99819	0.85515	0.84885	0.99737	0.92336	0.78849	0.90521	0.88745	0.87006
13	0.99813	0.99804	0.84407	0.83733	0.99716	0.91725	0.77303	0.89773	0.87866	0.86003
14	0.99799	0.99789	0.83314	0.82598	0.99694	0.91117	0.75788	0.89031	0.86996	0.85011
15	0.99784	0.99774	0.82235	0.81477	0.99672	0.90514	0.74301	0.88295	0.86135	0.84031
16	0.99770	0.99759	0.81169	0.80372	0.99650	0.89914	0.72845	0.87566	0.85282	0.83062
17	0.99756	0.99744	0.80118	0.79282	0.99628	0.89319	0.71416	0.86842	0.84438	0.82104

18	0.99741	0.99729	0.79080	0.78207	0.99606	0.88727	0.70016	0.86124	0.83602	0.81157
19	0.99727	0.99714	0.78055	0.77146	0.99584	0.88140	0.68643	0.85413	0.82774	0.80221
20	0.99713	0.99699	0.77044	0.76100	0.99563	0.87556	0.67297	0.84707	0.81954	0.79296
21	0.99698	0.99684	0.76046	0.75067	0.99541	0.86976	0.65978	0.84007	0.81143	0.78382
22	0.99684	0.99669	0.75061	0.74049	0.99519	0.86400	0.64684	0.83312	0.80340	0.77478
23	0.99670	0.99654	0.74088	0.73045	0.99497	0.85828	0.63416	0.82624	0.79544	0.76584
24	0.99655	0.99639	0.73129	0.72054	0.99475	0.85260	0.62172	0.81941	0.78757	0.75701
30	0.99569	0.99549	0.67625	0.66386	0.99345	0.81927	0.55207	0.77961	0.74192	0.70612
36	0.99484	0.99459	0.62536	0.61163	0.99214	0.78725	0.49022	0.74174	0.69892	0.65865
42	0.99398	0.99369	0.57830	0.56351	0.99084	0.75649	0.43530	0.70571	0.65842	0.61437
48	0.99312	0.99279	0.53478	0.51918	0.98954	0.72692	0.38654	0.67143	0.62026	0.57306
54	0.99226	0.99190	0.49453	0.47834	0.98824	0.69851	0.34323	0.63882	0.58431	0.53454
60	0.99141	0.99100	0.45732	0.44070	0.98694	0.67121	0.30478	0.60779	0.55045	0.49860
66	0.99055	0.99010	0.42290	0.40603	0.98564	0.64498	0.27064	0.57827	0.51855	0.46508
72	0.98970	0.98921	0.39108	0.37409	0.98434	0.61977	0.24032	0.55018	0.48850	0.43381
78	0.98884	0.98832	0.36165	0.34466	0.98305	0.59555	0.21340	0.52345	0.46019	0.40465
84	0.98799	0.98742	0.33443	0.31755	0.98176	0.57227	0.18949	0.49803	0.43352	0.37745
90	0.98714	0.98653	0.30926	0.29256	0.98047	0.54991	0.16826	0.47384	0.40839	0.35207
96	0.98629	0.98564	0.28599	0.26955	0.97918	0.52841	0.14941	0.45082	0.38472	0.32840
180	0.97444	0.97324	0.09564	0.08559	0.96132	0.30240	0.02831	0.22452	0.16678	0.12395
270	0.96191	0.96013	0.02958	0.02504	0.94255	0.16629	0.00476	0.10639	0.06811	0.04364
365	0.94886	0.94649	0.00857	0.00684	0.92312	0.08846	0.00073	0.04836	0.02647	0.01450

FIGURE 7-4 Future Value of Annuity of $1

Period	(1) 5.25% Daily	(2) 5.50% Daily	(3) 5.25% Quarterly	(4) 5.50% Quarterly	(5) 8.00% Daily	(6) 8.00% Monthly	(7) 8.00% Quarterly	(8) 10.00% Monthly	(9) 12.00% Monthly	(10) 14.00% Monthly
1	1.00000	1.00000	1.00000	1.00000	1.00000	1.00000	1.00000	1.00000	1.00000	1.00000
2	2.00014	2.00015	2.01312	2.01375	2.00022	2.00667	2.02000	2.00833	2.01000	2.01167
3	3.00043	3.00045	3.03955	3.04144	3.00066	3.02004	3.06040	3.02507	3.03010	3.03514
4	4.00086	4.00090	4.07944	4.08326	4.00132	4.04018	4.12161	4.05028	4.06040	4.07055
5	5.00144	5.00151	5.13298	5.13940	5.00219	5.06711	5.20404	5.08403	5.10101	5.11804
6	6.00216	6.00226	6.20035	6.21007	6.00329	6.10089	6.30812	6.12640	6.15202	6.17775
7	7.00302	7.00317	7.28173	7.29546	7.00460	7.14157	7.43428	7.17745	7.21354	7.24982
8	8.00403	8.00422	8.37731	8.39577	8.00614	8.18918	8.58297	8.23726	8.28567	8.33440
9	9.00518	9.00543	9.48726	9.51121	9.00789	9.24377	9.75463	9.30591	9.36853	9.43164
10	10.00648	10.00678	10.61178	10.64199	10.00987	10.30540	10.94972	10.38346	10.46221	10.54167
11	11.00791	11.00829	11.75106	11.78832	11.01206	11.37410	12.16872	11.46998	11.56683	11.66466
12	12.00950	12.00995	12.90529	12.95041	12.01448	12.44993	13.41209	12.56557	12.68250	12.80075
13	13.01123	13.01176	14.07467	14.12848	13.01711	13.53293	14.68033	13.67028	13.80933	13.95009
14	14.01310	14.01372	15.25940	15.32274	14.01996	14.62315	15.97394	14.78420	14.94742	15.11284
15	15.01511	15.01583	16.45968	16.53343	15.02304	15.72063	17.29342	15.90740	16.09690	16.28915
16	16.01727	16.01809	17.67572	17.76077	16.02633	16.82544	18.63929	17.03996	17.25786	17.47919

17	17.01958	17.02051	18.90771	19.00498	17.02984	17.93761	20.01207	18.18196	18.43044	18.68312
18	18.02202	18.02307	20.15587	20.26630	18.03357	19.05719	21.41231	19.33348	19.61475	19.90109
19	19.02462	19.02579	21.42042	21.54496	19.03753	20.18424	22.84056	20.49459	20.81090	21.13327
20	20.02735	20.02866	22.70156	22.84120	20.04170	21.31880	24.29737	21.66538	22.01900	22.37982
21	21.03023	21.03167	23.99952	24.15527	21.04609	22.46093	25.78332	22.84593	23.23919	23.64092
22	22.03326	22.03484	25.31451	25.48740	22.05070	23.61066	27.29898	24.03631	24.47159	24.91673
23	23.03643	23.03816	26.64677	26.83785	23.05554	24.76807	28.84496	25.23661	25.71630	26.20743
24	24.03974	24.04164	27.99651	28.20687	24.06059	25.93319	30.42186	26.44692	26.97346	27.51318
30	30.06265	30.06564	36.47521	36.82549	30.09554	33.08885	40.56808	33.92352	34.78489	35.67390
36	36.09076	36.09509	45.64390	46.18003	36.13843	40.53556	51.99437	41.78182	43.07688	44.42280
42	42.12408	42.13000	55.55874	56.33334	42.18926	48.28514	64.86222	50.04132	51.87899	53.80226
48	48.16260	48.17037	66.28045	67.35363	48.24807	56.34992	79.35352	58.72249	61.22261	63.85774
54	54.20634	54.21619	77.87468	79.31492	54.31484	64.74271	95.67307	67.84687	71.14105	74.63795
60	60.25530	60.26749	90.41245	92.29757	60.38959	73.47686	114.05154	77.43707	81.66967	86.19513
66	66.32426	66.32426	103.97054	106.38879	66.47234	82.56625	134.74868	87.51689	92.84602	98.58527
72	72.36888	72.38651	118.63198	121.68324	72.56310	92.02533	158.05702	98.11131	104.70993	111.86843
78	78.43352	78.45424	134.48656	138.28365	78.66186	101.86913	184.30600	109.24662	117.30372	126.10894
84	84.50339	84.52746	151.63138	156.30155	84.76865	112.11331	213.86661	120.95042	130.67227	141.37583
90	90.57850	90.60617	170.17145	175.85797	90.88348	122.77414	247.15666	133.25174	144.86327	157.74305
96	96.65886	96.69038	190.22029	197.08429	97.00635	133.86858	284.64666	146.18108	159.92729	175.28993
180	182.33709	182.44938	720.42086	776.94883	183.57733	346.03822	1716.04157	414.47035	499.58020	605.78627
270	275.29116	275.54653	2499.65247	2831.50569	278.11760	752.04267	10445.82000	1007.96286	1368.15166	1878.37939
365	374.72348	375.19503	8813.92574	10555.57000	379.95392	1545.77202	68820.41000	2361.34187	3678.34343	5826.07659

basis. A prime example of this is IRA accounts. If a customer who is 36 years of age opens an IRA account into which she wants to deposit $500 at the end of every quarter, how much money would she have at age 60? The period of time is 24 years which would result in 96 periods. Assuming 8 percent over 96 periods compounded quarterly, the future value factor is listed in Period 96 and Column 7. The factor is 284.64666. $500 times 284.64666 is $142,323.33. That is the amount of money our customer will have at age 60. This is a tidy sum for retirement since there would be no taxation of this amount, leaving the full $142,323 available for her use.

The same $500 deposited periodically, with 2 percent interest paid every quarter but not compounded, would yield only $48,960. Compounding the rate triples the total. The compounding of interest coupled with periodic payments can substantially increase the amount available for a saver. Maybe Prime Minister Disraeli was right.

PRESENT VALUE OF AN ANNUITY

The present value table in Figure 7–5 is again a reconfiguration of the basic formula. By adding up the amounts in Figure 7–3, the factors shown in Figure 7–5 can be generated, just as was done for Figures 7–2 and 7–4.

The present value of an annuity allows you to determine the monthly payment necessary for mortgages or other loans. The present value of an annuity calculates how much money should be disbursed now assuming certain periodic payments over the future at a prescribed interest rate. You could solve for the present value, similar to what you solved for in the past, but you could also solve for the interest rate or the payments, if any three of the four variables are known.

Assume for example that a customer wants to borrow $8,000 for a new automobile. The institution is willing to lend money at 12 percent annual percentage rate (APR) for 48 months. What is the customer's monthly payment? In Column 9 of Figure 7–5, you can read a 12 percent rate compounded monthly. The present value of $1 received over the next 48 months, at a 12 percent interest rate, is $37.97396.

You now divide this factor into the $8,000 principle you plan to lend on the auto loan. This results in a monthly payment of $210.67. This is the amount of money that the customer would have to pay every month to pay off an $8,000 principal at an interest rate of 12 percent. This payment might be a bit high for a customer, since it is over $200. Perhaps you could lower it.

If your institution were willing to go 60 months at the same interest rate of 12 percent, the monthly payment would be $177.96. The longer term substantially lowers the customer's monthly payment.

However, your institution would be taking on more risk for lending money one year longer and should be compensated. You may want two percentage points more, or 200 basis points more, for this additional risk. The monthly payment would now be calculated by going to Period 60 at 14 percent monthly (Column 10). The factor is 42.97702. When divided into $8,000, a monthly payment of $186.15 is calculated. This gives your institution a higher yield, and may still satisfy the customer since the payment is still below $200. This is a good demonstration of how present value can be used to determine appropriate pricing to meet the needs of both the customer and the financial institution.

As an aside, present value can be used as evidence to prove that only men, strong men, could be loan officers in the past. Before calculators, volumes and volumes of books were necessary which listed every imaginable interest rate from less than 1 percent to over 20 percent and every imaginable payment period ranging from one month up to 25 years. These books of tables were calculated by mainframe computers, and before that by hand, from the formulas shown in this chapter. You can imagine the volumes of pages that were necessary to include all the hundreds of interest rates and all the hundreds of periods that were possible. Most banks had these books sitting on a shelf in their offices. The only ones who could lift these books were big, strong muscle-bound men. So no women needed to apply.

But thanks to NASA and the space program, there are now little tiny calculators which contain the four basic present value formulas, and the books are no longer necessary. Now women, through the use of a tiny calculator, can calculate monthly payments and yields on loans. Therefore women can now be loan officers. This may be an extremely good result because potentially the fairer and weaker sex may spend more time with their present value calculations to overcome the less than insightful application of these tables by the muscle-bound loan officers, who have approved tanker ship loans, real estate investment trust loans, and energy credits.

FIGURE 7–5 Present Value of Annuity of $1

Period	(1) 5.25% Daily	(2) 5.50% Daily	(3) 5.25% Quarterly	(4) 5.50% Quarterly	(5) 8.00% Daily	(6) 8.00% Monthly	(7) 8.00% Quarterly	(8) 10.00% Monthly	(9) 12.00% Monthly	(10) 14.00% Monthly
1	0.99986	0.99985	0.98705	0.98644	0.99978	0.99338	0.98039	0.99174	0.99010	0.98847
2	1.99957	1.99955	1.96130	1.95949	1.99934	1.98018	1.94156	1.97527	1.97040	1.96554
3	2.99914	2.99910	2.92294	2.91935	2.99869	2.96044	2.88388	2.95069	2.94099	2.93134
4	3.99856	3.99849	3.87212	3.86619	3.99781	3.93421	3.80773	3.91804	3.90197	3.88600
5	4.99784	4.99774	4.80900	4.80019	4.99671	4.90154	4.71346	4.87739	4.85343	4.82966
6	5.99698	5.99684	5.73374	5.72152	5.99540	5.86245	5.60143	5.82882	5.79548	5.76243
7	6.99597	6.99578	6.64651	6.63035	6.99387	6.81701	6.47199	6.77238	6.72819	6.68444
8	7.99482	7.99458	7.54745	7.52686	7.99212	7.76524	7.32548	7.70815	7.65168	7.59582
9	8.99353	8.99322	8.43672	8.41120	8.99014	8.70719	8.16224	8.63618	8.56602	8.49670
10	9.99209	9.99172	9.31446	9.28355	9.98796	9.64290	8.98259	9.55654	9.47130	9.38718
11	10.99051	10.99006	10.18084	10.14407	10.98555	10.57242	9.78685	10.46930	10.36763	10.26739
12	11.98879	11.98825	11.03599	10.99292	11.98292	11.49578	10.57534	11.37451	11.25508	11.13746
13	12.98692	12.98630	11.88007	11.83025	12.98008	12.41303	11.34837	12.27224	12.13374	11.99748
14	13.98491	13.98419	12.71321	12.65623	13.97701	13.32420	12.10625	13.16255	13.00370	12.84760
15	14.98275	14.98193	13.53555	13.47101	14.97373	14.22934	12.84926	14.04551	13.86505	13.68790
16	15.98046	15.97953	14.34724	14.27473	15.97023	15.12848	13.57771	14.92116	14.71787	14.51852
17	16.97801	16.97697	15.14842	15.06755	16.96651	16.02167	14.29187	15.78958	15.56225	15.33956

18	17.97543	17.97426	15.93922	15.84962	17.96258	16.90894	14.99203	16.65083	16.39827	16.15113
19	18.97270	18.97140	16.71977	16.62108	18.95842	17.79034	15.67846	17.50495	17.22601	16.95334
20	19.96983	19.96839	17.49021	17.38207	19.95405	18.66590	16.35143	18.35202	18.04555	17.74630
21	20.96681	20.96523	18.25067	18.13275	20.94945	19.53566	17.01121	19.19208	18.85698	18.53012
22	21.96365	21.96192	19.00128	18.87324	21.94465	20.39967	17.65805	20.02521	19.66038	19.30489
23	22.96035	22.95846	19.74217	19.60369	22.93962	21.25795	18.29220	20.85145	20.45582	20.07073
24	23.95690	23.95485	20.47345	20.32423	23.93437	22.11054	18.91393	21.67085	21.24339	20.82774
30	29.93322	29.93004	24.66646	24.44683	29.89832	27.10885	22.39646	26.44704	25.80771	25.18996
36	35.90438	35.89984	28.54392	28.24509	35.85443	31.91181	25.48884	30.99124	30.10751	29.25890
42	41.87039	41.86423	32.12958	31.74454	41.80272	36.52705	28.23479	35.31470	34.15811	33.05430
48	47.83125	47.82324	35.44540	34.96869	47.74319	40.96191	30.67312	39.42816	37.97396	36.59455
54	53.78698	53.77686	38.51169	37.93919	53.67585	45.22345	32.83828	43.34181	41.56866	39.89678
60	59.73756	59.72510	41.34722	40.67600	59.60071	49.31843	34.76089	47.06537	44.95504	42.97702
66	65.68301	65.66797	43.96936	43.19750	65.51780	53.25337	36.46810	50.60806	48.14516	45.85017
72	71.62334	71.60547	46.39417	45.52064	71.42710	57.03452	37.98406	53.97867	51.15039	48.53017
78	77.55854	77.53760	48.63651	47.66101	77.32864	60.66789	39.33019	57.18555	53.98146	51.02999
84	83.48862	83.46437	50.71009	49.63299	83.22243	64.15926	40.52552	60.23667	56.64845	53.36176
90	89.41358	89.38579	52.62763	51.44984	89.10847	67.51418	41.58693	63.13958	59.16088	55.53677
96	95.33344	95.30185	54.40086	53.12375	94.98677	70.73797	42.52943	65.90149	61.52770	57.56555
180	177.67723	177.56763	68.90337	66.50225	176.47659	104.64059	48.58440	93.05744	83.32166	75.08965
270	264.80573	264.56174	73.93685	70.90605	262.13836	125.05661	49.76181	107.23362	93.18871	81.97366
365	355.55934	355.11799	75.53751	72.22961	350.74475	136.73171	49.96370	114.19669	97.35334	84.47153

This little aside does have a point. It is no longer necessary to have tables of present value formulas printed in book form. Small calculators can do the job nicely, and they not only produce the same result but have greater flexibility to adjust for things such as balloon payments and variable payment terms.

SUMMARY

Present value is the use of four simple algebraic formulas to determine the current or future value of money. These are basic formulas for the pricing of rate-related financial services such as loans, investments, and deposits. It is fundamental for a pricer of financial services to understand them and to be able to manipulate them with ease. Failure to thoroughly understand all four present value formulas will severely restrict the pricer of financial services from being creative in the pricing of financial services.

8

Asset and Liability Management Considerations and Risk Assessment

The Latin verb intereo *means "to be lost;" a substantive form,* interisse, *developed into the modern term "interest." Interest was not profit but loss.*

—Sidney Homer, *A History of Interest Rates*

Asset and liability management is a planning procedure which accounts for all assets and liabilities of a financial institution by rate, amount, and maturity. Its intent is to quantify and control risk. The focus is on the risk management of the net interest margin for profit.

Since rate is involved in asset and liability management (ALM), pricing becomes both a critical input to and an important result of the process. Financial marketers can no longer forge ahead in booking loans with the assurance that deposits and funding will magically be available. The converse is also true. Booking deposits with the assurance that they will be employed profitably can no longer be done. The preplanning of the deployment of liabilities and the funding of assets must be taken into consideration, and asset and liability management encompasses the basic principles under which this is accomplished. Thus, ALM must be part of pricing any rate-related financial service.

Asset and liability management is both an art and a science, and is a relatively new exercise for most financial institutions. Until the early 70s, little information was available on the necessary skills to manage assets and liabilities. But in the past ten years, interest in analyzing and matching assets with liabilities has increased dramatically due to three reasons.

First, inflation caused tremendous volatility in rates and very high absolute levels of rates. The prime lending rate in the late 70s and early 80s fluctuated considerably and reached levels as high as 22 percent.

Another reason for interest in asset and liability management is deregulation. As the cost of the basic money supply of financial institutions became deregulated due to the phasing out of Regulation Q, protection for the long-sacred strategy of lending long and borrowing short disappeared. As many financial institutions, especially savings and loans, saw their deposit structures erode from short-term, low-, or no-rate deposits into money market rated deposits and were unable to restructure their earning assets of mortgage loans to match, net interest margin narrowed and even turned negative. This development was an excellent incentive to develop asset and liability management skills.

Finally, with deregulation came a new form of competition. No longer were depository financial institutions competing only with one another; they were also competing with security firms and nonbank firms such as Sears, J. C. Penney, and even at one time Parker Pen. This competition became global in scope, as the movement of money became easy and quick across country lines. For example, the primary commercial paper market, or the lending and borrowing of money between major corporations, was about a $50 billion market domestically in the early 70s. This market, in the past few years, has grown to well over $200 billion. Where did this growth come from? From corporations who borrowed and lent among themselves internationally without the assistance of a bank intermediary.

All these reasons underly the strong current interest in asset and liability management. What exactly does the "management" of assets and liabilities attempt to accomplish? The basic purpose of ALM is to measure the risk/reward ratio when planning for profits.

When performing this analysis, a time frame first must be selected. An institution might select 30, 90, or 180 days, or any other time frame desired. Within this time frame, all elements of the balance sheet and income statement are analyzed.

ELEMENTS OF ASSET
AND LIABILITY MANAGEMENT

The elements to be analyzed are:

- Cash flows
- Profits
- Rates
- Balances
- Time

Cash Flows

Asset and liability management begins by tracking cash flows, both into and out of the financial institution. Lump sum flows such as loans, investments, and deposits are all tracked. In addition, interim flows of cash which change every day are also tracked in the form of reserves and cash items in the process of collection. Finally, long-term or occasional flows such as stockholders equity are tracked.

Profits

The second element of asset and liability management is an orientation toward profits. The vast majority of profits for a financial institution come from the difference between its earning assets and its paying liabilities. In assessing and attempting to manage risk, the institution's purpose is to maneuver itself into a position to obtain the maximum profits for the minimum risks.

Rates

The third element of asset and liability management is rates. There are three types of rates to consider, defined by whether they are fixed or variable within the time frame chosen. First, contractual rates are fixed for the period of time of concern. Second, variable rates fluctuate within the period of time chosen. Finally, nonrate assets or liabilities are those balance sheet items which have no rate associated with them, such as reserves, correspondent balances, or cash items in the process of collection (float).

Balances

Balances are the fourth element of asset and liability management. Balances can be divided into two categories, again defined by the length of time for which they remain stable. First, contractual balances are fixed for the chosen period of time. Second, liquid balances fluctuate over the period of time chosen. For example, if the chosen time frame were 30 days, a 90-day deposit would be fixed for that period of time. Other types of balances which would normally be considered fixed would be defined as liquid, such as bonds, loans, or deposits, if they mature or are withdrawn or deposited in the institution within the chosen time period.

Time

Finally, the last element of asset and liability management is time, meaning the maturity of various loans, investments, and deposits, and the period of time these balances are maintained in the institution. Many deposits or loans have specific contractual time frames, or maturities, such as government bonds, loans, or deposits. Some of these have call features which can cause them to be paid off or liquidated before their actual stated maturities. Other deposits, especially transaction deposits such as checking accounts, NOW accounts, and MMDA accounts, have no specific time frame associated with them. However, even these transaction accounts have a typical time for which the balances stay with the institution, depending on the behavior of the institution's customers.

The above elements are then analyzed to assess their risk by using one of two methods. First, "gap analysis" measures the differences between various pools of similar types of funds, and attempts to manage these differences. "Duration analysis," on the other hand, is a present value cash flow technique which analyzes the flow of funds and their related rates and market yields. Our discussion of these methods will identify how price is affected during the process of asset and liability management and risk assessment.

GAP ANALYSIS

In March of 1975, in the *Bank Administration Institute Magazine,* John Clifford, in an article entitled, "A Perspective on Asset-

FIGURE 8–1 Classical Gap

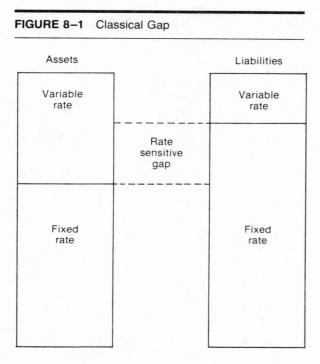

Liability Management," indicated that banks needed to structure the information on their balance sheets differently. Financial accounting techniques were increasingly unsuitable as the industry approached a more competitive and deregulated environment and wrestled with the problems of inflation. In this article, asset and liability management was defined as managing the differences between various pools of similar funds, and the now classical approach to gap management was introduced.

Shown in Figure 8–1 is what Mr. Clifford defined as the "gap." Assets are in the left-hand column and liabilities are in the right-hand column. Both assets and liabilities are divided into two pools of funds, either variable rate funds or fixed rate funds. The "rate sensitive gap" is the difference between the variable rate assets and the variable rate liabilities. This same gap is also, of course, the difference between the fixed rate assets and the fixed rate liabilities.

If interest rates declined, those variable rate assets supported by variable rate liabilities would retain their spread. But if the rates of the variable rate assets supported by fixed rate liabili-

FIGURE 8–2 Controllable Gap

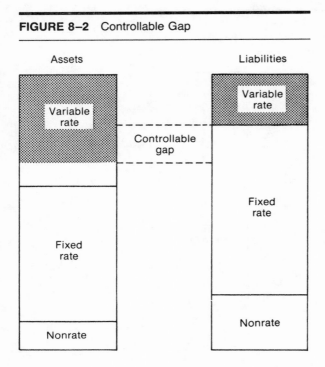

ties—those assets within the rate sensitive gap—began to drop, cost of funding would remain fixed and margins are squeezed. The objective of performing this simple gap analysis was to prevent the gap from getting too large and exposing the institution to fluctuating interest rate risk. The next three gaps presented below are refinements of this classical gap.

The rate sensitive gap can be refined into what is called a controllable gap, depicted in Figure 8–2. Within the rate sensitive gap, only a portion of the variable rate assets and liabilities can be controlled or managed within the time period of concern. The rest of the variable rate items would be contractually fixed for a longer period of time than that under consideration. The purpose of determining a controllable gap is to form a measure of the assets and liabilities that can be dealt with on a day-to-day basis to restructure the balance sheet. It measures those assets and liabilities which are close to cash equivalency and which can be restructured, either by rate or maturity, depending on management's perspective of the future rate environment.

FIGURE 8–3 Nonrate Gap

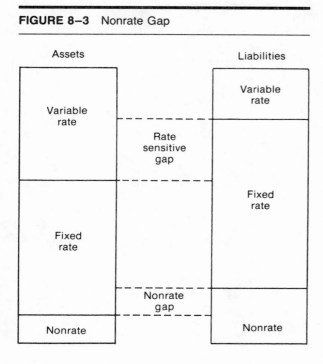

In Figure 8–3, the pools are grouped into the three categories—variable rate assets and liabilities, fixed rate, or nonrate. This structure produces the nonrate gap. Many depository institutions have high level nonrated liabilities in the form of checking accounts and/or equity. (Equity does of course have a cost—a cost of capital—but for simplicity's sake in this analysis, equity or capital is assumed to be a nonrate item). In the example shown in Figure 8–3, some fixed rate assets are being supported by nonrate liabilities, protecting their spread no matter what happens to the interest rates. If the reverse were true, if nonearning assets were being supported by fixed rate liabilities, the spread would always be negative and detrimental.

It is also useful to group income statement items by rate. In Figure 8–4, the income statement is grouped according to sources of income or expense. Income can be defined as variable rate interest income, fixed rate interest income, or nonrate or fee income. Expense can be defined in the same way. Noninterest income is netted with noninterest expense; in the example, expense is greater than income, as is usually the case, so the result

FIGURE 8–4 Income Gap

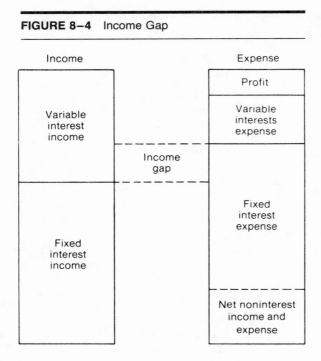

is placed in the expense column. The difference between total income and total expense is profit (or loss); in the example, a profit is realized, which is depicted on the expense side since then expense is less than income. Loss would be depicted on the income side, as expense would be greater than income. This analysis produces an "income gap," or measurement of how much more income is associated with one pool of funds on the balance sheet than with another.

A handy way to implement gap analysis is to segregate all the various asset and liability balances—based on whether the balance is fixed or variable for the given time frame and whether the rate is fixed or variable—into sections of a matrix, called an asset and liability matrix, or AL Matrix. Shown in Figure 8–5 is the AL Matrix for the three types of rates and the two types of balances. Each of the line items on a balance sheet would be placed into one of these six sections and totals would be generated for each section.

Doing this, the various gaps can be identified for management information purposes. Shown in Figure 8–6 is the rate

FIGURE 8–5 AL Matrix

	Balances	
Rate	Fixed	Liquid
Fixed		
Variable		
Nonrate		

sensitive gap. The crosshatched sections represent the balances which constitute the rate sensitive gap. The section for fixed balance-variable rate includes commercial loans or variable rate auto loans. The liquid balance-variable rate could include Fed

FIGURE 8–6 AL Matrix—Rate Sensitive Gap

	Balance	
Rate	Fixed	Liquid
Fixed		
Variable		
Nonrate		

FIGURE 8–7 AL Matrix—Controllable Gap

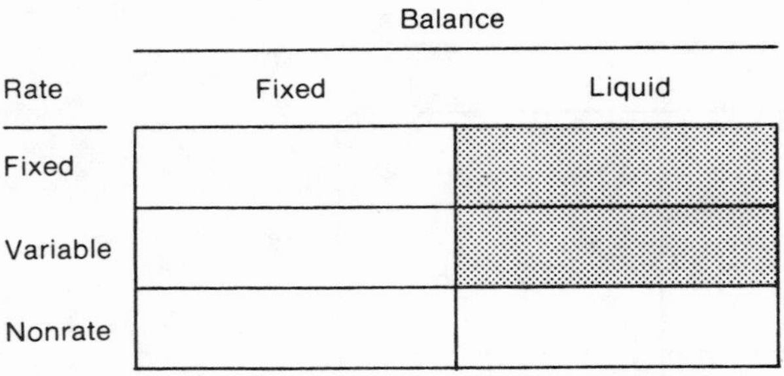

	Balance	
Rate	Fixed	Liquid
Fixed		
Variable		
Nonrate		

Funds purchased or sold. And the liquid balance-fixed rate section includes maturing certificates of deposit or bonds.

In Figure 8–7, the controllable gap can be calculated. Only those assets and liabilities having liquid balances are of concern, so the section from the former AL Matrix for the fixed balance-variable rate is excluded. Now, only items of cash or near cash which could be used to restructure the balance sheet are of interest.

Finally, in Figure 8–8 is depicted the nonrate gap, which subtracts nonearning assets, such as cash items in the process of collection and reserves, from nonpaying liabilities, such as checking account balances and capital.

FIGURE 8–8 AL Matrix—Nonrate Gap

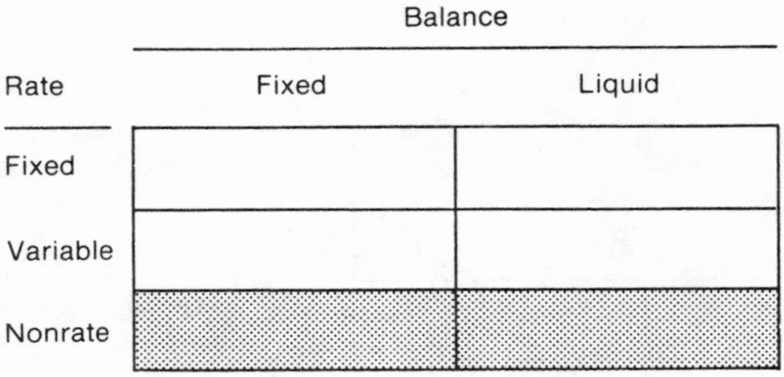

	Balance	
Rate	Fixed	Liquid
Fixed		
Variable		
Nonrate		

Gap analysis defines various pools of funds by rates and balances. It attempts to manage these pools to achieve a satisfactory level of profitability and an acceptable level of risk. To do this analysis, it's crucial to know into which pool of funds a particular deposit, loan, or investment belongs. Identification of the correct pool for a particular rate-related item will enable determination of overall profitability and, in some cases, whether a particular service should be marketed at all.

The disadvantages of using gap analysis are that the collection of data on all balances by maturity and by rate is no easy matter, and this is a continuing problem when performing gap analysis. In addition, gap analysis shares a difficulty with any type of asset and liability management analysis in that the institution is forced to predict what interest rates will do in the future, a notoriously inaccurate exercise.

DURATION ANALYSIS

Duration analysis is the second method for performing asset and liability management. It is a present value technique which measures the "duration" or average maturity of assets and liabilities. Duration analysis avoids the definitional problems of identifying pools of funds with which the gapist wrestles constantly. One of the clearest definitions of duration is provided in an article appearing in the Federal Reserve Bank of Chicago's *Economic Prospectives*. George G. Kaufman, professor of finance and economics at Loyola University in Chicago and a consultant to the Federal Reserve Bank of Chicago, defined duration as follows:

Duration is a measure of the average life of a security. In its simplest form, it is computed by multiplying the length of time to each scheduled payment by the ratio of the present value of that payment to the total present value or price of the security and summing, or

$$D = \frac{\sum_{t=1}^{n} t \cdot PVF_t}{\sum_{t=1}^{n} PVF_t}$$

where:

where:

D = duration

t = length of time (number of months, years, etc.) to the date of payment

PVF_t = present value of the payment (F) made at (t), or $F_t/(1 + i)^t$

$\sum\limits_{t=1}^{n}$ = summation from the first to the last payment

This measure of duration is referred to as Macauley's Duration, and is named after Fredrick Macauley, who first computed it in 1938 in his seminal study of the history of interest rates in the United States. Duration is a single number that is measured in units of time, e.g., months or years. For securities that make only one payment at maturity, duration is equal to maturity; for all other securities, it is shorter than term to maturity.[1]

Duration measures the cash flow that is generated from a particular investment, loan, or deposit by weighting the present value of the cash flow according to the periods of time when that cash flow is received. The result is an average date when that cash flow is received. The idea is to match the duration maturities of cash outflows with cash inflows. If, for example, the average cash inflow dates are later than the average cash outflow dates, that means that the assets have to be refinanced on average before they mature. The institution would then be at risk in a rising interest rate environment. The durationist can attempt to immunize the balance sheet by trying to establish an equilibrium between the duration maturity of assets and the duration maturity of deposits.

Duration calculations, although they can be and are done for individual assets or liabilities, are especially useful when used in the aggregate. The durationist has considerable flexibility in determining the composition of the group of assets on which the duration will be calculated, so as to match the asset group most efficiently to the duration of a group of various liabilities.

Duration is a far more analytical technique than gap analysis, and can precisely identify the risk to which a particular institution is subject according to the structure of its assets and liabilities. From a management perspective, duration is simple to administer once data is available to calculate the present value of cash flows.

---
[1]"Measuring and Managing Interest Rate Risk: A Primer," George G. Kaufman, *Chicago Economic Perspectives,* January–February 1984, p. 16.

The critical element in a duration calculation is the interest rate. Much has been written on duration, and the major confusion centers around what rate to use to discount the cash flows from a deposit, investment, or loan. Some use the particular asset's or liability's current yield. Others use a coupon equivalent yield derived from secondary market rates and other money market related rates and yields for a similar security. There are numerous rates and yields that can be used.

Another critical element of duration is its high informational demands. Data needs to be obtained concerning the cash flows from all assets and liabilities or at least from categories of similar assets and liabilities. In addition, rates and yields need to be identified which can be used to discount the cash flow.

Also, from a product perspective, various marketing structures for services can not always be designed to comply with the requirements of the duration form of asset and liability management. For example, zero coupon CDs are not necessarily readily marketable to many consumers. Yet from a duration perspective, this is an extremely viable form of pricing to associate with earning assets; since there is only one cash flow to calculate, the duration of a zero coupon CD is the same as its maturity.

Finally, although many assets and liabilities have stated maturities, many do not. For some assets or liabilities, such as checking account balances or savings accounts, it may be difficult to even estimate maturities. This difficulty, of course, can seriously hamper the durationist, although a gapist has similar problems.

Duration can be an extremely valuable technique for pricing purposes. However, a frequent criticism of the practical implementation of duration is that the actual application can be overwhelming when considering the establishment of the duration of an entire portfolio of loans, investments, or deposits. One way to approach this is for the institution to identify the duration of individual securities or loans and manage them on a micro level, such as calculating only the duration of a specific type of auto loan. Then, the institution can calculate duration for the specific funding source for that loan. These duration calculations of individual assets and liabilities over time will aggregate to the management of *all* of its assets and liabilities on a duration basis.

In the future, duration will be used more and more by financial institutions as software and systems of data collection are developed to handle the heavy informational demands of duration asset and liability analysis.

IMPACT ON PRICING

Asset and liability management is important for pricing because the analyses used identify the profit earned from various assets and liabilities and the risk associated with the return that is generated. Profit is a result of pricing, and risk assessment is a function of the bottom line.

When using gap analysis, it is important that the pricer of financial services correctly identify the pool for a particular earning asset so it is associated with the correct paying liability to accurately calculate the profit generated by and the risk inherent in that particular asset and liability mix.

When using duration analysis, it is important that the correct rate be identified since this is the driving factor with which to discount cash flows to determine average maturities or durations of investments, loans, and deposits. Duration is a technique which could be used for individual assets and liabilities to identify the actual duration of particular earning assets and paying liabilities. Over time it can be used to aggregate these durations in a portfolio approach to calculate the duration of an entire institution's assets and liabilities. Thus, duration could be used as an effective pricing tool by identifying the actual duration maturity of a particular service. Once this is known, it could then be offset with the corresponding asset or liability. The management of the entire balance sheet can be approached by analyzing individual services piecemeal and pricing them based on duration analysis.

SUMMARY

Asset and liability management is a planning procedure which takes into account rates, balances, and time to assess the risk associated with profitably managing the net interest margin of a financial institution.

There are two methods for accomplishing the analysis of asset and liabilities to effectively manage their relationship. First, gap analysis segregates the balance sheet into a series of pools of similar maturity assets and liabilities, and then manages the gaps within these pools. Second, duration analysis is a present value technique which measures the average life of a security based on the cash flow that is produced from the security, whether it is an investment, a loan, or a deposit. Duration will, in time, become the leading technique because it accurately assesses the risk associated with the management of the net interest margin. However, in the interim, because of the heavy informational demands of duration, gap analysis is a viable tool which generates a very close approximation of the risk associated with the relationship between assets and liabilities for most financial institutions.

As a pricing principal, asset and liability management is a integral part of the elements necessary to effectively achieve optimal levels of pricing.

9

Account Analysis

The Invoice of Financial Services

Why should I send them an account analysis?
I can make more money if I keep them in the dark.

—Anonymous Bank President

Account analysis is a procedure which assists the financial institution to equate fees and balances. It provides a supporting structure to implement pricing decisions for financial services. It also explains, to a large degree, why the Sears and Merrill Lynches of the world want access to the deposit-taking and loan-making functions of financial institutions.

Our discussion will be divided into several major sections. We will present the basics, such as definitions, and will address the importance of account analysis. Then, the various individual components of account analysis, many of which are misunderstood or misused by financial institutions, will be examined. Finally, the policy issues as they may apply to your institution as well as the proper implementation of account analysis in the marketplace will be presented.

INTEREST FROM COMPETITORS

Firms such as Sears and Merrill Lynch are competing with financial depository institutions for two reasons. First, these firms

146

want access to deposit insurance, which eliminates the risk associated with the collection of funds and the paying of interest to the consumer and, in some cases, to money brokers for large corporations. With the FDIC or FSLIC insuring deposits, consumers' perceptions are that the full faith and guarantee of the Federal government stands behind their deposits, even though from a technical perspective this insurance is highly leveraged. It is provided from a pool of premiums collected over time from financial institutions, and represents 1 percent or less of the total outstanding deposits in financial institutions in the United States. Nonetheless, most consumers consider leaving money with a depository financial institution as riskless.

Therefore, from a pricing perspective that trades on this feeling of comfort of the consumer, a financial institution can offer a lower price for its deposits than a nonfinancial competitor can. Thus, an interest rate offered on deposits supported by FDIC insurance can be lower than if a firm were to hang its shingle out as a private uninsured financial institution such as Merrill Lynch and Sears.

The second reason competing firms want to be in the financial depository institution business is because of the uniqueness of the payment mechanism available to banks and thrifts. This additional payment mechanism is founded on the concept of fees and balances covered in Chapter 6, and forms the foundation of account analysis.

If a consumer buys brokerage services from Merrill Lynch or a shirt from Sears, he can use a variety of payment methods. He can pay for the shirt with a charge card, coin, currency, a check, or a credit from a prior purchase that was returned. Brokerage services can additionally be paid for through the use of a margin account or a loan.

However, a bank or savings and loan can also accept balances to pay for services, and that is the uniqueness of banking. Not only can a financial institution offer all of the payment mechanisms available to any other business, it can also accept deposits which it can invest sufficiently long to pay the fee for the purchased services. This has classically come to be known as buying services with "hard dollars" (fees), or "soft dollars" (balances).

These, then, are the two fundamental reasons behind the keen interest in financial services. And at the core of this interest is account analysis.

Account analysis is the procedure used by financial institutions to equate hard dollar fees and soft dollar deposit balances and to evaluate customers' payment positions with regard to services rendered. Account analysis is, therefore, nothing more than the "invoice for financial services rendered," presented periodically to the customer.

COMPARISON TO PROFITABILITY ANALYSIS

It is important to note that account analysis is not a "profitability analysis" of the customer. Profitability analysis and account analysis are often equated, but they are quite different.

Profitability analysis is for the internal use of the institution and calculates the profit earned by the financial institution on an individual customer. Account analysis is for the external use of the customer and calculates the fees for services used and the payment required or the credit earned; it is the customer's "invoice."

A useful analogy is a grocery store purchase, where one buys goods and receives an invoice listing the goods purchased, the prices for each good, and the total payment that has to be made. The grocery store does not reveal its costs and how much profit it has realized on milk or meat or a loaf of bread. The invoice merely states what was purchased and the price for those goods.

Account analysis is exactly the same as a grocery store invoice. It states what has been purchased and what is owed or credited.

One additional item is included on an account analysis which is not included on a retail store invoice because of the unique nature of banking. That is the listing of balances maintained and the calculation of the value of those balances, a value which is applied to the fees for services purchased.

Profitability analysis, on the other hand, in addition to evaluating all of the above information, is structured to include costs, and therefore allows the calculation of profit. Thus, profitability analysis can determine whether a particular product or customer is profitable for the institution.

Account analysis is contrasted to profitability analysis for the same customer in Figures 9–1 and 9–2. In Figure 9–1 is shown an accounting of purchased services from a financial institution and the balances left to pay for those services. The balances are earning a rate equivalent to money market rates,

FIGURE 9–1

ACCOUNT ANALYSIS
Acme Manufacturing Company
December 31, 1985

Ledger balances, checking		$15,000
Less: Float		4,000
Reserves		1,000
Investable balances		10,000
Earnings credit		× 8.4%
Monthly credit		$70.00
Services:		
Checks	$30.00	
Deposits	5.00	
Items deposited	25.00	
Monthly maintenance	10.00	
Total		$70.00
Net		–0–

adjusted for reserves and items in the process of collection (float). Account analysis for this customer shows that the balances left are just sufficient to pay for the services used.

Profitability analysis, on the other hand, depicted in Figure 9–2, shows that while this customer has satisfied the payment of the services used, the cost of the products used has not allowed any profits for the institution. Pricing of the products is below

FIGURE 9–2

PROFITABILITY ANALYSIS
Acme Manufacturing Company
December 31, 1985

Bank services revenue:		
Checks		$30.00
Deposits		5.00
Items deposited		25.00
Monthly maintenance		10.00
Total revenue		$70.00
Bank costs:		
Labor	$30.00	
Material	10.00	
Overhead	50.00	
Total cost		$90.00
Net loss		($20.00)

FIGURE 9–3 Differences between
Account Analysis and
Profitability Analysis

Profit Analysis *Elements*	*Account Analysis* *Elements*

Services used
  × Prices
	Services used
	  × Prices

Balances
  × Earnings credit
	Balances
	  × Earnings credit

Costs
  Interest expenses
  Noninterest expenses	

---

cost, and therefore these products are not profitable to the institution.

Acme Manufacturing, however, should not be notified that they are not "paying their way" because they are. They are paying the prices as stated according to their account analysis. The profitability of the services used is a separate issue. They may have been priced incorrectly, or they may be bundled into an overall relationship so another service or product furnishes the profitability of the relationship.

This fundamental difference between profitability analysis and account analysis is critical. Financial institutions often do not differentiate the two analyses, confusing staff and customers alike.

Account analysis includes the services used, the prices of those services, and the balances required to pay for those services. Profitability analysis includes all of the above *and* the costs of the services used.

FEES VERSUS BALANCES

The foundation of account analysis is the concept of equating a fee with a balance or vice versa, as discussed in Chapter 6. The major components of account analysis are: An earnings credit rate, adjustments such as float and reserves, fees, and balances.

Changing The Components

What is the effect on balance requirements of changing the elements of account analysis? Figure 9–4 shows the relationships.

FIGURE 9–4 How Changes in Account Analysis
Factors Affect Balance Requirements

Fees	Earnings Credit	Adjustments	Effect on Balance Requirements
Increase			Increase
	Increase		Decrease
		Increase	Increase
Decrease			Decrease
	Decrease		Increase
		Decrease	Decrease

An increase in fees will have a direct impact on increasing balance requirements. An increase in the earnings credit rate increases the value of balances and therefore decreases the balances required. An increase in adjustments decreases the earnings credit rate and therefore increases the balances required. Decreases cause similar adjustments. A decrease in fees decreases the required balances, a decreased earnings credit rate increases balances required, and a decrease in adjustments decreases the level of balances required.

Based on this interrelationship of factors, let's look at each one individually in greater detail.

Float

Float consists of cash items in the process of collection, and is a line item in the cash section of the balance sheet for financial institutions. Some institutions have opted to extract float from both the cash section of the balance sheet and from deposits, which reduces assets and thereby capital requirements, although the banking and accounting regulators frown on this practice.

Float is the component which makes up the difference between ledger and collected balances and can be a major adjustment in an inefficient institution. Float is important not only for analysis purposes but also for all other balance-related pricing such as the rate set on interest-bearing deposits. Float can be calculated in a variety of ways and can be actual or estimated. If actual, every item making up every daily customer deposit is read to match the check transit number with the institution's current availability schedule for items deposited. A float factor in days is then assigned to each item, summarized by account and by customer, and reported on the account analysis.

Estimating float can be accomplished by using SWAG ("scientific wild a—guess"), which consists of simply picking a daily float factor which "feels right." Float can also be estimated through periodic sampling. To sample float, the institution chooses a day or week or some other defined time span and tracks all items deposited by transit number, compares this to an availability schedule for those transit routes, and then makes a determination of the universal float factor to be assigned to all transit checks or to subgroups of transit checks determined by transit routes.

The difference between actual and estimated methods can be significant for large and/or out of district depositors; this then can have a strong impact on the level of collected balances and ultimately the balance equivalent or price you charge the customer.

Some institutions intentionally increase the float estimate above the actual in order to be able to show a low service price structure. Float is an adjustment which directly affects the balance equivalent for service fees. As depicted in Figure 9–4, an increase in float, as part of adjustments, will increase required balances and thus fees. Hence, an institution can enjoy high balances while appearing to keep prices low. Ultimately, however, the price charged by the institution is the same.

Funds Advanced

When customers withdraw balances before they are collected, the financial institution is left with a positive ledger balance but a negative or overdrawn collected balance. This situation is common when a customer moves funds daily. If the institution honors these collected balance overdrafts, it has "advanced funds."

If a customer were to overdraw his account on a book basis or a ledger basis, creating a ledger overdraft, the institution is technically required to credit the customer's deposit account and debit a loan account called overdrafts, which is essentially unsecured credit. When a customer is overdrawn on a collected balance basis, the same procedure should take place as with ledger overdrafts, but it seldom does.

Shown in Figure 9–5 are two examples of account analysis. In both cases, a five-day month is used for the sake of brevity. Case A is the classical analysis where the negative balances of the days when overdrafts occur are netted with the positive balances of other days to produce one summary collected balance at month-end. Reserves are netted out on a daily basis for the overdrafts, and, of course, the available balance is decreased on a daily basis.

In total, the customer had a $400,000 ledger balance for the month and a collected balance for the month of $100,000. On average, the customer had $20,000 daily collected balances. Netting out the total of reserves, available balances total $88,000 and average daily available balances are $17,600.

In Case B, the concept of "funds advanced" is applied. When an overdraft occurs on any given day, no netting with subsequent days occurs. Instead, each overdraft is treated individually and funds are advanced against that overdraft sufficient to bring the daily balance back to zero. This creates a loan which is charged to the customer at his usual borrowing rate.

Although the total and average ledger balances are the same in this second case, notice how differently the adjusted collected and available balances are treated. When an overdraft occurs on a collected basis, funds are advanced and the collected balance is adjusted back to zero. Now the total collected balance for the month is $200,000 rather than the $100,000 of Case A, and the average daily collected is $40,000 rather than $20,000. Average daily reserves are now calculated to be $4,800. Finally, totaling the adjustment due to funds advanced gives an average daily available balance that is twice what it was in Case A.

Notice that since funds advanced is a loan, the balance in the deposit account is increased. Although the institution gives balance credit for these funds, it must also charge for them. The effect is the difference between the lending rate and the institution's cost of funds. Also note that reserves must increase to cover the higher deposit amount.

Funds advanced is an important part of account analysis which, if ignored, will cause an institution to understate the balance credit to the customer. It will also miss an excellent opportunity to increase profitability by recognizing the use of the institution's funds when a customer is overdrawn on a collected balance basis.

FIGURE 9–5 Funds Advanced

CASE A

Day	Ledger Balance	Less Float	Collected Balance	Less* Reserves	Available Balance
1	$100,000	$ 50,000	$ 50,000	$ 6,000	$ 44,000
2	50,000	100,000	(50,000)	(6,000)	(44,000)
3	100,000	25,000	75,000	9,000	66,000
4	50,000	100,000	(50,000)	(6,000)	(44,000)
5	100,000	25,000	75,000	9,000	66,000
Total	$400,000	$300,000	$100,000	$12,000	$ 88,000
Average	$ 80,000	$ 60,000	$ 20,000	$ 2,400	$ 17,600

CASE B

Day	Ledger Balance	Less Float	Collected Balance	Funds Advanced	Adjusted Collected	Less* Reserves	Available Balance
1	$100,000	$ 50,000	$ 50,000	–0–	$ 50,000	$ 6,000	$ 44,000
2	50,000	100,000	(50,000)	$ 50,000	–0–	–0–	–0–
3	100,000	25,000	75,000	–0–	75,000	9,000	66,000
4	50,000	100,000	(50,000)	50,000	–0–	–0–	–0–
5	100,000	25,000	75,000	–0–	75,000	9,000	66,000
Total	$400,000	$300,000	$100,000	$100,000	$200,000	$24,000	$176,000
Average	$ 80,000	$ 60,000	$ 20,000	$ 20,000	$ 40,000	$ 4,800	$ 35,200

*Reserve Requirement assumed to be 12%.

This component is part of account analysis for both a commercial and a consumer customer. If an institution is open late Friday afternoon, and a customer comes in to cash a paycheck by depositing the check and getting some of it back in cash, when does the institution get reimbursed for the funds which have been advanced to the customer? Probably not until Tuesday morning. So the institution has just made a loan to the customer if the amount of cash back exceeded the collected balance in the customer's account. Use of funds advanced would eliminate this problem.

Reserve Requirements

The reserve requirement is that amount required of all financial institutions to be deposited with the Federal Reserve. Banks required to maintain reserves prior to deregulation have finished the phase-out of the old reserve requirements, and all other institutions are phasing in the reserve requirements through September of 1987.

The present regulations require that for the first $28.9 million of all transaction accounts, defined as DDA, NOW, and ATS accounts, 3 percent must be reserved with the Fed. Twelve percent is required on all balances thereafter.

The reserve requirement can be either averaged or "stated." If averaged, the institution calculates the amount at 3 percent and the amount at 12 percent and weights the amounts accordingly. "Stated" reserves are simply estimated.

Averaging is most accurate, and since account analysis is performed after month-end the information is available to calculate reserves accurately. The stated method is best suited for institutions with less than $28.9 million in transaction balances. Large institutions must choose between the two methods. If an institution uses a larger than required reserve rate, balance requirements increase and, ultimately, so do the prices for services.

GENERAL POLICY ISSUES

The following policy issues should be considered when determining an account analysis procedure:

1. Full disclosure;
2. Accuracy;
3. Indifference between payment of fees and balances;
4. Netting.

Full Disclosure

Full disclosure means periodically telling customers about each of the services they are purchasing from the institution. Therefore, account analysis should be communicated to the customer on a frequent, periodic basis and in a form that is readable by the customer. Since account analysis is the invoice of banking services, customers should know what services they are buying and the prices of those services. This is true for both commercial and consumer customers.

This raises the issue of what to do with customers who are not aware of leaving excess balances with you. Should these customers be told of this excess, which might then prompt them to reduce the balances? The answer is yes. If the customers are not told of excess balances, sooner or later they will figure it out for themselves, perhaps with the help of a friendly rival down the street.

When customers find out they have been leaving excess balances, their reaction is predictable:

1. They may be angry that they have not been informed of the situation, which could encourage them to leave the institution.
2. They may reduce their balances and invest the excess, hopefully within the institution but maybe with another, and simultaneously become price sensitive for all services that are provided them in the future.
3. They may not care and leave the situation as status quo.

All of these reactions have been encountered by institutions when their customers realize they have excess balances. The best reaction, from the present institution's viewpoint, is of course the third one. The other two alternatives are exactly what institutions which do not practice full disclosure are trying to avoid. However, it is highly unlikely that the customer will remain uninformed, and the situation you most want to avoid is having the customer enlightened by the competition.

A full disclosure policy is one in which customers are made aware of the services they are buying and the associated prices on a periodic basis. In addition, this communication should be in a form that is readily available to and fully understandable by the customers. To try to hide an excess balance position or to consolidate information to avoid understanding by the customer is inappropriate and will create relationship problems.

Accuracy

The second principle guiding account analysis should be accuracy. To overstate float, understate prices, or misstate any item on an account analysis creates a situation that can only lead to poor customer service. Accurate disclosure of all of the major components of account analysis is essential to enable customers to accurately comprehend the institution's services, prices, and pricing structure.

Customers' understanding of account analysis can actually work to the benefit of the institution. If customers have little business that is transacted outside of the institution's market area, they would have a small amount of float. If the institution is able to track float for each individual customer and reports it on the account analysis, then those customers will have the benefit of an accurate statement of items in the process of collection. If the institution does not have the ability to individually track float, an accurate estimate of float can still give customers an approximation of collected items and thus still be of value to them.

To state float, as some institutions do, in terms of an excessive number of days, such as greater than three days, is an inaccuracy that customers will not tolerate and which may eventually cause a relationship problem.

Indifference Between Fees and Balances

The third major policy guideline is to create an indifference as to whether customers pay in fees or balances. This requires the institution to accurately price services based upon value and the institution's internal cost structure and desired profit in order to be able to equate the value of balances to fees collected for services rendered.

Accurate pricing requires accurate cost analysis to determine the minimum prices for the institution's services to allow a profit margin. This cost analysis may, in some cases, indicate that prices on some services will not produce sufficient profit for the institution's normal investment returns. However, this may be a service that the institution has to offer in order to have the opportunity to provide other more profitable services.

An example would be where an institution may not be able to charge a sufficiently high price on "items deposited" to make this a profitable service. But it will continue to offer this service at a reduced price in order to maintain checking account relationships with commercial customers and enjoy profits on other services such as wire transfers.

Ultimately, the institution wants to structure pricing policy so as to be able to offer profitable services to its customers regardless of whether these customers pay with fees or equivalent balances. The institution may thus have customers who pay entirely in fees, those who pay entirely in balances, or those who pay with a combination of both.

Theoretically, customers will be better off paying for financial services with fees because of the built-in "friction" in the banking system due to reserves. Reserves are an adjustment to balances and are an added cost when pricing balances; therefore, customers are getting less "bang for the buck." Sophisticated corporate customers commonly compensate their banks with fees instead of balances because of this friction from reserves.

Netting

Finally, there is the issue of netting. Netting is the procedure which allows a shortfall in one period to be netted with an excess in a subsequent period. This process can be done if the institution has the operational system to track this situation and display it on an account analysis. The use of this procedure should be limited to a specific time frame which should not exceed one year; otherwise, the tracking of balances becomes too much of an administrative burden. In addition, institutions should factor in that the value of money varies from period to period; they could still end up with a shortfall in value due to a shrewd customer who underpays with balances in a high interest rate period and makes up the deficit with balances in a low interest rate period.

A cousin of netting is double counting. This is a pricing technique allowed by institutions where one amount of balances pays for multiple services. In general, if all balances available to pay for all services adequately compensate the institution, then double counting can be justified. However, in most cases, double counting is used by customers to lower the price of services used. When this occurs, no justification for this procedure exists other than the inability of the institution to control the situation.

SUMMARY

Account analysis can be done for all customers including retail consumers. The use of account analysis can be an important pricing procedure to use as a defensive strategy to compete with financial institutions who by regulation cannot accept deposits. Account analysis is a way to implement relationship pricing strategies by using the unique mechanism of fees and balances to maximize value not only to the customer but to the institution itself. An abbreviated form of account analysis may be more appropriate for the retail consumer, but the principles and procedures as outlined in this chapter are the same.

10

Pricing Constraints
Laws, Regulations, and Operations

"Whose head is this, and whose inscription?" "Caesar's," they replied. At that he said to them, "Then give to Caesar what is Caesar's, but give to God what is God's." Taken aback by this reply, they went off and left him.

—Matthew, Chapter 22, verse 20–22

All businesses operate under constraints in the form of governmental regulations and local and national laws. In addition, operational constraints are usually present because of the limitations of manual and data processing systems.

In this chapter, we will discuss the various constraints to which financial services are subject. The discussion will be divided into two areas. First, regulations and laws will be dealt with briefly. There are many excellent sources on the specific details of regulations governing banking activities, such as the Federal Reserve Bulletin. The purpose of this chapter is to provide an overview of the laws and regulations affecting pricing, and to focus on the specific ones of most concern. Later on in the chapter, operational constraints will also be discussed.

LAWS AND REGULATIONS

The Constitution of the United States gave Congress the power to regulate commerce. Based on this power, Congress created the Bank of the United States, a central bank, in 1791. Because of fear of concentration of power (similar to the present opposition to interstate banking), this bank was eliminated in 1811. However, a central bank was needed, and in 1816, the Second Bank of the United States was created, only to be forced to close again in 1836.

For the next quarter century, banking was handled almost entirely by the individual states. Bank failures were common, and paper money varied from state to state. The Civil War created demands for a stable and uniform currency, and the National Bank Act was passed in 1863. This Act created federally chartered banks, which created the dual banking system in the United States, meaning that banks could be chartered by either states or the Federal government. The dual banking system operated under the guideline that state regulations would prevail unless a national law was passed which superceded state law.

Then, in 1913, the Federal Reserve System was created, which gave the United States once again a central bank. The Federal Reserve Bank maintained a low profile until the 30s, when it became an active regulator. Also in 1933 and 1934, in response to the Depression, before which there were 30,000 banks and after which there were 15,000, numerous security and investment acts were passed, including the Glass-Stegal Act, the FDIC Act, and the FSLIC Act, followed in subsequent years by the Bank Holding Company Act and the Douglas Amendment to this Act.

In March of 1980, the Depository Institutions Deregulation and Monetary Control Act (DIDMC) was passed. The purpose of this Act was two-fold. It was meant to gradually deregulate banking, and specifically to phase out the interest rate restrictions of Regulation Q by April 1, 1986. Secondly, it was meant to allow the Federal Reserve greater control over the banking system and the monetary supply by requiring all banks to be members of the Fed. It also gave thrift institutions consumer lending powers, and established the Depository Institutions Deregulation Committee (DIDC) to implement the phase-out of Reg Q.

In September of 1982, the Garn-St Germain Depository Institutions Act was passed to augment the 1980 Monetary Control Act. The Garn-St Germain Act covered a wide spectrum of issues, including granting the FDIC and FSLIC short-term additional powers, such as extraordinary acquisitions, to assist failing banks and thrifts.

The Monetary Control Act and the Garn-St Germain Act have had major impacts on banking activities in the 1980s. Both these acts are discussed in greater detail later in this chapter.

Banks today are subject to regulation by either state or federal regulators or both. Each state has a Commissioner or Supervisor which charters and supervises state-chartered banks. In addition, there are a number of major federal agencies which regulate banks:

1. The Office of the Comptroller of the Currency, created in 1863.
   The Comptroller is part of the Treasury department and charters and supervises national banks.
2. The Federal Deposit Insurance Corporation (FDIC), created in 1933.
   This agency insures all federally chartered banks and most state chartered banks. It also regulates all state banks which are not members of the Fed but have FDIC insurance. Those state banks which do not have FDIC insurance are regulated by their states.
3. The Federal Savings and Loan Insurance Corporation (FSLIC), created in 1933.
   This agency insures all federally chartered member savings and loan institutions.
4. The Federal Home Loan Bank Board, created in 1932.
   This agency regulates all federally chartered savings and loans and savings banks, which must be members of the agency. It also regulates all state chartered thrifts who either have FSLIC insurance or who are members of the agency.
5. The Federal Reserve Bank, created in 1913.
   The Fed regulates state banks which are members of the Fed and all federally chartered banks, which must be members of the Fed, as well as all bank holding companies. Since the Monetary Control Act of 1980, all depository institutions are required to keep reserves with the Fed.

In addition, the DIDC has regulatory powers, but the Committee will dissolve in 1986. Banks are subject to the state law in which they are located unless Federal law is specifically passed to supercede state law.

Interstate Banking

The prohibition on interstate banking is an excellent example of the priority in which laws regulate. Banks are prohibited from interstate full-service branching by state law, not federal. This prohibition has been enacted by all states in some form, and is a direct constraint on pricing. Prohibiting banks from locating physically close to markets restricts them from effectively serving those markets. Therefore, the banks already located in those markets have a freer hand in pricing and are less subject to competition. This form of controlling competition always raises prices.

FEDERAL RESERVE REGULATIONS

These regulations, by custom, are coded by alphabetical letter. The regulations below are those which most directly exercise restrictions on pricing.

Regulation D

This regulation specifies reserves to be maintained by all financial institutions. All depository institutions became required under the Depository Institutions Deregulation and Monetary Control Act to maintain reserves with the Fed. This is an expansion of the 1913 Federal Reserve Act which had required only member banks to keep reserves with the Fed. Total net transaction accounts up to and including $28.9 million are subject to 3 percent reserves; transaction accounts over $28.9 million are subject to 12 percent reserves.

This fractional reserve system was intended to maintain control over economic activity by controlling the monetary aspects of the economy. One of the results of the reserve requirement, a result which is examined in detail in Chapter 6 on Fees Versus Balances and in Chapter 9 on Account Analysis, is that it creates friction in the system which prevents the full use of all deposit dollars.

More specifically, holding reserves means that for every dollar the institution takes in through deposits, it must set aside 3 cents or 12 cents. Therefore, the institution cannot lend out $1; it can only lend out 97 cents or 88 cents. This reduces the value of the deposits to the institution, which in turn reduces the credit for the deposits the institution can pass on to the customer. The direct impact on the pricing of financial services is to raise the price.

Regulation J

This regulation covers the collection of checks, or items in the process of collection. This is popularly called the float regulation. It governs the collection of money among depository institutions in the United States, and deals with such issues as holding periods of checks and notification of insufficient funds to the bank of first deposit. The purpose of this regulation is to allow money to move most efficiently by standardizing collection procedures.

The impact of the guidelines specified in this regulation on the pricing mechanism is very similar to that of reserves. Friction is created because money that is deposited may not be collected at the time of deposit, and therefore cannot immediately be lent out or invested. In fact, most money is not collected at the time of deposit and will take anywhere from one to three days to become collected (usually one day). The result is that since the depository institution cannot employ the funds immediately, the customer has to wait before earning any value for deposits left with banks, either in earnings credit or in interest. The result of Regulation J, again, is that value is lowered for deposits and therefore prices rise.

Regulation Q

This regulation is probably the most famous of all regulations and the most well known to consumers of financial services. It governs the payment of interest on deposits, and is slowly being phased out per the Monetary Control Act of 1980. The Depository Institutions Deregulation Committee (DIDC) was created in part to oversee this phase-out, and by March of 1986 Regulation Q will have been completely phased out.

Reg Q allowed the Federal Reserve to establish the level and type of interest rate that could be paid on specific types of deposit accounts. With this artificial ceiling, interest on deposit accounts for years did not accurately reflect the open market value of money. Interest rates offered by financial institutions were substantially below what could be obtained in the marketplace. Since the cost of funds for depository institutions was kept low, these institutions could lend out money at lower rates and still maintain their spreads. Thus, this regulation kept the price of all financial services artificially low, both to those saving money in the form of deposits and to those borrowing money in the form of loans. The result was that borrowers really were subsidized by the government through the form of lower interest rates at the sake of savers or depositers.

Regulation Z

The Truth in Lending regulation was initially enacted in May of 1968 as part of the Consumer Credit Protection Act. It mandated that certain disclosures be made to the consumer regarding consumer credit. In the past, until the DIDMC was enacted, the amount of regulations governing the compliance procedures was enormous. The DIDMC simplified this, as did the Garn-St Germain Act of a few years later.

The influence of this regulation was far reaching by making the decision processes of lenders more transparent to consumer borrowers. In many cases, unfair practices were curtailed and/or eliminated due to the enactment of this law and subsequent regulations. However, this regulation is the embodiment of the statement that there are no free lunches. Consumer credit costs increased due to the added time necessary to comply with the regulation. While the regulation did eliminate abuse, it also substantially increased the cost of providing credit, and subsequently raised the price of credit to the consumer.

Regulations G, T, U, X

These four regulations deal with the financing of securities transactions. G governs credit extended by parties other than banks, brokers, and dealers for the purchase of securities. T governs credit extended to securities brokers or dealers for the purpose of purchasing or carrying margin securities. U limits the amount of credit a bank may extend for the purchase or carrying of margin stock if the credit is secured directly or indirectly by stock. X broadens the provisions of G, T, and U to specific cases of extensions of credit for purchase or carrying of securities and requires borrowers to comply with margin requirements in securities transactions.

The result of these four regulations on pricing is to limit the value that can be obtained through a security, thereby reducing the return on securities. A higher return could be realized without these regulations by using credit as leverage to buy the security, or by leveraging the security itself by pledging it as collateral and then using the resulting credit to reinvest for additional return, in effect arbitraging between the revenue generated by investing the borrowed funds and the cost of that borrowing.

The eight regulations described above are the specific ones that constrain the pricing efforts of financial institutions. Reserve requirements, check collection guidelines, restrictions on interest for deposits, and consumer lending disclosures impose the greatest restrictions on pricing. The overall result of these regulations is that prices are increased. The offsetting benefit is supposedly increased social equality and standardization controlled by the government.

STATE REGULATIONS

All 50 states have various regulations governing financial services. All states will charter depository institutions and license security transactions and other financial services. It is not possible in this limited space to summarize the regulations of the individual states, but the overall regulation by state authorities can be grouped into two basic areas.

States often will regulate the earning asset side of most financial institutions through usury laws which cap the rate that can be charged for borrowing. In many cases, the amount of borrowings and other terms such as maturity are also restricted under usury laws. The DIDMC overrode some usury laws for selected consumer services for a limited period of time. Also, numerous legislative amendments to the DIDMC since 1980 have continued to change the usury laws. For the most part, the usury laws are fading because of federal action, but there is still a strong desire by some states to maintain usury ceilings for borrowing.

States will also get involved in areas where they perceive possible social ills. For example, in 1984 the Massachusetts Legislature passed "1865 Checking." This law requires depository institutions to offer free checking to consumers 18 years old and to consumers over 65. Also, "lifeline checking," or the mandate to provide basic financial services to those who cannot afford them, is a major current issue supported by numerous consumer groups in a number of states. Finally, check holding laws have been passed by some states to control the amount of time a bank can withhold payment of funds to allow time for physical collection.

The major result of usury laws and other state laws pertaining to financial services, as is the case with most restrictions on market forces, is to increase the price of financial services. Prices of a particular financial service may be reduced for a particular group such as senior citizens, but the overall result is that other groups will have to bear the cost of providing this service below cost.

SPECIFIC REGULATIONS

Depository Institutions Deregulation and Monetary Control Act of 1980

The deregulation of the financial services industry that everyone talks about is primarily due to this Act, which was briefly described earlier. The Act was signed by President Carter on March 31, 1980, and was the first major piece of legislation to reform financial services since the 1930s. The objectives of this Act are straightforward:

Sec. 202.(a) The Congress hereby finds that—
(1) limitations on the interest rates which are payable on deposits and accounts discourage persons from saving money, create inequities for depositors, impede the ability of depository institutions to compete for funds, and have not achieved their purpose of providing an even flow of funds for home mortgage lending; and
(2) all depositors, and particularly those with modest savings, are entitled to receive a market rate of return on their savings as soon as it is economically feasible for depository institutions to pay such a rate.
(b) It is the purpose of this title to provide for the orderly phase-out and the ultimate elimination of the limitations on the maximum rates of interest and dividends which may be paid on deposits and accounts by depository institutions by extending the authority to impose such limitations for 6 years, subject to specific standards

designed to ensure a phase-out of such limitations to market rates of interest.

The Act has many different titles regarding numerous different financial service topics. A brief review of those affecting pricing will highlight the importance of this Act:

1. Reserves were reduced by the Act and became required of all financial institutions, not just nationally chartered institutions.
2. Federal Reserve services such as check clearing were required to have explicit prices which are charged to the financial institution user, essentially unbundling Fed charges.
3. Negotiable order of withdrawal (NOW) accounts, which had been enacted in the New England region, were made legal for the entire nation.
4. Deposit insurance was increased from $40,000 to $100,000 for all types of deposits.
5. Allowable interest rates on credit union loans were changed and somewhat liberalized to reflect economic conditions.
6. The lending power of savings and loans was expanded to allow consumer lending to a maximum of 20 percent of total assets and could include credit cards and auto lending.
7. Trust activities were allowed for savings and loans.
8. As previously noted in the section on State Regulations, usury laws were overridden for a number of consumer services.
9. Regulation Z, dealing with consumer lending disclosure, which had become very complicated, was substantially simplified.

While the clear intent of this Act is for Reg Q to die, the Act doubles as a monetary control act, and in fact, the regulators placed more importance on that aspect of the Act than the interest rate aspect. The requirement for reserves on all deposits and the open pricing for all federally provided banking services is definitely a direction the regulators took to heart.

Garn-St Germain Depository Institutions Act of 1982

In September of 1982, Senator Garn and Representative St Germain produced what is now called the Garn–St Germain Act. This was an omnibus banking bill that further clarified the Depository Institutions Deregulation and Monetary Control Act and specifically addressed additional aspects of deregulation which would aid the ailing housing industry and savings and loans who were suffering because of the effects of deregulation and high interest rates. The important aspects for pricing purposes are summarized as follows:

1. The Act allowed thrifts to offer a commercial demand deposit account (checking account) if it were tied to a loan relationship with the thrift.
2. Overdraft loans were allowed for all customers of thrifts.
3. The lending powers of thrifts were extended to commercial lending.
4. The amount of consumer lending allowed was increased from 20 percent of total assets to 30 percent.
5. The deposit interest rate differential that had existed for 20 years between thrifts and banks was phased out.
6. Probably the most important aspect of this bill as perceived by consumers was the directive to the DIDC to create a money market demand account that was competitive with the money market funds. This account, now called the MMDA, came into being on September 14, 1982. The account allowed a market rate of interest to be paid on deposits of $2,500 or more with a phaseout of this minimum over the next three and a half years. By the end of 1984, a little over two years after the start of this account, close to $400 billion of deposits was in this type of account.
7. A controversial aspect of the Act was the clarification of enforceability of the "due on sale" clause in many mortgages. This clause usually stipulated that the mortgage became due when real estate was sold, which had the effect of ending the onerous low-rate mortgages which hobbled savings and loans. However, because the lower mortgage rate frequently made a house more saleable, sellers often tried to pass the low rate on to the

buyer in spite of the clause. The Garn–St Germain Act stipulated that due on sale clauses were enforceable regardless of state law and that they were governed solely by the loan contract.

8. The legal lending limits for national banks were increased from 10 percent of capital and surplus to 15 percent.
9. Various lending restrictions for national banks on real estate lending were eliminated.
10. Further simplifications were made to Truth in Lending.
11. NOW accounts were extended to allow public money deposits.

The result of the Garn–St Germain Act was to further deregulate the depository institution industry. Prices were allowed to reach competitive levels, which at the time of this Act were very high. Many institutions suffered because of this Act since low fixed-rate or no-rate deposit money moved to high rate money market funds. However, these dollars proved to be stable and provided a good source of funds for most institutions.

In summary, the result of regulation is to inhibit the free market price mechanism. In a capitalistic free market society, price is the mechanism whereby millions of decisions can be made on the allocation of resources. When government restricts the pricing mechanism, it creates artificial barriers to the efficient flow of resources. Therefore, placing restrictions on financial institutions, which by their very nature are intermediaries in the turnover of money, seriously restricts the flow of funds in the entire marketplace. The result of the Depository Institutions Deregulation and Monetary Control Act and the Garn–St Germain Depository Institutions Act is primarily to reduce the pricing constraints faced by financial institutions.

OPERATIONAL CONSTRAINTS

The processing of day-to-day work in a financial institution is called "operations." John Naisbitt, author of *Megatrends*, indicated that banking is information in motion. Operations is the physical embodiment of this statement. The smoother the operations procedures are in a financial institution, the more easily information is moved, both internally and in communications with the customers.

Operations in most financial institutions is completed in one of three ways:

1. In-house data processing and bookkeeping systems;
2. Service bureau systems;
3. Correspondent banking systems.

Most financial institutions will use a combination of these three forms of operational systems. The larger the institution, the greater the tendency to have its own data processing and book-keeping systems controlling and servicing the entire operational and production needs of all services and products that are offered.

Data Processing Constraints

The data processing and bookkeeping systems of a financial in-stitution are frequently the same. The major purpose of these intertwined systems is to account for financial transactions. Since accounting records for financial institutions, unlike other com-panies, must balance every day, the system and operational sup-port required is enormous.

The data processing systems and support procedures are dy-namic rather than static. Software must be created and support provided to new or already existing software for mainframe or smaller data processing systems. The requirements on the soft-ware are constantly changing, and most large institutions and some small institutions employ numerous programmers, either directly or under contract, who constantly change, modify, and correct the software. Large capacity mainframe computer sys-tems, which all large financial institutions have, require skillful technicians working in a closely structured environment.

However, different departments have different needs for data processing support, and all feel their needs are most important. Priorities need to be established for the requested modifications of software, and it must be determined which information is most urgently needed. Pricing changes, while appearing minor to a marketer, can constitute major changes in software programs which affect numerous applications and which highly structured DP departments may resist.

One of the major constraints, then, faced by marketing man-agements of financial institutions is the establishment of prior-ities for any changes requiring an application modification of a data processing system, which certainly includes all pricing changes. A marketing manager can conduct thorough analyses, including market research of needs of customers, identifying costs, and comparing competitive aspects of the proposed service, and then wind up waiting for months before the price can be changed on the software.

Manual System Constraints

Manual systems still reflect a considerable portion of financial data tracking and processing. Because of inefficiencies inherent in a manual system, it can be difficult to input and track the data necessary to the pricing of various services.

A good example of a service that is tracked manually, if at all, is balance inquiries. Most financial institutions have a small number of customers who call daily about the level of their balances or transaction activity in their accounts. These customers are generally small in number but can be very costly to service. Most institutions would like to charge or at least track the activity of these customers. However, this tracking would have to be done manually, and the input of data for these customers would require a use of resources which can exceed any revenue collected. Therefore, many financial institutions forego collecting fees for balance inquiries because the cost to collect the data and charge the customer is more than the revenue that could be earned.

Customer Information File Constraints

A very important operational constraint is imposed by the type of customer information file (CIF) used by a financial institution. These files, consisting of various compiled information on customers, such as name, address, and services and products used, generally concentrate at the account or customer level. However, as we discussed in Chapter 3 regarding the household nature of financial relationships, the relationship a customer has with an institution cannot be viewed at the account or customer level; it must be viewed on an aggregate basis, combining the use of all services and products by a particular household.

In the past, many financial institutions have concentrated their financial service tracking efforts at the product level. But this disregards that a customer may use more than one product. A customer may run a checking account very frugally, yet have a profitable relationship with the bank because of other services being purchased. So many banks started using CIF systems which collect information at the next more general level, the customer level. However, this is not accurate either because several customers make up a household. A wife may run her accounts frugally, but her husband, in the same household, may leave generous balances in his account. You don't want to start charging the wife when the husband's accounts are profitable, because the total household is profitable for the financial institution.

However, herein lies the operational constraint. Most CIF systems stop at the customer level and forget about households. Operationally, they may be incapable of combining data at the household level, and are therefore not suited to marketing or pricing requirements. They are designed to nail down every aspect at the customer level, but they forget about the household relationship while it is the household relationship that is critical to appropriately pricing financial services. It is thus essential that financial institutions concentrate their efforts on expanding their CIF systems or replacing them with ones that have the capability to collect data efficiently on a household basis.

An auxiliary problem is being created because of the use of small in-house computers. Many financial institutions which use outside service bureaus and correspondents to process their transaction data are trying to reduce the cost of these services or add system capability through the use of personal computers. An institution may take a computer application such as safe deposit box billing, a particular type of loan, or CDs and start tracking the data on personal computers. While the institution may realize a short-term cost reduction, this solution totally disrupts the main system's capability to collect information at the household level. To do this, the main system must have access to all products and services as well as all accounts of the institution so that it can combine them.

The main applications, such as checking accounts and most loans, are still run on mainframe units, either on service bureau or correspondents' computers or on in-house units. Therefore, all direct customer applications such as loans, deposits, and fee-based services should remain on the same system, or the main system must have the capability to periodically update from distributed systems that are operating on other computers.

All indirect applications such as word processing, general ledger, or communications such as wire transfers, that are not directly related to customer data collection can be put on a mini-computer or personal computer.

Financial institutions should not be misled by data processing companies or "techies" who hype state of the art technology in personal computers but do not understand the strategic importance of data collection and marketing information files.

In summary, operations provides the data on which marketing and pricing is based. However, priorities, manual data collection, and customer information file problems can pose serious constraints on the pricer of financial services. Financial institutions should be aware of these factors and try to mitigate them as much as possible to keep their constraints to a minimum.

SUMMARY

Legal, regulatory, and operational factors pose very real constraints on the pricing of financial services. Laws and regulations tend to inhibit the free flow of market forces, and thereby end up increasing the cost of financial products. These costs are passed on to consumers in the form of higher prices. Since the early 1980s, various laws such as the Depository Institutions Deregulation and Monetary Control Act and the Garn–St Germain Depository Institutions Act have helped to reduce some of the impact regulations have had on financial institutions and the services that they offer.

Financial institutions are also subject to the constraints of their own and outside providers' operational systems. The establishment of proper priorities can be difficult and the costs of manually collecting some data can outweigh the benefits. The problems inherent in customer information file systems in particular are often not consciously recognized until serious damage is done and the ability of the institution to service and price customers appropriately is hampered.

The pricer of financial services should be aware of the regulatory, legal, and operational constraints. This awareness would be a large step toward the managing of these constraints and the proper and efficient pricing of financial services to the consuming public.

PART 3

Pricing Strategies

The Theory of Quadratic Pricing:

The Integration of Pricing Strategies

The four stages of a woman are: up to 14, when she needs good parents and good health; 14 to 40, when she needs good looks; 40 to 60, when she needs a good personality; and over 60, when she needs cash.
—Mary Kay Ash, Mary Kay Cosmetics, Inc.,
"One on One," ABC, 6/21/83

Four basic strategies can be followed for pricing financial services. While there are many tactical considerations and different approaches to pricing products and services, they can be grouped into these four basic strategies:

- Cost
- Competition
- Relationship
- Value

In this chapter, we will present a unique way of integrating these four strategies, relating them to the demand for financial services in a "Quadratic Pricing" scheme. We will also review a number of products associated with each strategy to illustrate how to move products and prices within the Pricing Quadrants.

COST-PLUS PRICING STRATEGY

Cost-plus is perhaps the most common pricing strategy. Many financial institutions, especially banks and savings and loans, do most of their pricing using cost-plus. This strategy requires that a cost analysis be performed for the particular product or product line being priced. The cost analysis, as discussed in Chapter 5 under cost considerations, should concentrate on fully absorbed cost and include both interest and noninterest expenses. After performing this cost analysis, the pricer needs to determine the yield that is required in order to achieve the desired return on investment or profit percentage. An increment is then added to the cost of providing the product to get that desired return, and that is the price.

The advantage of using the cost-plus approach is two-fold. It's a very simple pricing strategy, and it's very analytical. The data collection required for implementation, while somewhat complex in nature, is specifically identifiable. The analysis can be performed in a relatively short period of time on any type of financial service or product offered by an institution. Also, the price can be precisely identified by tying it to the cost and a profit margin. The execution is also very simple, in that a margin is simply added to the cost of providing the product.

The disadvantage of the cost-plus strategy is that it's very myopic. It completely ignores the customer and market demands. A tremendous amount of confusion can be created when this strategy is used in isolation from other strategies. Presidents, marketing directors, and cashiers scratch their heads and wonder why the customer won't pay the price they have set. The problem, of course, is that cost-plus pricing concentrates on a totally internal perspective and ignores what's happening in the marketplace and, most important, ignores what the customers' needs are.

COMPETITION PRICING STRATEGY

Competition is a second strategy for pricing financial service products. Competition is also a very popular approach and, in fact, cost-plus and competition strategies constitute the vast majority of approaches to pricing used by most financial institutions. Following a competition pricing strategy is simply finding out what the other guy is doing and pricing accordingly. It's the "binocular theory of pricing." Hidden away in every financial institution, sitting somewhere on a shelf, are binoculars. At least once a week, and generally on Tuesday morning, the binoculars are taken out and competition all around the market is scanned for current rates and service charges on competing products. Then, based on the "long-term strategic plan" of the financial institution, prices are set.

The advantages of this form of pricing are that, once again, it's a very simple method and very easily executed. There is little analytical work to be done, with the least amount of data collection required of the four strategies, usually limited to a "shopping survey" to determine competitive prices. The execution is also fairly straightforward in that the institution merely decides whether it wants its prices to be higher than, lower than, or in between the competition.

The disadvantage of the competitive pricing strategy is that it is also extremely myopic. It focuses totally on what competitors are doing and once again forgets the needs of the customer. In addition, it also forgets the needs of the institution. The competition's cost structure or strategic direction may differ dramatically from your own. To take a simple example, the competition could be a low cost producer, and your financial institution might be a high cost producer. Setting the price based on this competition would result in your earning little or no profit.

RELATIONSHIP PRICING STRATEGY

A third pricing strategy is called relationship pricing. This strategy is based on the realization that banking is a relationship business, not a transaction business. Most service products bought from financial institutions, especially transaction accounts like checking accounts or NOW accounts, are part of a relationship and are bought on an ongoing basis. This concept was discussed in depth in Chapter 3 on the intangible nature of financial products. Customers do not generally sign up for an account, run it for one month, and then close the account. They tend to establish relationships with a banking institution.

Relationship pricing is based on this understanding of the nature of financial products and takes into account all of the services that are purchased by a household or a business. It would be inappropriate to focus on the single account or product. If a particular consumer household has several different products, such as a checking account, a savings account, a CD deposit, an auto loan, and a safe deposit box, the profitability (or loss) of one or more of these services could be combined to produce over-

FIGURE 11–1 The Household
Pyramid

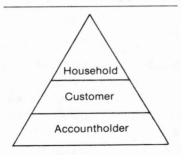

SOURCE: © 1985, G. M. Moebs
& Associates.

all profitability for the customer. It would also be inappropriate, however, to focus on the individual customer, as a number of customers usually share the same household. Appropriate pricing takes place at the household level, defined as "common last name, common address." This orientation is graphically illustrated in Figure 11–1, The Household Pyramid. The financial institution should orient its pricing at the top of the pyramid.

In the commercial market, this relationship orientation is called bundling of services and usually pertains to the coordination of price setting between the commercial loan department and the commercial deposit department where cash management services are sold. In 1972, *Unbundling Full Service Banking*, written by Bryan and Clark, had a tremendous impact on the commercial banking industry, as already discussed in Chapter 6. Its basic premise was the suggestion that bankers should price individual products to get a better grasp on what their products cost them. The idea was to stop giving products away in the mistaken assumption that they cost the bank nothing. This book caused many of the large banks to rethink their pricing of commercial products. Bundling became a dirty word around most money center banks, and the concept of unbundling became a bandwagon onto which most large institutions jumped. However, the concept of bundling or unbundling was misunderstood. Bundling, one of the foundations of the relationship pricing strategy, is neither good nor evil in and of itself. It is a tactic used for relationship pricing, and it can be used very effectively.

In the consumer end of the business, relationship pricing is called packaging. The first package of financial services was introduced in 1973 with the Wells Fargo Gold Account. This was a checking account bundled with travelers checks, cashier's checks, money orders, a safe deposit box, a MasterCard, accident insurance, a check cashing card, and printed checks, into one package of services for one monthly fee. This account was later copied by Merrill Lynch in its asset management account and renamed the Cash Management Account. There are many products on the market now that package financial services into one "account" for the consumer, and they are basically all the same, even though their creators would like you to believe there are very distinct differences. The orientation can be different, in that the account can be focused toward a deposit relationship or a loan relationship, but the concept, tactical implementation, and overall strategy used is that of a relationship.

The advantage of relationship pricing is that this approach mirrors the services that are provided to the customer. Financial products are truly services, and an ongoing relationship is established with the customer. Market research surveys reveal that customers feel they are not purchasing individual services as much as they are purchasing an overall relationship from their financial institution.

The disadvantage of relationship pricing is that it can lower profitability if not executed properly. When individual product statements are created for each of the service products used in a relationship, it may become clear that a number of these products are being sold below their cost, producing a loss for the individual product. This was the primary reason why Bryan and Clark recommended against bundling. But if the overall relationship, when all products are aggregated, produces a profit, then relationship pricing is justified and appropriate. The institution must be careful, however, when using this strategy. If too many of the products are sold at a loss, without taking into consideration where the profit is coming from, then, when the relationship is consolidated, the overall relationship also produces a loss.

It becomes clear, then, that one of the major requirements for implementing relationship pricing is a good operational system. This is another disadvantage of relationship pricing; it has high data collection requirements and may be difficult to implement because of the requirement of consolidating all products used by a relationship. Many institutions have not achieved the level of data collection and reporting capability that is required to successfully implement relationship pricing. However, if an institution has the ability to collect data on all the services that a household or business uses, and can summarize this data into management reports suitable for pricing purposes, then relationship pricing can be used very effectively.

VALUE PRICING STRATEGY

Value pricing can be the most appropriate pricing strategy, but it is also the most difficult to implement. Value is what is perceived by customers as the worth of the financial service that is being bought. Identification of value perception is a subjective process which identifies the needs of customers, matches those with the services of the institution, and thus attempts to determine how the institution and its services are perceived.

Value pricing is neatly illustrated by a situation I found myself in several years ago. I was driving home late one night from a business trip in southern Illinois, and just south of O'Hare Airport in Chicago, about 10 miles from home, my car ran out of gas. I had been trying to make a round trip without refueling and had run into bad weather. So there I sat about a mile away from an oasis (a travel stop-over area) where I could get fuel. It was raining and it was dark. I got on my CB radio, and within half an hour a MinuteMan arrived, which is the Illinois equivalent of emergency road service. The friendly service person proceeded to tell me that I had several options. I could walk to the oasis where diesel fuel for my Oldsmobile was $1.09 a gallon. This was not a very attractive alternative, as weather conditions were awful and there was the unpleasant but distinct possibility that a car might hit me. My next alternative was that he could tow my car to the oasis where I could get fuel for the same $1.09 a gallon, but the towing charge would be $49.95. My third option was to get help from someone else, which was no option. And, finally, my fourth option was that this service person just happened to have a gas can with 5 gallons of diesel fuel in it. However, his diesel fuel would cost me $5 a gallon. Which option do you think I took? Is there any doubt I gladly paid the $25 for the fuel? This is value pricing!

The advantage of value pricing is that it focuses very closely on customer needs. Because the customers' perceived value of worth is identified, the probability of establishing a price acceptable to them is excellent. This type of pricing is also most likely to establish an optimal price for the institution.

The disadvantage of value pricing is that it concentrates too much on marketing and may forget that the firm needs to make a profit. If the perceived value of a checking account is zero, but it costs the institution $80 a year to provide this service, it cannot price the checking account, by itself, at zero without eventually pricing itself into bankruptcy. In addition, the ability to identify the perceived value held by customers is a subjective process prone to considerable error. Extensive market research may be necessary to establish the value that the customer perceives; thus the data collection requirements of this strategy can be demanding and expensive. Even then, the process of identifying value is still very subjective and subject to the fickle nature of customers and the many biases inherent in market research. In addition, the implementation can be difficult, because even if worth is established, value is very difficult to quantify and price.

THE QUADRATIC PRICING MATRIX

Each of the strategies of cost-plus, competition, relationship, and value have advantages and disadvantages. The primary point to remember in considering which of these strategies to use is that each taken in isolation from the others is inappropriate for pricing financial products. Each of the strategies must be integrated with the others in determining price.

Shown in Figure 11–2 is the Quadratic Pricing Matrix, which integrates the individual strategies together with a demand curve. Each of the four sides of the square represents one of the four pricing strategies. Cost-plus pricing is on the lower axis, with its own scale indicating high cost to the left and low cost to the right. Competition pricing is on the right-hand axis, with low competition being at the top and high competition at the bottom. Relationship pricing is on the upper axis, with strong relationships at the left and weak relationships at the right. Finally, value pricing is on the left-hand axis, with high value being at the top and low value at the bottom.

FIGURE 11–2 The Quadratic Pricing Matrix

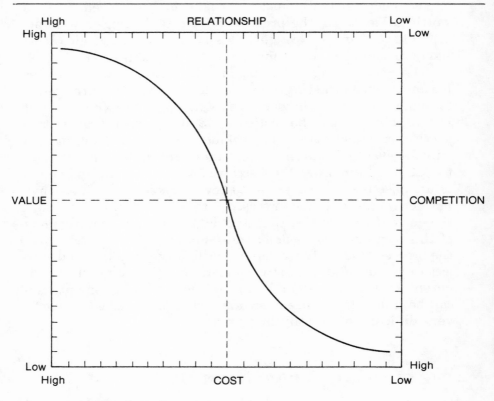

SOURCE: © 1985, G. M. Moebs & Associates.

Price is related to these scales. For the cost-plus pricing strategy on the lower axis, when costs are high, prices should be high to cover the costs. For competition, when competition is high, prices will be forced down to a lower level. For relationships, when relationships are strong and a customer has all her services with one institution, making it harder for her to leave, the institution can price the relationship higher. Finally, when value is perceived to be high, prices can be higher.

The interrelationship between the extent to which each of the strategies is in force determines a demand curve, which is drawn through the center of the square. As with all demand curves, it is assumed that price is on the vertical axis and volume is on the horizontal axis. The demand curve represents the combination of price and volume with the four pricing strategies.

FIGURE 11–3 The Quadrants

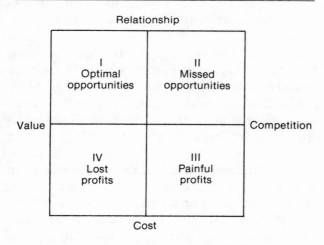

Relationship

I Optimal opportunities	II Missed opportunities
IV Lost profits	III Painful profits

Value / Competition

Cost

SOURCE: © 1985, G. M. Moebs & Associates.

This Quadratic Pricing Matrix closely relates to the principles discussed in Chapter 4 on Economics.

The Quadratic Pricing Matrix can be used for pricing anything, whether it be a financial service or hot dogs. The total demand curve for financial services is ratchet shaped, or in the shape of a propeller, because of the way the four strategies interact with one another. For a different industry, specific product, or specific market, the shape of the curve may be different.

PRODUCT POSITIONING

If an institution can configure a service in such a way as to place the service at the upper left of this curve, it is in the best position. This is the quadrant of *optimal opportunities*, and is Quadrant I in Figure 11–3. This is the best quadrant in which to be. Relationships are very strong, value is high, and competition is low or nonexistent, although cost may be high in order to achieve these other positionings. Prices can be positioned very high when this situation exists. Pricing strategies within this quadrant, since relationships are high and perceived value is high, usually focus around these two strategies.

As competition increases, perceived value decreases and relationships weaken, costs tend to be more tightly controlled, and prices decrease. This process continues until, in the center of the Matrix, price wars can occur. The shape of the demand curve is very steep, indicating that it will take a large change in price to affect volume.

At the lower right of the curve, pricing becomes transactional and of a commodity nature. Cost is now quite low as firms have to be low-cost producers to survive, competition is very high, value is perceived to be low, and relationships are weak or non-existent. A product is now in Quadrant III, the quadrant of *painful profits*. Here again, a small reduction in price will result in a large increase in volume for a particular financial institution. Pricing strategies within this quadrant are often a combination of cost-plus, emphasizing a position as a low-cost producer, and competition, as firms try to counter or undercut the competition.

Positioning the price of a service within the upper right quadrant, Quadrant II, will result in an unstable price. The price is higher than demand, and is in disequilibrium. Here relationships are weak, but competition is also weak. Cost is low, but perceived value is high. The usual pricing strategy encountered here is competition, as institutions lazily match the competition without giving pricing too much further thought.

This is the quadrant of *missed opportunities*. If competition is weak, the institution could easily build relationships. If cost is low but value is high, the institution could go to value pricing and significantly increase its spread and/or profit.

A service within Quadrant IV will also be inappropriately priced. This is the quadrant of *lost profits*. Perceived value is low, but cost is high. Although relationships are strong, competition is also high. Within this quadrant, it is very difficult for an institution to raise prices, although the strong relationship orientation helps somewhat. Pricing strategies often encountered in this quadrant are cost-plus, as institutions try only to cover their high costs. This is the least desirable quadrant, and an institution should work at increasing the perceived value of any service in this quadrant to enable it to raise prices, or it should reduce operating costs to recognize a profit.

THE POSITION OF SPECIFIC PRODUCTS

Although no financial service fits precisely into any one quadrant, individual services can be matched to the Quadratic Pricing Matrix as a way to better understand the integration of the four pricing strategies and the optimal establishment of price. Four products will be analyzed which have particular pricing problems and which are often priced inappropriately by being situated in the wrong quadrant. The four we will deal with are:

• Passbook savings accounts
• Basic checking
• ATMs
• Small business loans

Passbook Savings Accounts

Passbooks are an excellent example of a product that is often inappropriately priced. This product is often placed in the lower left-hand quadrant and is operated at a loss. Institutions perceive that it has low value yet high cost and has insignificant relationship value. Many of them offer it because they think they have to, yet they work diligently at trying to move the customer toward statement savings to gain profitability for the institution.

But what about customer needs and market demands? A price positioned in Quadrant IV, don't forget, is below market demand. Institutions are not asking the basic marketing question—does the customer want a passbook? This question was discussed in detail in Chapter 3 in the section on tangibility. And the answer is yes, the customer does want passbooks. The perceived value is low only in the minds of the financial institutions.

The pricing technique usually used for this account, since it is thought to be positioned in Quadrant IV, is cost-plus, as institutions try only to cover the high costs they believe this account carries. But the two fallacies in this disequilibrium are first, the value of this account is high. Most consumers save for a variety of different purposes, all important to the consumer, such as for an emergency, retirement, or a "rainy day" in the future. Is rate most important to these people? No, value and the assurance of a safe place for their money is more important than the pure rate that is given on the account.

Second, it is uncertain whether passbook savings really are more expensive than statement savings. According to the Functional Cost Analysis produced by the Federal Reserve, it is actually less expensive. (See Figures 5–18 and 5–19.) If, because of the inaccuracies believed by some to make the Functional Cost Analysis less than reliable, institutions still choose to believe that passbooks are more expensive to offer, then they should trade on the perceived value of the account to maintain profitability. Institutions can offer a decreased interest rate on passbooks. Do you have to have 5.5 percent compounded daily? No. Many consumers would be happy to have passbooks that offered 5 percent, 4.5 percent, or less. In fact, a number of institutions around the country are still only paying 3 or 4 percent on their passbook dollars, and some of those are showing increases in passbook savings. These bankers understand perceived value and have the correct cost for producing their services; they coordinate the two to give the consumers what they want and achieve a high level of profitability for the institution.

Changing these two perceptions of high cost and low value into lower cost and high value moves this product into Quadrant I, where institutions most want to be and where profits are highest.

Basic Checking

The market environment of a basic low-cost or no-frills checking account is one of high competition, because institutions see these accounts as one of the best ways to gain market share. But the value of a checking account is perceived to be quite low. Also, usually the cost of producing a checking account is fairly low, due to efficient operations for this common product. This pricing profile places this account in the lower right-hand quadrant of the Quadratic Pricing Matrix. Although this is an equilibrium position, and the product could comfortably remain in this quadrant, can this product be offered more profitably?

Pricing techniques used for basic DDAs (demand deposit accounts) are usually cost-plus, as institutions just try to cover costs in order to offer this essential product for the lowest cost possible or even for below cost when the account is used as a loss leader. The other popular pricing strategy for basic checking is competition, as institutions try to match what their neighbors are doing or try to outdo the competition.

However, the original reason for offering basic checking, as a loss leader to bring new customers into the institution, is quite valid, and the product can be more profitable than it presently is if certain configurations are considered.

First, all exceptions to an account must be priced separately and profitably. This includes items such as NSFs (nonsufficient fund checks) and overdraft lookups. These items need to be priced so that customers do not abuse the low-cost checking privilege. Separate pricing should also apply to all ancillary services associated directly with a checking account. These services are often complimentary; this practice should be stopped.

In addition, a good sales effort must be performed by the new accounts people to take advantage of possible new customer accounts enticed in by the loss leader checking account. Other services need to be sold to these new customers such as savings and deposit accounts, fee-based services such as safe deposit boxes, and loans such as auto loans and home equity loans. If no efficient cross-sell effort is maintained, the checking account will simply stay as it started, as an isolated unprofitable loss leader.

Finally, it is important that the institution project an image counteracting the valueless perception associated with a low-cost account. This requires efficient and accurate operations and a strong sales effort to increase perception of value.

Approaching low-cost checking in this fashion makes it a viable product for an institution. It also moves the product up the demand curve into an area where value is perceived to be higher, relationships are strengthened, and competitive advantage is secured, all combining to enable the institution to raise prices and remain profitable.

Automated Teller Machines

There has been much written and discussed about automated teller machines (ATMs). Access to an ATM is usually one of the ancillary services attached to a checking account. Recall from the discussion about checking accounts above that all ancillary services associated with low-cost checking should be individually priced and charged. Of all the institutions offering ATMs, 75 percent offer this service for free. Of those that do charge, 75 percent charge a transaction fee and 25 percent charge an annual fee.

How much do people value what they've gotten for free? Think of how easy it is to squander the winnings from a lottery ticket. Or how quickly an allowance given to, rather than earned by, a son or daughter disappears. Human nature is such that anything free is perceived as being of low value.

Offering ATM services for free places this product solidly in the lower left-hand quadrant of the Matrix, the quadrant of lost profits where the firm least wants to be. The only way to compete in this quadrant is to be the low-cost producer. But this is difficult because, although the perceived value of ATMs is low, the cost of providing them is high. Therefore, what the institution wants to do is to raise the perception of value.

This gets somewhat into the chicken-and-the-egg dilemma. Do you raise value perceptions first and then raise the price, or do you raise price first and hope that value perceptions follow? It has been the experience of financial institutions that if they charge for the ATM service, the perception of value will follow. These institutions are saying that it is costly for them to offer ATMs, yet they want to provide this service to the customer. ATMs are advantageous to the consumer because of their emergency nature and the proximity that can be offered with a lot of different locations. But if the institution wants to continue to offer these things of value to customers, then it has to charge a fee.

While no market research has been done, it appears that those institutions that are charging for their ATM usage have more successful programs, measured both in usage and in profitability. It appears that the very act of charging customers for the use of a product raises the value of the product in their eyes. The concept of value and the worthlessness of something free could be at the heart of customers' attitudes toward ATM usage. Many financial institutions find that they can only get one third of their customers to use ATMs. This could be because two thirds do not perceive any value in what they have been given.

Small Business Loans

Loans to small businesses are a good example of a service positioned in Quadrant II, the quadrant of missed opportunities. This product has little competition because very few institutions are interested in offering credit to companies under $5 million in sales; they feel there is no profit to be made. Cost would be relatively low for providing this credit. The relationship aspect is low because the institutions that do offer credit to this market generally do not attempt to cross-sell.

Yet financial institutions ignore the important fact that credit is very valuable to the small business. Because no one is interested in giving them credit, small businesses find they have to actively sell their demand. What do they seek? They seek access to credit, service, and flexibility. They tend not to be price-sensitive because they value access, service, and flexibility more highly than rate to accommodate the usually volatile nature of a small business. This would be a golden opportunity for an institution to use the value pricing strategy.

In addition, there are excellent opportunities to cross-sell to the small business. Small businesses are usually short on staff and therefore require all kinds of financial support. The financial institution could assist them with cash management and treasury, including money market accounts, lockboxes, automatic tax payments, and investments.

Recognizing the high value of credit to the small businessman and emphasizing the additional services required by a small firm can move the pricing of this product to the left in the Matrix, enabling the institution to raise prices.

IMPACT OF MARKETING COMPONENTS ON A LOAN PRODUCT

It is interesting to see how altering one of the components of the marketing mix—price, place, promotion, and product—can affect where a product is placed within the Quadratic Pricing Matrix. Place, or distribution channel, and promotion, or method of communicating, can have strong impacts on the price of a product. An excellent example of this would be auto loans.

A direct auto loan is one where the financial institution directly originates the loan with the consumer. Relationships are usually strong and perceived value is high. Cost is also high because of the high personnel interaction required. This profile places direct auto loans in Quadrant I, high on the demand curve, and with an associated high price and relatively high profitability.

An indirect auto loan is one where the financial institution has bought the loan from the originating institution. In an indirect loan situation, relationships are nonexistent since the ultimate consumer may not even be aware of your institution. Consequently, value is also low. Cost is low, since procuring the loan simply involves buying the paper. And finally, competition is high; there are a very large number of competitors in the indirect auto paper market.

Because of this product profile, prices are low and margins are very thin. This places the product in Quadrant III in the lower right-hand corner of the Matrix.

How can you move this product up the demand curve to improve profitability? You can alter two of the components of the marketing mix—the distribution channel and the promotion method. If you buy auto paper, you have no direct distribution channel to the end user. Also, your promotion is limited to industrial marketing to the originating financial institutions. However, you also have a very valuable piece of information that allows you to influence the distribution channel and the promotion method. You have a name and an address.

With a name and address, you can market to the end-user household in the future. You can change your distribution channel from contact with the originating financial institution to contact with the consumer. You can direct market to the end user. When the auto loan matures, you could approach the household with other credit offerings. In this way, you can cross-sell to the household and establish a recognizable identity with the consumer. These tactics create a relationship, strengthen perceived value, and perhaps raise cost. This changes the product profile sufficiently to enable you to move up the demand curve toward Quadrant I where higher profitability can be enjoyed.

SUMMARY

There are four basic pricing strategies. They are cost-plus, competition, relationship, and value. The understanding of these four strategies is essential to pricing any product or service.

The Quadratic Pricing Matrix integrates the four strategies with the microeconomics of a demand curve. The financial pricer must understand the dynamics of the interrelationships between the four strategies. The Matrix will enable the pricer to establish a level of prices which would be optimal for both the consumer and the institution. Correctly determining where a product is positioned within one of the four quadrants, and which pricing strategy, or combination of pricing strategies, is most appropriate, can spell the difference between profitability, missed opportunities, and lost profits. If a product is positioned within an unprofitable quadrant, one or more of the components of the product profile should be changed to move the product toward another quadrant.

PART 4

Implementing Prices

12

Methodology for Implementing Prices

Do what you can, with what you have, where you are.

—Theodore Roosevelt

In the previous chapters, we have presented the theory and financial principles underlying the pricing of financial service products and applied these to the four common strategies for pricing services and products.

In this chapter, we will use all of the previously presented principles to create a methodology for properly implementing prices. Numerous consultants in the field offer various steps to follow and basic approach guidelines to implement price changes, and there have been many "How To" cookbooks published on the subject of implementation, a few of which are listed in the bibliography. For detailed guidance, we suggest you consult these references listed. However, the following 12 steps are a compilation of some of these approaches and cover the basic areas of concern:

- Establish a price list of all services.
- Conduct a cost analysis.
- Evaluate competition.
- Determine current household/parent company positions.
- Determine market position of the institution.

- Prepare product line financial statements.
- Conduct an operational assessment.
- Review applicable regulations and operating policy.
- Make a management decision.
- Train staff.
- Communicate properly.
- Monitor results.

While the order of the above steps does not necessarily have to be followed, there is a logic to this order. It has been found that following the steps in order substantially reduces the risk of implementing an improper price. For example, conducting the cost analysis after evaluation of competition or market position is not a critical departure from the methodology. But making a management decision before the analyses enumerated in the previous steps have been completed would be an error. Also, communicating to the customers or training the staff before making a decision and doing proper analysis for that decision would also be an error. Therefore, although some flexibility does exist in implementing these steps, a systematic approach will give the institution the best results.

ESTABLISH A PRICE LIST

Establishing a price list of all services is a two-step process. First, a task force should be set up of people who are knowledgeable about all the services and products of the financial institution. This task force is not a committee in that when its task is done, it is dissolved. Financial institutions, like other organizations, love to set up committees. But these often get bogged down in procedural and bureaucratic details. So we suggest a short-lived task force to better focus on the immediate issues at hand. Then, one person or a few people from the task force should stay with the entire price implementation process to provide continuity and control.

The appropriate people on the task force can come from an assortment of functions. Six areas, however, should be included on the task force:

- Finance/asset and liability management.
- Marketing.
- Training.
- Loans/investments.

- Operations/bookkeeping.
- Policy and planning.

Each of the representatives from these functional areas has an important contribution to make to the establishment of a price list as the first step in implementing prices.

The financial representative brings to the task force particular expertise in the area of cost and asset and liability management. This person would be responsible for cost collection and the analysis of the fixed or variable nature of products. In addition, interest rate related asset or liability considerations would also be the responsibility of this person. The establishment of the cost of funds and appropriate funding using some of the techniques presented in Chapter 8 such as gap analysis or duration is an important contribution to this effort. This person would be the profit conscience of the task force.

The marketing representative would bring expertise in all areas of marketing such as product configuration, pricing, distribution of the product, and communications and promotion of the product. Also, the marketing person would have information concerning relationships and should have access to research on the value that current customers or prospective customers attach to the financial institution and its products. In addition, the competitive position of the firm is usually monitored by the marketing department. Thus, the marketing representative brings not only expertise in the area of marketing but also a considerable amount of analytical and informational resources.

The employees' perspective is represented on the task force by the training person. The training person must have an understanding of the institution's products because employee training generally is product-oriented. Also, when prices are actually implemented, training is a key element of communicating the efforts of the task force to the employees and thus to the customers. The training person also has an understanding of employees' individual abilities and can furnish insight into who might be most successful in implementing price changes.

The representative from the loan and investment functions is an essential part of the task force, since these are the main revenue-producing areas of financial institutions. Also, this individual, especially if he or she comes from the loan area, usually has a very good handle on corporate and commercial customers and the unique needs of those customers. Someone with knowledge of the investment function is also critical because this function has access to market information on financial rates such as Fed Funds, commercial paper, government bills, and bonds. This information is important in establishing funding rates which assist in determining product profitability.

Finally, someone who is knowledgeable about the institution's policies and who has decision-making power is one of the most important members of the task force. All too often a group of individuals who are not in the mainstream of policy determination and implementation formulate prices for financial services which conflict with the overall strategies and plans of the firm. Having an executive from the institution familiar with these plans and strategies involved is crucial. In smaller firms, this representative may very well be the CEO, while as the size of the institution increases, a senior member of management would be sufficient.

This group of six individuals could be larger or smaller. The important point is that all functions are represented. In smaller firms, several functions may be represented by one individual. In larger financial institutions, several individuals may represent a particular functional area. For example, the marketing function may be represented on the task force by one person who is responsible for pricing, one for research, and a third for product development. Each of these individuals would bring specific viewpoints, information, and resources to the task force. In addition, areas such as finance, control, and asset and liability management might be represented by three or more individuals. However, the task force could get unwieldy if it is much larger than ten people.

Once the task force is assembled, its objective is to create a list of all services offered by the institution and their respective prices. This list would include products for which prices have been established as well as those for which they have not. For example, services such as photocopies or notary are often provided free. These should be listed as services that are being offered to the customer. All too often, services are given away without regard to their perceived value and internal cost to the financial institution. The exercise of generating a list of services is an opportunity to reexamine instances where services are being offered but not charged.

Once the price list is generated, the task force could follow a number of courses. First, it could stay with the process and assist with the analytical steps and actual implementation. This may be the practical approach when prices have not been reviewed in a number of years and the pricing effort is a major one.

Second, the main task force could be dissolved, and one person or small group of people could be given responsibility for implementing and monitoring the pricing efforts of the firm. This individual, who would probably be a marketing person, should have extensive knowledge of the financial institution, the necessary analytical tools, and the communications ability to present the results of the task force findings to management, employees, and customers. Placing the responsibility with one individual would assist in eliminating the bureaucratic problems that occur when pricing committees become unwieldy and which lead to compromises that cause lower profitability or delays in implementing prices on a timely basis. Giving responsibility to one individual provides continuity and control over the pricing implementation program.

CONDUCT A COST ANALYSIS

Chapter 5 reviewed all aspects of cost as they influence pricing. Remember that costs must be analyzed so that prices can duplicate cost behavior to eliminate the risk inherent in having price behavior differ from the underlying cost behavior. Also, keep in mind that cost is not directly related to price, but that the two are interrelated through profitability.

In conducting a cost analysis for the purpose of implementing prices, the costs of all services must be analyzed to determine the behavior and the profitability of the service. This review can be done in several ways. One way would be to review each product with in-house personnel and resources. This would require some expertise in accounting and cost analysis. Smaller institutions may not have this expertise; they may want to use the second approach, which involves the hiring of an outside service such as a consulting firm to analyze the firm's cost. Using an outside service can also allow the institution to learn how to review costs for the future. Either approach should result in establishing the costs of products, which may be a first-time effort, and creating a permanent procedure to track costs. A third way to achieve a cost review is to participate in the Federal Reserve's Functional Cost Analysis. As noted in Chapter 5, this is now available to savings and loans as well as to banks. Participating in this survey would furnish an institution with the methodology necessary to review costs in the future. Finally, the aid of the task force which created the list of services could be enlisted, and the experience and the insights of the members concerning product behavior can be used to estimate costs. While this is a subjective approach and subject to errors, for many small firms it may be the easiest way, or the only way, to achieve a cost analysis. Therefore, the ends here could justify the means.

EVALUATE COMPETITION

Evaluation of competition is accomplished in two ways. First, a shopping survey of competitors' prices is performed. No set format is best for this, and information can be obtained in a variety of ways. The shopping survey could be performed by one of the members of the task force, or an outside service can be engaged to do it for the institution. In addition, various consulting firms and newsletters publish pricing data on a periodic basis. Also, the firm's advertising agency or market research firm could assist in obtaining competitive price information.

Second, an analysis of the financial position of the competition should be performed. Analyzing the strengths and weaknesses of the competition aids in identifying where potential pricing opportunities could exist. For example, Figure 12–1, the U.S. Bank Performance Profile done by the Bank Administration Institute, analyzes up to 8 different banks by 60 or more different financial ratios. Line 5, for example, indicates great variance among the five banks shown in the level of their noninterest income. Noninterest income as a percent of assets varies from .31 percent to over 1 percent. Further analysis could be done to identify why these banks have these different financial characteristics. For example, why does Bank 2 have such high noninterest income, and why do Best Bank and Bank 3 have such low noninterest income? Analyzing the competition in this way gives very good insights into the relative strategies that each of the competitors is following. This financial information is readily available for depository institutions such as banks, savings and loans, savings banks, and credit unions.

DETERMINE HOUSEHOLD OR
PARENT COMPANY POSITIONS

Data on household position is vital for the establishment of any type of relationship pricing. Shown in Figure 12–2 is a cross-sell report for a particular financial institution and nine of its products.

A cross-sell report such as this one differs from a customer information report (CIF report) in that it is a household report which combines all the account and customer activity of a particular household. Analyzing cross-sell information from just the customer aspect forgets about the interrelationships that customers have within the household. In most households there are at least two major financial service decision makers, and analyzing these people individually rather than collectively can result in improper recognition of the total profitability of a household. Recall our Household Pyramid, Figure 11–1, which depicted the relative positions of account holders, customers, and households, with households at the top of the pyramid.

In Figure 12–2, the services and products that are analyzed are as follows:

DDA = Checking accounts
Sav Bk = Savings passbooks
Sav Stm = Statement savings accounts
Sav Xmas = Christmas club accounts
Sav IRA = Individual retirement accounts
CDR = Regular CDs
CDMM = Money market CDs
MPL = Monthly payment loans
Mtg = Mortgage loans

The information shown is for consumer households. The same information could be gotten for commercial companies by analyzing the parent company and subsidiaries, sales offices, outlets, and warehouses.

Starting at the row marked DDA, under the total households column, there are 9,997 households that have checking accounts. The second line of the next column, marked DDA, lists that the 9,997 households have a total of 10,870 accounts.

FIGURE 12-1 Comparative Financial Report

Operating performance—percent of assets	Best Bank	Bank 1	Bank 2	Bank 3	Bank 4	Rank
1) Interest income (FTE)	9.24	10.09	7.97	8.89	8.69	2d
2) Interest expense	4.55	4.64	4.39	4.99	5.15	2d
3) Net interest margin	4.68	5.45	3.57	3.90	3.54	2d
4) Loan loss provision	.24	.20	.03	.01	.36	4th
5) Noninterest income	.32	.82	1.31	.31	.48	4th
6) Salaries and benefits	1.43	1.99	1.45	1.50	1.41	2d
7) Occupancy and furniture and equipment expenses	.33	.31	.48	.42	.37	2d
8) Other noninterest expense	.69	.99	.47	.82	.58	3d
9) Tax equivalent adjustment	.91	.83	1.10	.60	.74	4th
10) Tax provision	.12	.44	.00	.03	−.10	4th
11) Return on assets—operating income	1.25	1.48	1.33	.80	.64	3d
12) Return on assets—Net Income	1.21	1.48	1.24	.77	.62	3d
13) Return on equity—Net Income	16.70	26.21	13.86	13.55	9.06	2d
Yield and rates						
14) Effective tax rate—operating income	9.29	23.17	.00	3.79	−21.29	2d
15) Cash dividend percent operating income	25.52	21.34	25.33	38.38	41.04	3d
16) Capital formation ratio	12.29	20.62	10.09	8.17	5.17	2d
17) Operating income per employee	12345	10678	13539	8007	6401	2d
18) Noninterest income percent noninterest expense	13.24	24.82	54.37	11.36	20.43	4th
19) Tax equivalent yield on earning assets	10.17	11.08	9.74	10.02	9.53	2d
20) Yield on loans	10.50	11.45	9.74	11.44	10.61	4th
21) Net charge-offs percent average loans	.37	.22	−.02	.01	.66	4th
22) Loan loss provision percent average loans	.51	.29	.09	.03	.71	4th
23) Yield on investment securities (FTE)	9.99	9.63	9.32	8.09	8.14	1st
24) Rate on time and savings deposits	6.11	6.69	6.48	6.61	6.59	5th
25) Rate on total interest funds	6.16	6.96	6.60	6.80	7.03	5th
26) Break-even yield	7.64	8.04	6.76	8.39	8.12	2d
Balance sheet data						
27) Earning assets percent assets	90.81	91.11	81.82	88.77	91.15	3d
28) Cash and due (noninterest) percent assets	6.15	5.46	16.44	7.94	6.26	2d

	(1)	(2)	(3)	(4)	(5)	Rank
29) Investment securities percent assets	41.74	20.88	42.67	37.91	39.99	2d
30) Loans percent assets	47.50	69.09	35.87	49.67	50.79	4th
31) Reserve percent year-end loans	1.01	.60	1.03	.69	.67	2d
32) Loans percent deposits	51.96	78.43	41.21	55.73	59.99	4th
33) Demand deposits percent assets	17.56	24.99	22.84	19.32	18.46	5th
34) Savings deposits percent assets	44.02	34.61	33.20	32.25	33.50	1st
35) Money market CDs percent assets	10.31	9.15	7.21	8.33	13.03	2d
36) Time deposits over 100M percent assets	3.01	11.34	13.64	13.97	5.16	5th
37) Other time deposits percent assets	16.49	7.99	10.12	15.23	14.48	1st
38) Total deposits percent assets	91.41	88.09	87.04	89.13	84.65	1st
39) Borrowing percent assets	.33	3.72	2.88	3.71	7.40	5th
40) Equity capital percent assets	7.24	5.65	8.94	5.73	6.84	2d
41) Large liability dependence	.00	12.47	6.50	6.00	10.02	5th
42) Employees per million assets	1.01	1.38	.98	1.00	1.01	4th

Growth statistics

	(1)	(2)	(3)	(4)	(5)	Rank
43) Income before security transactions 1-year	14.30	25.74	17.45	7.82	−28.97	3d
44) Net income 1-year	12.95	31.75	10.04	4.15	−27.60	2d
45) Average assets 1-year	8.39	7.00	−6.56	−2.41	−2.99	1st
46) Income before security transactions 5-years	89.48	154.85	35.64	.00	87.79	2d
47) Net income 5-years	82.83	155.32	30.94	.00	50.89	2d
48) Average assets 5-years	50.75	76.30	33.05	.00	27.99	2d

Loan types percent average loans

	(1)	(2)	(3)	(4)	(5)	Rank
49) Real estate—residential	22.05	15.88	22.96	29.55	39.47	4th
50) Real estate—other	35.29	14.67	21.41	10.09	30.79	1st
51) Commercial and industrial	23.95	46.94	24.17	31.32	13.11	4th
52) Agricultural	.00	.00	.00	.00	.00	1st
53) Personal loans	17.02	21.19	25.39	18.08	15.30	4th
54) All other loans	.20	1.30	5.56	7.20	1.29	5th

Miscellaneous

	(1)	(2)	(3)	(4)	(5)	Rank
55) Trust income percent assets	.01	.09	.00	.10	.06	4th
56) Service charge on deposits percent assets	.24	.59	.87	.14	.27	4th
57) Foreign and domestic deposits percent assets	91.41	88.09	87.04	89.13	84.65	1st
58) Foreign deposits percent total deposits	.00	.00	.00	.00	.00	1st
59) Public funds demand deposits percent total deposits	.06	.05	.07	.08	.37	4th
60) Public funds time deposits percent total deposits	.78	5.25	3.25	8.74	3.43	5th

FIGURE 12–2 Cross-Sell Account Report

Service	Total Households	DDA	Sav Bk	Sav Stm	Sav Xmas	Sav IRA	CDR	CDMM	MPL	Mtg
DDA	9,997	9,997	4,242	1,948	293	117	909	234	1,173	303
		10,870	6,478	2,047	366	152	1,743	290	1,441	316
		100.000	42.432	19.485	2.930	1.170	9.092	2.340	11.733	3.030
Sav Bk	13,595	4,242	13,593	517	310	120	1,187	274	1,067	314
		4,650	17,702	563	394	148	2,196	334	1,301	326
		31.207	100.000	3.803	2.280	0.632	8.732	2.015	7.849	2.310
Sav Stm	4,296	1,948	517	4,296	46	17	109	38	349	53
		2,291	867	4,405	60	27	178	46	431	54
		45.344	12.034	100.000	1.070	0.395	2.537	0.884	8.123	1.233
Sav Xms	474	293	310	46	474	9	80	10	46	10
		370	541	53	584	10	183	11	64	11
		61.814	65.400	9.704	100.000	1.898	16.877	2.109	9.704	2.109
Sav IRA	192	117	120	17	9	192	44	9	27	16
		142	228	17	9	239	85	11	35	16
		60.937	62.500	8.854	4.687	100.000	22.916	4.687	14.062	8.333
CDR	2,021	909	1,187	109	80	44	2,021	118	149	65
		1,046	1,893	117	107	56	3,392	155	198	68
		44.977	58.733	5.393	3.958	2.177	100.000	5.838	7.372	3.216
CDMM	416	234	274	38	10	9	118	416	37	16
		281	486	44	16	12	255	494	46	16
		56.250	65.865	9.134	2.403	2.163	28.365	100.000	8.894	3.846
MPL	3,933	1,173	1,067	349	46	27	149	37	3,933	130
		1,402	1,739	383	64	34	234	41	4,452	137
		29.824	27.129	8.873	1.169	0.686	3.788	0.940	100.000	3.305
Mtg	800	303	314	53	10	16	65	16	130	800
		353	576	59	14	23	113	16	167	824
		37.875	39.250	6.625	1.250	2.000	8.125	2.000	16.250	100.000
Sngl Serv Hshlds		3,610	8,166	2,255	81	36	568	75	2,229	328
		36.110	60.075	52.490	17.088	18.750	28.104	18.028	56.674	41.000

SOURCE: Urban Data Processing, Burlington, Mass.

In the next column, for savings passbooks, the first line lists that, of the 9,997 DDA households, 4,242 have a savings passbook. In the second line, these 4,242 households have a total of 6,478 passbook savings accounts. On the third line under savings passbooks in the DDA row is listed that 42.432 percent of DDA households have a savings passbook.

Taking another example, the cross-sell report shows that 3,933 households have monthly payment loans (MPL). Of these, 1,173 households have a checking account with the bank. These households have a total of 1,402 DDA accounts. Also, 29 percent of monthly payment loan households have a DDA service, or less than one third of the customers who have a loan with the bank have a checking account. This is important for relationship pricing considerations since checking account deposits could be used to increase total profitability. The 29 percent that do have a checking account with the bank could be further analyzed to see how profitable they are for the bank as opposed to the 71 percent who do not have a checking account but do have a monthly payment loan.

Finally, the last row indicates single service households under each of the services. Under the DDA column is listed that 3,610 households have only a checking account with the bank, and these households represent 36.11 percent of all DDA households. A total of 8,166 households have only passbook accounts with the bank, or approximately 60 percent of the savings passbook base. This indicates that savings passbook customers tend to have only one service with the bank whereas DDA households tend to have more than one service. This is important information for determining a relationship position and recognizing potential pricing opportunities within those relationships.

This type of relationship information is produced in an automated fashion by Urban Data Processing out of Burlington, Massachusetts, which uses automated collection procedures to determine marketing cross-sell information. Urban Data can assist any financial institution in collecting their information and putting it into a cross-sell report, as well as generating other types of marketing reports. However, some firms may not have the resources to devote to this automated collection process and may prefer to conduct a manual sample of their account base. They can then determine relationship profiles based on the sample.

Sampling can be done by taking a random selection of all accounts to obtain the name and address of a household or commercial business. All services and products used by this name and address are then analyzed. By doing this randomly, the institution could then say that the results are statistically valid and that the sample results represent the true results of the total population of all the bank's households and commercial businesses. Valid decisions can then be based on the sample results.

Regardless of how the information is collected, whether by taking a sample or by analyzing the entire population of households in an automated fashion, the understanding of the household profile is an important step in pricing services.

DETERMINE MARKET POSITION

The current market position of the institution can be determined in two ways. First, a tremendous amount of secondary information is available for all markets. The Census Bureau collects a lot of data for specific markets. This demographic information, pertaining to housing, income, marital status, and other characteristics, can give tremendous insight into the type of market in which the institution is operating. In addition, census information can usually be broken down by tract and block groups within the marketplace so that differences, if they exist, can be pinpointed and analyzed. Census information is readily available from your local Census Bureau office.

After examining the market in which the institution is interested, market position can be determined by conducting market research. Because of the regulated nature of the financial service industry in the past, many financial institutions were not inclined to do much market research. This has changed, and more and more institutions, both large and small, are collecting market information on attitudes and lifestyles and financial services needs of customers and prospects. This research can be used to supplement the demographic data from the Census Bureau.

Market research is extremely important in determining the value that customers and prospects see in the services of the institution and financial services in general. Without this information, an entire pricing strategy—value pricing—would be based solely on subjective interpretation.

PREPARE PRODUCT LINE
FINANCIAL STATEMENTS

Cost information can provide one component for the determination of product profitability. Revenue generated by products is also required to complete the profit picture. The cost and revenue information should be aggregated by product line or specific product. In larger organizations this may be difficult, as transfer pricing becomes necessary to determine interest and noninterest costs such as overhead. The creation of product line financial statements is important, however, to assess the profitability that individual products and services are contributing to the firm.

Some institutions may find that product line financial statements are not necessary for products for which there is little or no revenue. For example, notary services are usually given away free of charge by most institutions. Although there is a labor cost for performing this service, it is usually minimal. If a product line financial statement were drawn, it would become obvious that this service is losing money. Should we discontinue it? No. It is part of the total service relationship provided by the institution. More basic, should a product line financial statement be generated for this service? No. It takes very little of the firm's resources and produces little or no revenue. For services and products such as this, product line financial statements are not necessary.

In addition, smaller firms may find that product line financial statements, while of value, are difficult to generate and maintain. These smaller institutions may, because of limited resources and expertise, be limited to creating product line financial statements for the basic services only, such as checking accounts and installment loans.

CONDUCT AN OPERATIONAL ASSESSMENT

Pricing programs are often constrained by the operational capability of the institution, as discussed in Chapter 10 on constraints, which include both automated data processing capacity and manual bookkeeping systems.

Many financial institutions' data processing systems are very sophisticated and powerful and are more than capable of handling any type of pricing routine. But even these systems are subject to constraints; establishing priorities to get programs changed to comply with a new product configuration can be difficult. Other priorities may override the pricing schedule demands. In addition, some systems cannot cope with some forms of pricing, especially the sophisticated relationship pricing which requires that numerous accounts be analyzed together for a particular household. Reviews need to be done of the data processing capabilities to determine constraints in changing prices, and priorities need to be established for software changes.

Second, the capabilities of manual systems, such as manual bookkeeping, are even more constraining than automated systems. As mentioned in Chapter 10, numerous problems are associated with bookkeeping systems. For example, many depository institutions would like to assess a charge for that small group of customers who call up every day to find out what their balance is. However, the time required to fill out the necessary tickets to charge customers can more than offset any revenue generated from this service. Thus, the ability of personnel to handle manual assessment of charges must be reviewed in considering any price adjustment.

REVIEW APPLICABLE REGULATIONS AND OPERATING POLICIES

Chapter 10 reviewed many of the legal and regulatory constraints on pricing as well as some of the operational constraints mentioned above. Financial institutions must comply with regulations at both the state and federal level, and failure to comply can cause considerable problems and even dollar penalties for the firm.

Even more important is conformity with internal banking policies. Recently in California a foreign owner purchased a small independent bank. The bank had a policy, aggressively communicated to the customer at the time of account opening and recorded on signature cards, of offering free checking. The clincher was that this free checking was guaranteed for perpetuity to new customers when the bank first opened its doors. The new owners had not been told of this banking policy, and after gaining control of the institution started to charge everyone for banking services. This created quite an uproar, and the new owners were questioned by all the major TV networks at the door of their bank while being beseiged by customers, consumer groups, and other members of the local community. After checking the bank policies, the new owners had to reverse their decision on the price adjustment.

Most institutions who have been in business for any length of time have policies established for various accounts, loans, deposits, and fee-based services. Over time, these regulations are misplaced and forgotten. When a price change is made, an old customer will invariably remind management of this old policy, much to everyone's embarrassment. It is important to identify current and past bank policies, and to conform with what the bank has communicated as its procedures to consumers and commercial businesses.

This is not to say that these policies cannot be changed. But the change must be done with full knowledge of past policies and the future effect of the adjustments. Policies and procedures should be reviewed on a periodic basis to ensure that they are not forgotten.

MAKE A MANAGEMENT DECISION

Subordinates often collect the necessary data and do the analyses for price adjustments. The danger is that these subordinates will then proceed to implement the price adjustments without first consulting with management.

Management needs to place the full authority of the strategic plan of the institution behind the price adjustment. Only management involvement can give the prices the authority they need to be effectively communicated to and accepted by the consumer. Management should approve a price adjustment as well as confirm the time table for implementation. Disassociating management from the approval process, or ignoring the approval process altogether, can cause fragmented perceptions on the part of the consumer. It can also seriously hurt relationships as different parts of the institution communicate different underlying policies when price adjustments conflict with overall strategic plans.

A side issue in this discussion of the involvement of management is the underlying philosophy of many banking executives. During the many years under a regulatory environment, with prices and costs controlled, the only way to increase profits was to grow since prices could not be raised. Many financial institutions adopted the position that the most effective and fastest way to grow was to be all things to all people. This philosophy included never offending anyone, which resulted in extreme caution when contemplating policy changes, which included pricing changes. This mentality of serving all possible needs of the marketplace combined with not offending anyone in order to achieve high growth has resulted in an attitude toward pricing summed up as "When we change prices, we can't lose one customer."

This attitude ignores the question of whether the customers that are lost when prices are raised were profitable. They often were not. But all too often financial service marketers who have entered the business since 1980 have met with a tremendous amount of resistance from the old guard when attempting to adjust prices because of this concentration on growth. However, profits are a more realistic focus, and sometimes it is necessary to lose a few customers to make more money. Pricing is one of the tools of marketing which can assist in increasing profitability and eliminating unprofitable customers.

TRAIN STAFF

The ultimate control over effective price implementation rests in the hands of the employees who are on the front line dealing directly with the customer. These people need to be totally supportive of any price adjustments that are made to financial services. The lack of proper training of employees, or neglecting to properly communicate the intent of a price change to employees, can seriously undermine the desired effect of a price adjustment.

It is crucial for someone, hopefully the representative from the task force, to explain to the frontline employees why the price has been changed and what the impact will be. I once made a presentation to a group of bookkeepers concerning various price adjustments to some deposit products and fee-based services. The reactions of the bookkeepers were, "We were never told why prices were changing; we were just told to do it." They also responded, "You mean we finally get to charge some of these customers who have been getting away with murder?" These bookkeepers were made to feel that they were part of the decision-making process. They were advised how to deal with customer objections, and they were given the opportunity to generate more revenue from customers who they felt had been enjoying a free ride.

Using staff training as a form of motivation can be a powerful tool for successfully implementing a program. The lack of training can kill a pricing program.

Another way to motivate employees to support a price change program is to couple it with incentives and bonuses for employees. At a seminar in Texas, one of the participating bank presidents told me the following story. The supervisor of the drive-in facility had requested an additional person to handle the increased volume that the drive-in was experiencing. While the president was considering the request to hire this additional teller, a price adjustment program was implemented. This program was directed at eliminating the waiving of charges by many tellers and bookkeepers. An incentive was attached to the program in that 10 percent of all collected charges was returned to the tellers and bookkeepers.

The president forgot about the staff increase request while he was involved with the new price program. Two months later, the supervisor told him that one of the drive-in tellers was no longer needed and that staff could be reduced. The president then recalled the staff increase request and asked what the reason was for the reversal of staffing needs. It appeared that, after a few months of the new price program, the drive-in tellers figured out that they were going to collect only so much in fees. There were four tellers who worked the drive-in, and if one could be eliminated, more incentive could be earned by the remaining three! The fourth teller was eliminated, and the three proved more than capable of handling the work load.

Tying incentives to a pricing increase can produce a double benefit in both increasing revenue and decreasing costs. Properly understood and applied, incentives can be a powerful tool to help properly train and motivate employees to accept and implement pricing programs. More and more financial institutions, both in commercial and consumer areas, are using incentives in pricing programs, during product introductions, and as part of general compensation. Obviously, programs need to be monitored to prevent a few overzealous employees from trying to increase their bonuses at the expense of customer service. But in total, incentives, bonuses, and/or commissions tied to a pricing program are very effective means to assist in implementing prices.

COMMUNICATE PROPERLY

Staff and customers alike must receive adequate communication about any price adjustment. Staff communication has been discussed above, but customer communication is of equal importance. A price change that is not properly communicated can cause tremendous resentment and even lose customers. I recall a large money center bank changing its policy on charging for FDIC insurance based on the amount of balances left with the institution without anticipating objections. The account officers were kept busy for weeks calming down customers who were irate because they had to pay insurance for the balances they were required to keep.

Communication to customers is largely common sense. This is "bad news" time and as with any bad news, the communication should be kept short and to the point. You don't want to emphasize the price adjustment, and the communication medium should be "plain vanilla."

Numerous do's and don'ts have been published concerning specific communications with customers. For further details covering more specific advice, we refer the interested reader to the bibliography.

MONITOR RESULTS

Monitoring the results can be the most difficult part of a price adjustment implementation program. Many financial institutions go through the previous 11 steps and then forget or avoid this step. Monitoring is difficult because it often has to be done manually. Information must be collected from employees dealing directly with the customers, such as new accounts personnel, account officers, tellers, and bookkeepers. The collection of information from these sources is time consuming, especially when done manually, and subject to error. But for an institution to implement price changes and then not track the effects of its changes results in a serious loss of information about its customer base and its reactions to bank policy.

Why do many institutions forget about monitoring the results of price changes? Because it's difficult to do and because people often don't want to see the results. Remember how painful examinations in school were, or performance reviews on the job, both of which are forms of monitoring. However, if, in spite of your best efforts, the price change is not having the impact you had hoped, the only way you can modify it is to know about the true impact, and that can only be determined by monitoring.

There is no set way to do monitoring. You can survey the customers, talk to the employees, or analyze the resulting increased profits or reduced costs. The important thing is to remember to somehow track results.

SUMMARY

This chapter has outlined a methodology for implementing prices. Twelve primary steps were detailed which should be performed to successfully implement price increases or adjustments to financial service products. Although the steps do not have to be performed in strict order, the general order should be followed to assure that all necessary procedures have been performed.

PART 5

Tactical Pricing Considerations

13

Cases

I hear and I forget.
I see and I remember.
I do and I understand.

—Chinese Proverb

As with any body of knowledge, the final test comes with actually implementing the theory and principles presented. All of the elements necessary to understand effective pricing—service marketing principles, economic theory, pricing principles, pricing strategies, and a methodology for successfully implementing prices—have been presented and reviewed.

In this chapter, we will apply these principles to practical examples to pull together all of the ideas presented. Three cases will be presented, dealing with commercial deposit services, credit card, and safe deposit boxes. At the end of each case, a solution will be discussed, including the pricing components and principles illustrated by the case.

CASE A
Commercial Savings *(Deposit Pricing)*

As President of the bank, you are about to walk into a meeting between the head of commercial services and the head of marketing. You are to mediate a rather heated dispute created over the past month since the head of marketing joined your $100 million bank.

The head of marketing is claiming that the head of commercial loans is giving the bank away. The head of commercial loans claims that the head of marketing doesn't know anything about banking.

At the last meeting between these two, they agreed on the following customer as being typical of most commercial customers for a one-month period:

Friendly Joe's, Inc.

Average book balance	$80,000
Average float	$60,000
Account activity	
Checks	200
Deposits	22
Items deposited	440
Lock box items	400
Coin and currency monthly fee	$ 50
Monthly account fee	$ 10

The controller tells you that reserves are 20 percent and that the overhead rate is 60 percent. The following are activity prices for services:

Checks	$.20
Deposits	.50
Items deposited	.05 each
Lock box items	.10 each

You also learned that all services have a 20 percent profit markup. Finally, your own research indicated that Friendly Joe's, Inc. was overdrawn on average about $20,000 for the month and that all overdraft charges are waived.

Currently, the earnings credit rate, which is also the cost of funds, is 15 percent, which is about what it has been for the past three months and is expected to remain for the next six months. The prime lending rate is 18 percent. Friendly Joe's, Inc. rarely borrows, but when it does it is at prime.

You will probably have to have an analysis done to figure out who is right and who is wrong since profitability is very important. As you walk into the conference room, the head of commercial services and the head of marketing are on the floor wrestling with each other with their secretaries trying to pull them apart.

Required. As President, what action would you take immediately pertaining to the situation?

Although this case may seem far fetched, it actually happened. One vice president actually grabbed the tie of the other, and the two had to be physically separated. This only demonstrates that the area of pricing can be very sensitive, with strong feelings on all sides.

A very common accusation is that the commercial department is "giving the bank away." This is especially common when account analysis and/or profitability analysis has not been performed for some time, if ever. Usually, an institution prone to this situation tends to bundle all other services with loans, and offers these other services as loss leaders. However, in a study done several years ago, it was found that over 50 percent of all businesses do not borrow, cannot borrow, or do not need to borrow. Therefore, many of these institutions are servicing only half their market by focusing exclusively on loans.

This case illustrates some of the problems associated with commercial account analysis and commercial pricing. The combined account analysis/profitability analysis of this case, in Exhibit 13–1, indicates that there is a loss on the account of $75 (earnings credit of $440 less charges of $515). However, on a full cost basis, the account is actually making almost $11, and on a direct cost basis, it's making $78. Recall that the full-cost basis includes labor, material, and overhead, while direct cost includes only labor and material. What should the president do?

Some bankers may say that we've incorrectly stated our analysis. They would not have included funds advanced, and the customer would then be profitable for the bank, by $5, as shown in Column 2. But Friendly Joe's has withdrawn about $20,000 more than it had on a collected basis. As indicated in Chapter 9, these funds which were advanced should be added back as an adjustment to the collected balance. When this is done, and the

EXHIBIT 13–1   Case Study A Answer (Commercial Account Analysis)

		Account Analysis		Profitability Analysis	
Book balance		$80,000	$80,000	$80,000	$80,000
Float		60,000	60,000	60,000	60,000
Collected		$20,000	$20,000	$20,000	$20,000
Funds advanced		–0–	20,000	20,000	20,000
Adjusted collected		$20,000	$40,000	$40,000	$40,000
Reserves at 12%		2,400	4,800	4,800	4,800
Available (investible)		$17,600	$35,200	$35,200	$35,200
Earnings credit rate		15%	15%	15%	
Monthly credit		$220	$440	$440	

	Activity	Price	Price	Full Cost	Direct Cost
Funds advanced	18%	–0–	$300	$250.00	$250.00
Checks ($.20)	200	$ 40	40	33.33	20.83
Deposits ($.50)	22	11	11	9.17	5.73
Items deposited ($.10)	440	44	44	36.67	22.92
Lock box ($.15)	400	60	60	50.00	31.25
Coin/currency		50	50	41.67	26.04
Monthly maintenance		10	10	8.33	5.21
TOTAL		$215	$515	$429.17	$361.98
INCOME/(LOSS)		$ 5	($75)	$ 10.83	$ 78.02

funds advanced are priced at 300 basis points above the cost of funds, this produces the loss of $75.

How should an institution handle funds advanced? Over a yearly period, deficiencies and excesses can be netted, and the excesses can be carried over to the next period to cover the deficiencies. So it is possible that, over an annual period, Friendly Joe's is leaving us whole. However, our analysis is limited to one month, and for that month, taking into consideration the funds advanced to cover the balance deficiency, the account lost money. If the $75 is charged, the bank will be left whole and will make money.

If the institution decides to waive the $75, should it get rid of Friendly Joe's as being unprofitable? On a full-cost basis, this relationship is contributing about $11 to overall profitability. The answer would then be not to get rid of Friendly Joe's but to try to adjust the prices or collection procedure and increase the profitability. On a direct-cost basis, the bank is definitely making money.

This case illustrates the principle of fees and balances and the necessity to collect charges when there are balance deficiencies. Second, the case illustrates the application of the two costing methods in determining total profitability of a relationship and how to determine this profitability with appropriate pricing with fees or balances. Finally, the case demonstrates the application of an account analysis and the different ways a financial institution can interpret the resulting information.

CASE B
Unsecured Consumer Credit/Credit Card
(Loan Pricing)

As Glenda Gogettheer walks into her office on a fine fall morning, she is feeling pretty good about her job and recent accomplishments. As a vice president of a $20 billion dollar bank with eighty branches in a major metropolitan area, she was given the assignment a year ago to improve the profitability of the credit card function. Through a lot of hard work, her decision to improve the service's profitability succeeded.

She had cut expenses by streamlining procedures and reducing staff. While income had been limited because of a usury law, she had benefited from a steadily falling cost of funds for the bank over the past year. Both operational cost cutting and declining interest costs have played equally important roles in credit cards' first profitable year in the past three years.

As she sits down and glances over *The Wall Street Journal,* she notices that the prime lending rate has jumped a dramatic 150 basis points and is now a full point over the usury ceiling limiting the interest rate on cardholders. She remembers yesterday's interoffice memo from the marketing department indicating that retail consumers are flocking to a new variable rate (fluctuating daily) savings account recently permitted because of a regulatory change which allows any rate of interest (this bank opted to equal the best money market rate) with no minimum deposit level. Because of this shift, the cost of funds for the bank next month will increase for the first time in 13 months, and it will be a dramatic increase.

As Glenda looks up, Bill Risenlowerr, Senior Vice President of consumer lending (and her boss) walks in red-faced.

Glenda: Good morning, Bill.

Bill: Don't good morning me, Glenda Gogettheer!

Glenda: What's the matter?

Bill: I was just called in by the old man who handed me my head!

Glenda: Why?

Bill: He wanted to know what kind of plan exists to maintain the profitability of all consumer lending. I told him with the rise in cost of funds we're unable to maintain profitability. He said that was totally unacceptable, and if I didn't want to go back to the branches as an assistant branch manager, I'd better do something about it!

Glenda: Sounds like Burt Bananas is under pressure from the Board of Directors.

Bill: You betcha! What are we going to do?

Glenda: Hey, here comes Peter Pricem from the marketing department. Bill, you remember Peter; he's the product manager for credit cards, and he's just the man to help us!

Required. With the product profile from Exhibit 13–2, what would you recommend (higher prices, additional data collection, research, analysis, hara-kiri) to help their profit plight?

Credit card is a transaction product that settles and clears its transactions on a system which is separate from most item processing systems in banks. Although credit card is almost a stand-alone product, it should be regarded as an important integral product in the overall pricing of consumer financial services. It has important cross-sell characteristics to be used in a relationship.

The first thing that should be done by Peter Pricem is to properly fund the credit card portfolio to reduce the cost of funds. When general interest rates are high, the credit card product is very profitable. But when rates are low, the product tends to go into hiding because the margins have narrowed, caused primarily by incorrect funding for this product.

EXHIBIT 13–2   Case Study B Answer (National Credit Card)

Financial Profile

Total lines of credit to customers	$1,000,000,000
Average outstanding credit balances	222,500,000
Total sales (charges in the past 12 months)	600,000,000

Income (past 12 months):

Finance charges	$44,500,000
Other income*	–0–
	$44,500,000
Cost of funds	$33,000,000

Expenses:

Operating	
Variable	$ 2,000,000
Fixed	7,000,000
Credit losses	1,500,000
	$10,500,000
Net income	$ 1,000,000

Operational Profile

Make-up of credit card accounts

Rollovers (pay interest every month)	40%
Convenience (pay off balances every month)	40%
Inactives (do not use cards)	20%
	100%

Price of card
   Issued free.
   If balance is not paid in 25 days, interest is charged at 20%
   No other charges.

Number of credit card accounts = 1,000,000
Number of accounts delinquent per month = 20,000 ($2,000,000)
Number of cash advances per month = 10,000
All cards reissued every two years.
Cross-sell profile of credit card customers:

Accounts per household: Rollovers	1.9
Convenience	1.4
Inactive	3.9

*Interchange of 1 percent is credited back to customer as an additional service to increase sales volume.

Credit cards should be funded with two different pools. One pool would be of short-term 30 to 60 day funds to support those convenience customers who are using the card for a transfer of value. These customers pay off their balances every month and are truly short-term borrowers. But the second funding pool for credit cards should be intermediate to reflect the true longer nature of this type of credit. This funding would support the roll-over customers who do not pay off but rather have outstanding balances every month. In the case, this represents $222.5 million in average outstanding credit balances. These outstanding balances are not short-term; instead they range from one year up to four years. Calculated on a present value duration basis, the average credit card portfolio is about a year and a half.

Most banks fund credit cards with short-term deposits. They are misled by the tremendous volumes of business generated by convenience customers and forget the funding of the average outstanding balances. The net result of this inaccurate asset and laibility management is that credit cards are charged with a much higher rate of cost of funds than is warranted. Many managers of credit card departments long for the day when they can fund their own portfolios in the capital markets on an intermediate basis to prove that credit cards are profitable in all types of interest rate environments.

Second, credit cards basically consist of factoring or buying receivables from various institutions. A consumer owning a card issued by institution A could charge an item at a store which has its accounts with institution B. This charge receipt, then, is settled by institution B. Institution A pays institution B for settling one of its charge receipts, and this settlement fee is called an interchange fee. This interchange fee is usually a minimum of 1 percent of the total outstanding. In the case, the bank is a consumer card holding bank and therefore is getting paid interchange fees from other banks, fees it passes directly on to its customers.

This fee kickback is a foregone profit opportunity—1 percent of $600 million is $6 million and could substantially increase the profitability of credit card. This would be one area for the bank to consider to increase the profitability of credit card. However, a reason not to eliminate the kickback may be that this policy aids in the marketing of the credit card. Both these factors should be considered when contemplating altering this policy.

Another profit possibility would be to levy an annual fee. Until the late 1970s, annual fees were not charged for credit cards other than by travel and entertainment companies such as American Express, Carte Blanche, and Diners Club. These companies, however, required that customers pay off balances every month rather than rolling over balances. This form of pricing caught on with the bank cards, and it has become "banking tradition" that all bank cards charge an annual fee. But is this good pricing?

The cross-sell profile given for credit card customers can help with this question. This profile was gotten from an analysis similar to the one discussed in Chapter 12. Here can be seen that inactive customers have almost four accounts per household, three accounts other than credit card. Roll-over customers have about one other account, and only 40 percent of convenience credit card users have another account with the bank. If an annual fee is charged, all credit card customers are affected equally. The bank then runs the risk of irritating the inactive customers who are profitable to the bank because of their use of other services, or the rollover customers who are profitable to the bank because of their outstanding credit card balances. In Chapter 4, we presented the estimated demand curve for auto loans; all credit tends to display the same classical behavior. If price goes up, usage will go down, especially with a blanket fee such as this.

An alternative solution is to go to "date of posting." Interest is presently being charged after the 25th day. Date of posting means that interest would start accruing from the date the transaction is posted to the account. There would be no free 25-day period. The attractiveness of this alternative is that the customers who would be affected are the convenience customers on which the bank is making little or no profit as they are using the card as a transfer of value, as though it were a checking account. The roll-over customers would not be affected because they are already currently paying interest. The inactive customers would not be affected because they are not using the card. Therefore, only a percentage of the convenience customers may be eliminated, which could substantially reduce our costs.

However, all of the above profit possibilities, although significant and perhaps equal to the interest earned on this credit product, do not address the heart of the issue. The real solution is to find a way to increase the credit profitability. This is a highly profitable portfolio already. Credit losses amount to $1,500,000 for average outstandings of $200,000,000, for a loss ratio of about .67 percent, which is excellent. In addition, delinquencies are running at 20,000 accounts per month, or $2,000,000, for a delinquency rate of .9 percent, which is also excellent. The credit quality of this portfolio is very high; these card holders are good users of credit, and herein lies the real key to increasing profitability.

Where in the Quadratic Pricing Matrix does this product fall? With low credit losses and low delinquencies, the cost is relatively low compared to other credit card portfolios. Also, all financial institutions in the credit card business want this kind of portfolio, so competition is high. Finally, perceived value is probably relatively low, since, as is often joked about, it is exactly the people who don't need credit, and therefore don't value it highly, who are the best credit risk. This places this product in Quadrant III, the commodity quadrant of painful profits, where profitability is difficult. Generally, most high quality products fall in Quadrant III.

What is the strategy for moving out of this quadrant? The bank can try to move up the demand curve by emphasizing relationships. One way to empahsize relationships in a credit relationship is to increase the size of the credit. This also makes the institution more valuable to the customer. Operating under what is called the comfortable level of debt theory, lines of credit could be substantially increased.

This action is based on the theory that consumers will incur debt up to a certain percentage of a line, but never up to 100 percent of the line. They are fearful of the consequences of going over the line of credit, and they want a cushion of unused credit at which they feel comfortable for emergencies. If a credit user, who is not a credit abuser, gets an increase in his line of credit, he will usually incur additional debt up to the same percentage. For example, a good credit user who uses 90 percent of a $1000 line will also use 90 percent of a $2000 line. Therefore, probably the most important way to increase the profitability of this high quality portfolio is to offer more credit to the good credit users. Most costs for financial institutions are fixed, as we discussed in Chapter 5, so operating costs would remain fairly constant. Yet outstandings would substantially increase, improving profitability.

This case illustrates the interrelationships of the many elements of pricing. First, as we discussed in Chapter 5, pricing should reflect cost, and cost behavior must be properly understood and related to the true nature of the product. In order to properly understand this product, duration analysis which was explained in Chapter 8 was called into play to calculate the average life of the outstanding credit. This could determine the correct funding maturity and identify the correct funding pool, which in turn allows the establishment of the proper cost, and appropriate pricing. In addition, an understanding of relationships becomes important in analyzing the cross-sell profile of the credit card user, which has a direct bearing on a possible decision to impose an annual fee. Also, the economic behavior of the product is important to anticipate its reaction to a price change. Finally, it is highly useful to place a product in the Quadratic Pricing Matrix, to provide guidance in determining the appropriate strategies to price correctly and improve profitability.

CASE C
Safe Deposit Boxes *(Fee-based Pricing)*

As Director of Marketing for a nine-bank multibank holding company, you face a dilemma on the pricing of safe deposit boxes. Each of your separate institutions has been pricing safe deposit boxes individually. While the markets in which each bank operates are somewhat different, demand for boxes is generally high since the competition in all markets is very low. Also, research tells you that customers with boxes have a high cross-sell at each institution.

The president wants to know your recommendation for prices. When you left his office, he said, "Remember, we have to get profits up substantially, yet be fair to each customer."

You just collected some data—Exhibit 13–3. (Lack of an entry for a particular item means that either the bank doesn't have that size box or that service isn't being charged.)

The comptroller tells you that it costs $4 to replace a lost key and $30 to drill open an abandoned box. Also, he said that Bank 1 and Bank 5 have problems with the belly dancers at local nightclubs renting boxes, which all have one-year terms, for their belly stones (for security) during their two-week gigs and then abandoning the box, which then has to be drilled.

Required. What would you do as Marketing Director?

EXHIBIT 13–3 Case Study C (Present Safe Deposit Box Pricing Configuration)

Box Size	Bank 1	Bank 2	Bank 3	Bank 4	Bank 5	Bank 6	Bank 7	Bank 8	Bank 9
2 × 4 × 13	$ 5	$12	$10	$ 6	$ 5	$10	$10	$11	$ 7
2 × 5 × 22				9	9	10	12		8
3 × 5 × 21	10		10		12				
5 × 5 × 21		15		15	15	15	15	15	15
3 × 10 × 21	15		15		18				
5 × 10 × 21		20	20		20	20	20	20	
5 × 10 × 24	25			27	24				
10 × 10 × 21		25			27				
10 × 10 × 24	35		25	32	30	25	25	25	25
10 × 15 × 24		40			35				
Key deposit	1								
Lost key		15			5				
Box drilling		35	10		10	5			
Last priced (Months ago)	6	24	24	60	72	12	18	12	36

These different banks all have different product pricing profiles. The boxes are all different sizes. Prices at some institutions have been changed as recently as six months ago, while others have not been changed for six years. Some of the banks charge for key deposits, drilling the boxes, or losing the key, others do not.

Safe deposit boxes are an excellent example of understanding the nature of the product you are trying to price. First, the underlying economic and cost structure should be understood. As discussed in Chapter 4, safe deposit boxes demonstrate highly inelastic demand. The amount of the resource available is usually fixed; financial institutions have only so many boxes to go around. In addition, this product's underlying cost behavior is that of a semivariable cost, as described in Chapter 5. There is a fixed component and a variable component.

However, boxes are usually priced erratically, as in the case. Some have fixed fees, and some have only variable fees. But all boxes have a fixed cost component, based on capacity which is fixed. Also, there are two variable components, one based on the occasional activity of drilling or replacing keys, and the other based on time. Although presently boxes are rented for one year, they could be rented for any length of time.

Therefore, the pricing that is appropriate here would include both a fixed and a variable component. First, key deposit, lost key, and box drilling fees should be instituted at all banks. A variable fee would thus be attached to a variable activity, and income would be increased at all banks. You could, however, forego some of these fees if the customer has a profitable relationship with the bank.

Second, the banks may want to reconfigure the product pricing profile to make the rental period more flexible. There is no requirement that safe deposit boxes need to be rented for a period of one year. For a situation similar to the belly dancers, rental periods could be offered for a week or a month. Hotels routinely offer their safe deposit boxes for these short periods, and for a high fee.

Finally, the base of the fee could be changed. Presently the fee is on a per box basis. But the fee could be based on the total cubic inches of the box. So total pricing for the smallest box, 2 by 4 by 13, would be a small fixed charge plus 104 cubic inches times a variable charge. This pricing policy would allocate charges fairly between all banks and all sizes. One drawback with this form of pricing is that the perceived value of a box may not vary significantly between the smallest and the largest. The cost of a small box may be $25 while the cost for the largest box may be $300. The bank needs to ask itself if the perceived value of the larger box is that much higher.

A bank customer once approached me in a country club shortly after prices were changed on safe deposit boxes. He was a local businessman and well respected in the community. He asked me, "Are you the one who changed the prices on the safe deposit boxes at the bank?" I said I was. He stuck out his hand and said, "Congratulations! I've often wondered about the pricing at the bank. I have your largest box and was only paying $40. You raised that to over $200 a year." While he said he hated the price increase, he thought that it was worthwhile. For years he had paid annual membership fees at the country club, and had also had to pay $12 a month, or $144 a year, to rent a locker for his golf clubs. Yet he only paid $40 a year to keep most of his net worth in the bank's largest box. He really questioned the pricing rationale of the bank.

Safe deposit boxes are not just metal vault boxes; they represent high value. Many bankers tell me they have waiting lists for their large boxes. Changing the pricing to reflect the true higher value and charging on a cubic inch basis would allow the pricing mechanism to solve the supply/demand disequilibrium and would increase profitability for this product.

This case illustrates value and relationship pricing, and the importance of having the pricing accurately mirror the underlying economic and cost behavior of a product.

Bibliography

Bryan, Lowell L., and Simon G. McH. Clark. *Unbundling Full Service Banking*. Cambridge, Mass.: Harcomm Associates, 1973.

Davidson, Sidney, and Roman L. Weil. *Handbook of Cost Accounting*. New York: McGraw-Hill, 1978.

Friedman, Milton, and Rose Friedman. *Free to Choose*. New York: Harcourt Brace Jovanovich, 1980.

"Functional Cost Analysis." Federal Reserve Bank of New York, 1979, 1980, 1981, 1982, 1983, 1984.

Horngren, Charles T. *Cost Accounting, A Managerial Emphasis*. Englewood Cliffs, N. J.: Prentice-Hall, 1977.

Kaufman, George G. "Measuring and Managing Interest Rate Risk: A Primer." *Economic Perspectives,* Federal Reserve Bank of Chicago, January/February, 1984.

Levitt, Theodore. "Marketing Myopia." *Harvard Business Review* 53, no. 5 (September/October 1975), page 26–44 + .

Motley, Lawrence B.; Robert Penquite; and Alex Sheshunoff. *How to Significantly Increase Your Service Charge Income*. Unpublished course materials. Austin, Texas: Sheshunoff & Company, 1978.

Motley, Lawrence B. *Pricing Deposit Services, An Implementation Manual*. Unpublished course materials. Chicago: Whittle, Raddon, Motley & Hanks, Inc., 1979.

Naisbitt, John. *Megatrends*. New York: Warner Books, 1982.

"Pricing $trategy." Newsletter. Chicago: G. M. Moebs & Associates, 1984, 1985, 1986.

Samuelson, Paul A. *Economics*. New York: McGraw-Hill, 1976.

Stigum, Marcia L., and Rene O. Branch, Jr. *Managing Bank Assets and Liabilities.* Homewood, Ill.: Dow Jones-Irwin, 1983.

Thompson, Thomas W.; Leonard L. Berry; and Philip H. Davidson. *Banking Tomorrow—Managing Markets through Planning.* New York: Van Nostrand Reinhold, 1978.

Index

Absorption costing
  case study using, 219
  description of, 79
  tracking of nonearning assets, 102
Account analysis
  case study using, 217–21
  comparison to profitability
    analysis, 148–50
  components of, 150–51
  importance of, 146–47
  policies toward, 155–58
Adjustments
  component for figuring balance
    equivalent, 102–3
  component used in account
    analysis, 150
  effect of change on account
    analysis, 151
  examples for use in equating fees
    and balances, 104–5
  impact on competitive advantage,
    107
  as policy issue, 110
Advertising
  for financial products, 22
  image, 22
Advisory services, as part of life
    cycle, 17
Agencies; *see* Federal agencies
AL Matrix, 138–41
Allocation
  of overhead, 79

Allocation—*Cont.*
  of resources, 54, 59–60, 227–30
Allstate Insurance Company, as part
  of Sears distribution chain, 44
American Bankers Association, 17
American Express
  credit cards, 96
  distribution methods, 44
  use of demographic research, 17–
    18
  use of direct marketing, 21
Annualization factor
  component for figuring balance
    equivalent, 101–3
  examples for use in equating fees
    and balances, 104–5
Annuity
  example of calculating future
    value, 121, 126
  example of calculating present
    value, 126–27
  formula for future value of
    annuity, 115
  in present value calculations, 114
APR, definition, 19
Asset and liability management
  AL Matrix, 138–41
  case study using, 221–27
  controllable gap, 135
  duration, 141–43
  elements of, 133
  income gap, 137–38

Asset and liability management—
  Cont.
  influence on pricing, 13
  nonrate gap, 137
  part of planning, 26, 131
  rate sensitive gap, 135
  representation of on pricing task
    force, 197
ATMs
  distribution using, 20
  as form of payment, 96
  position in Quadratic Pricing
    Matrix, 189
  pricing of, 189–90
  proximity of, 42
  shared network, 44
  as substitutes for checks, 61
Attitudinal research, 17–18
Auto loans
  demand for, 61
  downpayment for, 91
  example of calculating payment
    for, 126
  indirect, 191–92
  offered by savings and loans, 168
  position in Quadratic Pricing
    Matrix, 191–92
  present value of annuity formula
    for, 116
Automatic Data Processing, 20

Balance inquiries, tracking of, 172
Balances
  as alternative payment
    mechanism, 11, 48, 97, 147
  as element of asset and liability
    management, 134
  component used in account
    analysis, 150
  difference between ledger and
    collected, 151
  double counting of, 159
  listing on account analysis, 148
  netting of, 158
  policy toward compensating
    balances, 112
Balances versus fees, 95; *see also*
  Account analysis

Balances versus fees—*Cont.*
  calculation for, 106–7
  case study using, 217–21
  examples for equating, 104–5
  formula for equating, 103–4
  policies toward, 107, 110–12
Bank Administration Institute, 17,
  120
  Bank Performance Profile, 200
Bank of America, 14, 72
Bank Holding Company Act, 161
Bank Marketing Association, 17
Bank of the United States, 160–61
Banking, unique qualities of, 11, 48,
  97, 147
Bartering, as form of payment, 95
Book balances; *see* Ledger balances
Borrowing; *see* Credit
Brick and mortar, tangible nature
  of, 38
Brokerage firms, use of the
  telephone, 22
Budgeting, as part of planning, 26
Bundling
  case study using, 217–21
  compensating balances as part of,
    112
  definition of, 180
  of Fed charges, 168
  Gold Account, 181
  price consciousness, 30
  reasons against bundling, 100, 181
  reasons for bundling, 99
  use of for marketing, 71–72

Capacity constraints, 59–60
Capital planning, as part of
  strategic planning, 25
Captive auto finance companies; *see*
  Finance companies
Carrying costs of products versus
  services, 34–35
Cash flow
  for duration analysis, 142
  as element of asset and liability
    management, 133
Cash management, as part of
  strategic planning, 27

Cashiers check, as form of payment, 95
Certificates of deposit
  example for equating fees and balances, 105
  FCA costs of, 89–91
  jumbo CDs, introduction of, 99
  zero coupon, 121
Certified check, as form of payment, 95
Chartering
  done by states, 166
  as form of regulation, 40
Check, as form of payment, 95
Check clearing
  hold periods, 164, 167
  profit impact, 27
  system, 20
Checking accounts
  3-2-1, 5
  adjustments to, 103, 110
  calculation of overhead, 85
  costs of, 6
  demand for, 63
  demand for printed checks, 60
  dime-a-time, 5
  example for equating fees and balances, 104
  FCA costs of, 84, 88–89
  free, 72, 166
  lifeline, 167
  as loss leaders, 72
  no-frills, 188
  offered by savings and loans, 169
  position in Quadratic Pricing Matrix, 188
  pricing of, 188–89
  tracking of, 173
  use of balances, 98
  use of as basis for earnings credit rate, 102
CIF; see Customer information files
Citibank
  distribution of products, 44
  introduction of jumbo CDs, 99
Classical gap; see Gap analysis
Clearing checks; see Check clearing
Coin and currency
  as adjustment to earnings credit rate, 102

Coin and currency—*Cont.*
  as form of payment, 95
Coldwell Banker, as part of Sears distribution chain, 44
Collected balances
  case study using, 217–21
  difference from ledger, 151
Comfortable level of debt theory, 226
Commercial deposit pricing, case study on, 217–21
Commercial paper, increase in, 132
Commissioner of Banks, 162
Communication
  advertising as part of, 22
  importance for pricing task force, 197
  of price changes, 211–12
  promotion as part of, 21
  public relations as part of, 22
Community, management commitment to, 28
Compensating balances
  double counting of, 159
  netting of, 158
  policy toward, 112
Competition
  evaluation of for pricing task force, 197
  from finance companies, 92
  from J. C. Penney, 132
  from Merrill Lynch, 146–47
  from nonbank sector, 20
  from Sears, 147
  increase in due to deregulation, 132
  interest in deposit insurance, 147
Competition pricing strategy
  advantages and disadvantages of, 179
  discussion of, 11, 178–79
  use in Quadratic Pricing Matrix, 183–84
  use for pricing basic checking, 188
Competitive pricing survey, 6, 179, 200
Compounding
  future value formula for, 115
  result of, 116–17, 120–21
Comptroller of the Currency, regulatory role, 162

Computers, personal, use of for tracking products, 173
Constraints on pricing
  customer information files, 172–73
  data processing, 171–72, 208
  Federal regulations, 163–66
  Garn-St Germain Act, 169–70
  manual systems, 172, 208
  Monetary Control Act, 167–68
  operational, 170–71, 181, 207–8
  regulatory agencies, 161–62
  state regulations, 166–67
Consumer financial services life cycles, 17
Continental Illinois, image of, 22
Contractual balances, as element of asset and liability management, 134
Contractual rates, as element of asset and liability management, 133
Contribution margin, in direct costing, 79
Controllable gap
  discussion of, 136
  use of AL Matrix to calculate, 140
Convenience
  importance of to customer, 24
  of location, 19
Correspondent balances, as adjustment to earnings credit rate, 102
Cost
  analysis, 178, 199–200
  behavior, 73–76, 226
  case studies using cost analysis, 217–30
  collecting data on for pricing task force, 197
  of functions in institutions, 85
  as part of Quadratic Pricing Matrix, 184
  relationship to price, 69, 73
  relationship to profit, 70
Cost of funds
  case study using, 221–27
  determination of for use by pricing task force, 197
  discussion of, 80–81

Cost of Funds—*Cont.*
  funding of assets, 131
  as part of rate sensitive gap, 136
  pools for gap analysis, 141
  as rate to use for earnings credit, 101
Cost-plus pricing strategy
  advantages and disadvantages of, 178
  appropriateness of, 72
  discussion of, 11, 177–78
  fallacies of, 68–70
  use by government, 70
  use for pricing ATMs, 190
  use for pricing basic checking, 188
  use for pricing passbook savings, 187
  use in Quadratic Pricing Matrix, 183–84
Counter trade, 95
Credentials, as form of regulation, 39
Credit
  comfortable level of debt theory, 226
  as form of payment, 96
  offered by savings and loans, 168–69
  overdraft loans, 169
  position of loans in Quadratic Pricing Matrix, 190
  pricing of small business loans, 190–91
  real estate lending, regulation of, 170
  representation of on pricing task force, 197
  sub-prime loans, 72
  tracking of loans, 173
  unsecured, case study on, 221–27
Credit cards
  case study on, 221–27
  electronic banking, 20
  as form of payment, 96
  increasing usage of, 225
  offered by savings and loans, 168
  position in Quadratic Pricing Matrix, 226–27
  solicitation for, 21
  use of direct marketing/mail, 21

Credit services life cycles, 17
Credit unions, rates on loans, 168
Crocker Bank, 21
Cross-selling
  case study using, 221–27
  report, 201–5
  use of for bundling, 72
Customer information files
  constraints of, 172–74
  use for tracking households, 172,
    201

Data processing constraints, 171–72
Dean Witter, as part of Sears
    distribution chain, 44
Demand
  for auto loans, 61–62
  for checking accounts, 63
  curve, as used in Quadratic
    Pricing Matrix, 184
  elasticity of, 59, 62, 229
  for money market deposit
    accounts, 64–65
  for passbook savings, 62–63
  for printed checks, 60–61
  for safe deposit boxes, 59, 229
Demand deposit account; *see*
    Checking accounts
Demographic research
  life cycle of financial services
    usage, 17–18
  use of for pricing implementation,
    206
Deposit insurance
  of interest to competitors, 147
  regulated level of, 168
Deposit pricing, case study on, 217–
    21
Depository institutions, chartering
    of, 40
Depository Institutions Deregulation
    and Monetary Control Act
  change in reserve requirements,
    99, 163
  constraint on pricing, 167–68
  highlights of each part, 168
  phase out of Reg Q, 164
  purpose of, 9, 161

Depository Institutions Deregulation
    and Monetary Control Act—
    Cont.
  regulation of interest rate ceilings,
    166
  simplification of Truth in Lending,
    165
  specific objectives, 167
Depository Institutions Deregulation
    Committee, 161
Deregulation
  effects of, 9, 10, 68, 132
  increasing competition, 132
Dime-a-time checking, 5
Direct costing
  case study using, 219
  contribution margin, 79
  description of, 78–79
Direct costs
  direct labor, 78–79
  direct material, 78–79
Direct marketing, 21
Discount brokerage, 72
Discounting
  example of, 120–21
  present value calculation, 114
  present value formula for, 115
Distribution
  of economic income, 57
  one on one method, 43
  personnel used for, 41
  price impact of method, 47
  of services, 34
  telephone, 20
  using mail, 20
  using personal delivery, 19, 43
Dividends, as part of capital
    planning, 26
Double counting, as account analysis
    policy, 159
Douglas Amendment, 161
Draft
  difference from check, 96
  as form of payment, 95
Due on sale clause in mortgages,
    169
Duration analysis
  definition of, 134, 141–42
  difficulties with, 143
  use for pricing, 144

Earnings credit rate
  component for figuring balance
    equivalent, 101, 103
  component used in account
    analysis, 150
  effect of change on account
    analysis, 151
  examples for use in equating fees
    and balances, 104–5
Economic behavior
  case study using, 227–30
  demand curves of products, 58–65
  of prices, 54–58
  underlying costs, 73–76
Economies of scale, 77–78
Elasticity of demand, 59, 62
Electronic banking, 20, 44, 61, 96
Employees
  representation of on pricing task
    force, 197
  training of for price
    implementation, 210–11
Equilibrium of supply with demand,
  59
Examination, as form of regulation,
  39
Expense control, as part of strategic
  planning, 26

Factor, use of in present value
  calculations, 116
FDIC
  Act, 161
  effect of Garn-St Germain Act,
    161
  insurance of interest to
    competitors, 147
  regulatory role, 162
Federal agencies
  Depository Institutions
    Deregulation Committee, 162
  Federal Deposit Insurance
    Corporation, 162
  Federal Home Loan Bank Board,
    162
  Federal Savings and Loan
    Insurance Corporation, 162
  Office of the Comptroller of the
    Currency, 162

Federal Deposit Insurance
  Corporation; see FDIC
Federal Drug Administration,
  regulation of products, 39
Federal Home Loan Bank Board,
  162
Federal Reserve Board Regulations
  Regulation D, 163–64
  Regulation G, T, U, X, 165–66
  Regulation J, 164
  Regulation Q, 32, 39, 132, 161,
    164
  Regulation Z, 39, 165, 168
Federal Reserve Functional Cost
  Analysis; see Functional Cost
  Analysis
Federal Reserve System, control
  over banking and monetary
  supply, 161–63
Federal Savings and Loan Deposit
  Insurance; see FSLIC
Federal Trade Commission,
  regulation of products, 39
Fees
  component for figuring balance
    equivalent, 101, 103
  component used in account
    analysis, 150
  on credit cards, 224–25
  dollar of fees equated to balances,
    106–7
  effect of change on account
    analysis, 151
  examples for equating to balances,
    104–7
  reasons against paying with, 100
  reasons for paying with, 99, 110,
    158
  on safe deposit boxes, 229
Fees versus balances; see also
  Account analysis
  case study using, 217–21
  factors for calculating, 100
  formula for equating, 103–4
  policies toward, 107, 110–12
Finance, representation of on pricing
  task force, 197
Finance companies, competing
  against, 92

Financial services,
  balances as payment, 48
  creating money, 48
  life cycle, 17
First National Bank of Chicago,
    offer of discount brokerage, 72
Fixed assets, as adjustment to
    earnings credit rate, 102
Fixed costs
  behavior, 74
  case study using, 229
  predominance in financial
      institutions, 76–77, 79
  relevant range, 74, 77–78
Fixed rates, as element of asset and
    liability management, 133
Float
  as adjustment to earnings credit
      rate, 102, 150–52
  case dealing with, 217–21
  as form of payment, 96
  how to estimate, 152
  regulation dealing with, 164
Four Ps, 4, 15
Friction
  of check collection procedures, 164
  of reserves reducing value of
      balances, 110, 163
Friedman, Milton, 54
FSLIC
  Act, 161
  effect of Garn-St Germain Act,
      161
  insurance of interest to
      competitors, 147
  regulatory role, 162
Full disclosure, as account analysis
    policy, 156
Functional Cost Analysis
  certificate of deposit costs, 89–90
  checking account costs, 84, 89
  installment loan costs, 91
  problems with, 83–84
  savings account costs, 88–89, 187
  use of for pricing implementation,
      199–200
  use of for tracking banking
      functions, 85
Funding; *see* Cost of funds

Funds advanced
  case study using, 217–21
  as element of account analysis,
      152
  example of, 153
Future value
  examples of calculating, 116–17
  factor, 116
  formulas for, 115

Gap analysis
  AL Matrix, 138–41
  basic definition, 135
  controllable gap, 136
  difficulties with, 141
  income gap, 137–38
  nonrate gap, 137
  rate sensitive gap, 135–36
  use of pools, 141
  use for pricing, 144
Garn-St Germain Depository
    Institutions Act
  constraint on pricing, 169–70
  effect on FSLIC insurance, 161
  highlights of each part, 169
  purpose of, 161
  simplification of Truth in Lending,
      165
General Electric, support of
    electronic banking, 20
Glass-Stegal Act, 161
Growth
  desire for, 41
  management orientation toward,
      28
  strategies for, 32

Hard dollar payment, 11, 97, 147
Harris Bank, use of promotions, 21
High performance positioning, 30
Households
  cross-sell report, 201–5
  how to determine, 201, 205
  nature of, 179–80
  pyramid, 180

Image advertising, 22

Incentives
   function of price for determining
      economic behavior, 55–56
   use of for implementing price
      changes, 211
Income distribution, function of
   price for determining economic
   behavior, 57
Income gap, 137–38
Indifference between fees and
   balances
   as account analysis policy, 157
   when equating fees with balances,
      107
Indirect auto loan, 191–92
Indirect costs; *see* Overhead
Indirect payment, 95
Inelasticity; *see* Elasticity of demand
Inflation, effect on asset and liability
   management, 132
Information, function of price for
   determining economic behavior,
   54–55
Installment loans, FCA costs of, 91–
   92
Installment payments, present value
   of annuity formula for, 116
Insurance firms, chartering of, 40
Insurance products
   image, 36
   life cycle, 17
   tangibility, 36
Intangibility of services, 43, 45
Interchange fee, for credit cards, 224
Interest rate
   on credit cards, 225
   differential between banks and
      savings and loans, 169
   effect on credit for balances, 104–
      6
   as element of asset and liability
      management, 131, 133, 143
   policy toward, 111
   rate ceilings, 39, 164, 166
   on savings accounts, 188
Interest receivable, as adjustment to
   earnings credit, 102
Interstate banking, effect of
   regulation, 163

Inventory of products versus
   services, 34–35
Investment firms, chartering of, 40
Investment products
   adjustments to balances, 103
   life cycle, 17
   representation of on pricing task
      force, 197
Invoice for financial services, 148,
   156
IRAs
   future value of annuity example,
      126
   use in cross-selling, 72

Kemper Insurance Company,
   tangible image of, 36

Laws; *see* Regulatory acts
Ledger balances
   case study using, 217–21
   difference from collected, 151
Legal lending limit per regulation,
   170
Legislation, as part of strategic
   planning, 24
Lehman Brothers, as part of
   American Express distribution
   system, 44
Lending; *see* Credit
Licensing, as form of regulation, 39
Life cycles for financial products, 17
Liquid balances, as element of asset
   and liability management, 134
Loan, auto; *see* Auto loans
Loan, installment, FCA costs of, 91–
   92
Loss leader
   bundling of with other products,
      71–72
   pricing of checking account, 189
   use of for growth, 41
Lost profits Quadratic Pricing
   quadrant, 186

Mail distribution method, 20
Manual operations systems
   constraints, 172

Margin; *see* Net interest margin, Profit margin, and Contribution margin
Margin account
  regulation of, 165
  use of as rate for earnings credit, 102
Market equilibrium, 59
Market position, determination of, 206
Market research
  attitudinal, 17–18, 206
  demographic, 17–18, 206
  observation, 16
  types of, 15–18
Marketing
  affected by capital planning, 24
  myopia, 28
  part of strategic planning, 10, 24
  products versus services, 32
  representation of on pricing task force, 197
  segmentation, 28
Marketing mix
  changing components of, 192
  components of, 4, 15
Marketing orientation
  lack of in banking, 40
  price impact of, 46
MasterCard; *see* credit cards
Maturity of assets and liabilities, 131
Merger and acquisition, part of strategic planning, 26
Merrill Lynch
  Cash Management Account, 19, 98, 181
  as competition, 146–47
  use of balances, 98
Microeconomics, theory of, 53
Missed opportunities Quadratic Pricing quadrant, 186
Money market deposit accounts
  creation of, 169
  demand for, 64
  effect of compounding rate, 117
  movement into caused by deregulation, 132, 170

Money market mutual funds, 21
Money orders, as form of payment, 95
Monitoring results of price changes, 212
Morgan Guaranty Bank, target customers of, 14
Mortgages
  due on sale clause, 169
  example of calculating payment for, 126
  net interest margin narrowing, 132
MPACT system, 44
Multiplier effect, 48
Mutual funds, use of mail and telephone, 20
Myopia in marketing, 28

NACHA, 20
National Bank Act, 161
Net interest margin
  calculation of, 80–81
  definition of, 80
  management of, 131
  narrowing of due to deregulation, 132
  rate sensitive gap, 136
  spread versus margin, 80–83
  use of, 82–83
Netting, as account analysis policy, 158
Nonaccruing earning assets
  as adjustment to earnings credit rate, 102–3
  causing friction in system, 110
Noninterest bearing checking account; *see* Checking Accounts
Nonrate assets, as element of asset and liability management, 133
Nonrate gap
  definition of, 137
  use of AL Matrix to calculate, 140
NOW accounts
  adjustments to, 103, 110
  creation of, 168

NOW accounts—*Cont.*
example for equating fees and
balances, 104–5
FCA costs of, 88–89
first offered, 99
types of deposits allowed, 170
use of as rate for earnings credit,
102

Observation, as form of market
research, 16
Office of the Comptroller of the
Currency, regulatory role, 162
Operations
assessment of for pricing
implementation, 207–8
constraints, 170–74, 207–8
support for marketing, 33
Optimal opportunities Quadratic
Pricing quadrant, 185
Overdraft loans, allowed for savings
and loans, 169
Overhead
allocation of, 79
FCA calculation of rates, 85

Ps, four, 4, 15
Packaging
case dealing with, 221–27
for consumer relationships, 181
of products versus services, 34
Painful profits Quadratic Pricing
quadrant, 187, 226
Parker Pen, as competition, 132
Passbook savings; *see* Savings,
passbook
Payment, forms of, 95
Penney, J. C., as competition, 132
Perishability of products versus
services, 34
Pershing, discount brokerage offered
through, 72
Place
change in affecting Quadratic
Pricing Matrix position, 191
as part of Four Ps, 4, 15
Planning; *see* Strategic planning

Point of sale devices, as form of
payment, 96
Policy issues
account analysis policies, 158–59
allocation of reserves, 110
compensating balances, 112
conformity with for pricing
implementation, 208–9
friction of adjustments, 110
indifference between fees and
balances, 107
interest rate as reduction to
earnings credit, 111
preference toward fees, 110
representation of on pricing task
force, 198
Preauthorized drafts, as form of
payment, 96
Premiums
as form of communication, 21
as form of promotion, 21
Present value
examples of calculating, 120–21
factor, 116
formulas for, 115
Price
component for figuring balance
equivalent, 103
consciousness of, 30
creating a list of, 196–99
economic role for determining
behavior, 54–57
elasticity, 59, 62
monitoring results of changing,
212–13
as part of Four Ps, 4, 15
as part of Quadratic Pricing
Matrix, 184
relationship to cost, 69, 73
relationship to profit, 70
sensitivity toward, 12
survey, 6, 179, 200
Price is the product, 19, 23, 53, 55
Pricing
of commercial deposit services,
case study on, 217–21
committee, 3, 8, 196–97
communication of philosophy, 13
of credit cards, case study on, 221–
27

Pricing—*Cont.*
as form of communication, 53
impact of service characteristics
on, 45
implementation of, 195–96
as part of marketing, 10, 13, 23
as part of strategic planning, 10,
209
of products, 32
representation of on pricing task
force, 197
responsibility for implementing,
199, 209
of safe deposit boxes, case study
on, 227–30
of services, 32
target marketing, 14
Pricing strategies
competition, 11, 178–79, 188,
183–84
cost-plus, 11, 68, 70, 72, 177–78,
183–84, 187–88, 190
relationship, 7, 11, 106, 179–84,
226
value, 11, 182–84, 191, 221–30
Printed checks, demand for, 60
Procter & Gamble
use of market research, 16
use of marketing talent, 32
Products
costing of, 88–91
design for financial products, 19
marketing of, 32
part of Four Ps, 4, 15
pricing of, 32
product line financial statements,
207
Products versus services, marketing
of, 32
Products versus services
characteristics
distribution, 42
marketing orientation, 40
price impact of, 45
proximity, 41
relationships, 45
regulation, 38
tangibility, 33
Profit margin, added to cost for cost-
plus pricing, 178

Profit motive, as incentive, 56–57
Profitability analysis
case study using, 217–21
comparison to account analysis,
148–50
definition of, 148
Profits
as element of asset and liability
management, 133
of individual products, 207
management orientation toward,
28
as outcome from profitability
analysis, 148–50
Promotion
change in affecting Quadratic
Pricing Matrix position, 191
as part of Four Ps, 4, 15
Proximity
necessity for services, 41
price impact of, 47
Prudential Insurance Company,
tangible image of, 36
Public relations, 22

Quadratic Pricing
four quadrants, 185–86
four strategies, 177–83
movement of products, 187–92,
226

Rate; *see* Interest rate
Rate sensitive gap
definition of, 135–36
use of AL Matrix to calculate,
138–40
Regulation
compliance with for pricing
implementation, 208
forms of, 39
history of, 160–63
impact on marketing, 40
management orientation toward,
30
necessity for, 11, 39
part of strategic planning, 24
price impact of, 46, 170
as characteristic of services, 38

Regulation—*Cont.*
by states, 166–67
Regulation D
contents of, 163
effect of, 164
Regulation G, T, U, X
contents of, 165
effect of, 166
Regulation J
contents of, 164
effect of, 164
Regulation Q
contents of, 164
economic impact of, 62–63
effect on asset and liability
management, 132
effect on marketing, 32
effect of Monetary Control Act on,
161, 164
example of regulation of services,
39
Regulation Z
contents of, 165
effect of, 32
example of regulation of services,
39
simplification of, 168, 170
Regulatory acts; *see also* Federal
agencies
Bank Holding Company Act, 161
Consumer Credit Protection Act,
165
Depository Institutions
Deregulation and Monetary
Control Act, 161
Douglas Amendment, 161
FDIC Act, 161
Federal Reserve Act, 163
FSLIC Act, 161
Garn-St Germain Act, 161
Glass-Stegal Act, 161
National Bank Act, 161
Regulatory agencies; *see* Federal
agencies
Relationship pricing strategy
advantages and disadvantages of,
181
discussion of, 11, 179–82
survey, 7
use of fees and balances, 106

Relationship pricing strategy—*Cont.*
use in Quadratic Pricing Matrix,
183–84, 226
Relationships
case studies on pricing of, 217–30
cross-sell report, 201–5
information on for pricing task
force, 197, 201, 205
nature of, 179–80
price impact of, 47
pyramid, 180
way to sell services, 45
Relevant range for fixed costs, 74
Research, market
as part of marketing, 15
attitudinal, 17–18
demographics, 17–18
observation, 16
Reserves
as adjustment to earnings credit,
102, 110, 155
defined, 155
effect of, 110, 163
regulation dealing with, 163, 168
Resource allocation, 60
case study using, 227–30
economic impact of, 59–60
Reward, function of price for
determining economic behavior,
57
Risk management, 131

Safe deposit boxes
case study on, 227–30
demand for, 59–60
Savings, passbooks
demand for, 62
FCA costs of, 88–89
position in Quadratic Pricing
Matrix, 187–88
pricing of, 37, 188
tangible nature of, 36, 46
Savings, statement
FCA costs of, 89
lack of tangibility, 36
Savings accounts
adjustments to, 103, 110
control of interest rates on, 164
effect of compounding rate, 116–17

Savings and loans, products offered by, 168–69
Savings products, life cycles of, 17
Schwab, Charles, discount brokerage offered through, 72
Sears
  as competition, 132, 146
  distribution of products, 44
  slogans for, 97–98
  use of balances, 97
  use of marketing talent, 32
Security and Exchange Commission regulation of products, 39
Security transactions, regulation of, 165
Segmentation marketing, 28
Semivariable costs
  behavior, 74
  case study using, 229
Sentry Insurance Company, tangible image of, 36
Services
  list of for pricing task force, 198
  marketing of, 32
  price impact of characteristics, 45–46
  pricing of, 32
Services, financial; see Financial services
Share draft account
  adjustments to, 110
  use as rate for earnings credit, 102
Shearson, as part of American Express distribution system, 44
Soft dollar payment, 11, 48–49, 97, 147
Spread
  calculation of, 80–81
  definition of, 80
  use of, 82–83
Stockholders, management commitment to, 28
Strategic planning, 24
  asset and liability management, 131
  pyramid, 28
  pricing and marketing, 10
  pricing strategies, 177–83

Super NOW accounts, adjustments to, 103, 110
Supply and demand curves, 53, 58
  definition of, 58
  integration into Quadratic Pricing Matrix, 184
  theory of microeconomics, 53
Survey, price, 6, 179, 200
SWIFT, 20

Tangibility
  cause of carrying costs, 34–35
  cause of other characteristics of services, 38
  cause of transportation costs, 34
  packaging, 34
  perishability, 34
  price impact of, 46
  of services versus products, 33–35
Telephone
  form of distribution, 20
  solicitation, 22
Time frame, as element of asset and liability management, 132, 134
Time value of money, 114
Training
  necessity for, 23
  for price implementation, 210–11
  representation of on pricing task force, 197
Transaction accounts; see Checking accounts
Transportation
  of products versus services, 34
  subsidy for services, 42
Treasury bills, 54
Trust services
  as loss leaders, 72
  offered by savings and loans, 168
Truth in Lending; see Regulation Z

Unbundling; see Bundling
University of Chicago, 39
Urban Data Processing, 205
Usury ceilings
  case study using, 221–27
  controlled by Monetary Control Act, 168

Usury ceilings—*Cont.*
  effect on pricing, 32
  set by state regulation, 166

Value pricing strategy
  advantages and disadvantages of,
    183
  case studies using, 221–30
  discussion of, 11, 182–83
  use for pricing small business
    loans, 191
  use in Quadratic Pricing Matrix,
    183–84
Variable costs
  behavior, 73
  case study using, 229
Variable rates, as element of asset
    and liability management, 133

Visa; *see* Credit cards

Waiting lists
  case study dealing with, 227–30
  for resource allocation, 59–60
Wells Fargo Bank Gold Account, 181

Yield
  result of compounding, 114–17,
    126
  target for cost-plus pricing, 178

Zero coupon certificate of deposit,
    121